A Life of My Own

A LIFE OF MY OWN

A Memoir

Donna Wilhelm

La
Reunion

Dallas, Texas

La Reunion Publishing, an imprint of Deep Vellum
3000 Commerce St., Dallas, Texas 75226
deepvellum.org · @deepvellum
Deep Vellum is a 501c3 nonprofit literary arts organization founded in 2013
with the mission to bring the world into conversation through literature.

First edition November 2019.

Printed in the United States of America.

ISBN: 978-1-941920-91-6 (cloth) · 978-1-941920-92-3 (ebook)

Library of Congress Control Number: 2019947675

Publication of this work has been supported in part with a grant from the
Texas Commission on the Arts and a grant from the Moody Fund for the Arts.

Cover Design by Justin Childress | justinchildress.co

Cover Photo: Kim Leeson and KERA, North Texas Public Broadcasting

Interior by Kirby Gann

Text set in Bembo, a typeface modeled on typefaces cut by Francesco Griffo for Aldo
Manuzio's printing of *De Aetna* in 1495 in Venice.

Distributed by Consortium Book Sales & Distribution.

*This book reflects the life experiences of the author, and for privacy concerns, some
names of persons have been changed or abbreviated.*

CONTENTS

To readers everywhere—celebrate your lives and share your stories with those you love while there is still time.

ACKNOWLEDGMENTS

I am indebted to the generous supporters of my memoir. Eminently, Kristin vanNamen, for more than a decade, has mentored me in the craft of storytelling and encouraged me to confront my truths with compassion, for myself and others. Her patience, skill, and fortitude during relentless editing revisions has nourished the manuscript's coherence and essence. She rescued when computer technology thwarted my ineptness, and she conceived the reliable format and documentation that kept us on track and productive. I am grateful to members of the Forest Lane Writers Group, especially Rita Juster, Lauren Embrey, Trea Yip and Jane Saginaw, for their honest, cogent critiques, their encouragement and most of all, their friendship. My son Nick's advice— "Just write your truths, Mom"—allowed me to reveal my parental angst without fear of invading his privacy. The input of beta readers, notably Bridget Boland, helped me define the narrative arc and deepen character development. In joint editing sessions, Beatriz Terrazas contributed journalistic skills, clarity, and best practices that fine-honed the manuscript for publication. Kay Cattarulla, a friend of more than fifty years who shared affinity as international corporate wives, generously read my entire manuscript pre-publication. Her feedback was perceptive and poignant. On the path to publication, my friends and published authors Jaina Sanga, Julie Hersh, and Rena Pederson gave wise counsel and magnanimously shared their networks. My publisher Will Evans and Deep Vellum have enabled a unique collaboration of mission and vision. Our partnership focused on the power of the literary art form to connect authors and readers across all geographic and cultural boundaries—an intent that superseded the core financial goal of commercial publishing and created an ideal match for my philanthropic identity. Finally, and with deepest gratitude, I acknowledge Julia Brown, my treasured personal assistant. Nothing in my daily life, my philanthropic life, and my writer's life would be manageable without her loyal discretion, her compassionate efficiency, and her line-by-line proofing along with down-to-earth feedback.

A Life of My Own

A Note about the Journey

When my teenage daughter was away for a year at boarding school, she began to ask questions about my past. I sent back edited answers that I hoped would inspire her to trust herself and feel the support of a nurturing family. When I became a mother, I vowed to give my children every comfort and concern for their wellbeing. A promise meant to reverse the neglect and disparagement of my childhood.

I grew up in an immigrant boarding house run by my Polish mother in Hartford, Connecticut—a bizarre outcome for Mother, who had once been the privileged daughter of a patrician family in the Old World. My father Juzo, who'd grown up in Poland among hardworking farmers, emigrated to the New World and forged his way into working class America.

When I was a teenager, my much-older sister lured me from Hartford with promises of a liberated life with her in the Arizona desert. However, Arizona brought trauma and instability, along with one joyful year and the kindness of remarkable strangers. At age nineteen, I fled from my dysfunctional family—and arrived in the New York City of the 1960s.

There my reinvention began—first as a stereotypical Madison Avenue office girl and then as a glamorous Pan American Airways stewardess. When I accepted a marriage proposal from a promising young executive, I returned to my parents to share my joyful news. Instead, they delivered a diabolic wedding gift—they were not my birth parents. My true birth mother had been a young, pregnant, unmarried boarder. After she gave birth, she surrendered her newborn to the care of her landlady. There was nothing official or legal about it.

For the next three decades, I buried my parents' revelations deep in my psyche. And I poured myself into all-consuming roles: international corporate wife, aspirational career woman, and mother of two adopted children. Until all sense of my authentic self nearly disappeared. At age fifty-seven, I made the hardest decision of my life—to leave my thirty-two-year marriage in order to save myself. When aloneness overwhelmed me, I finally began to search for the one person who might love and rescue me. My birthmother.

Letters to my daughter had revealed only the surface of my past. Plagued by unfinished business, I spent years examining, writing, and reckoning with flaws and weaknesses, adversity and growth, vulnerability and strength—in myself and others. Revelations shaped into stories. Confronting truths deepened my compassion and helped make sense of my peripatetic life. Revisiting my past gave me the chance to fulfill longings: to hold the small hand of the lonely child in an adult world; to hug the courageous young woman who fled and reinvented herself; to comfort the unfulfilled wife who nearly lost herself. And to nurture the insecure mother who dismissed her self-worth. I've honored my journey by giving my stories a place to belong—in *A Life of My Own, A Memoir.*

Today, I give away millions of dollars of my personal money to humanitarian causes. Why I've pursued altruism as a mission remains a mystery to me. I have no guidelines to offer, only stories to share, and a message to the reader:

If you choose to travel with me, I hope my journey will inspire you to celebrate your life. By acknowledging the people, the experiences, and the transformations that shaped us, we honor who we are, we confirm why we are here, and we define where we are going. These are gifts that only we can give to ourselves.

Boarding House Life

360 Fairfield Avenue

Hartford, Connecticut, where I grew up, was founded by immigrants who never stopped coming. In the 1600s, Dutch and English settlers arrived, and for three centuries, others followed from all over Europe and beyond. In the early 1900s, my father Juzo and my mother Hania, more than a decade apart in age and from different social backgrounds, joined streams of refugees fleeing oppression in the Old World and seeking freedom in the New World. At Ellis Island, New York, they were processed, documented, and sent forward to their unknown futures. Many traveled onward to nearby cities like Hartford, where broad industries and small business opportunities flourished, and where immigrants found work and clustered by ethnic affinities. Hartford was the city where Juzo and Hania would meet and eventually marry.

Young and determined Juzo worked his way up the assembly line as a mechanic at Pratt & Whitney Aircraft Company. His young wife Hania saw an opportunity to meet the needs of immigrants for cheap, temporary housing. During the next half-century of her life in America, she would convert successive family homes into Boarding Houses #1, #2, and #3—an enterprise that would shape her life and the futures of vulnerable souls whom she chose to rescue.

Immigrant Hania in America, 1911

In the 1920s, itinerant down-at-the-heels Irish and off-the-boat Eastern Europeans came knocking at the door of Boarding House #1, aka "Polish Hania's on Webster Street." If they didn't speak Polish or basic English, they'd negotiate renting a room by hand gestures and offers jotted down on scraps of paper. By any standard, the Webster Street house was large— US Census data indicates that as many as twenty-one people had lived there at once, including my sister Edith, who was thirty years my senior and grew up on Webster Street in a different generation.

When I was born in 1943, Mother was by then fifty-one years old, Dad was sixty, and my parents had sold Boarding House #1 to the Farley Funeral Parlor. Its warren of rooms would continue to house short-term residents, only none of them came by choice.

Boarding House #2 was where I grew up. It was a three-story brick with dark green awnings spanning the long front porch of 360 Fairfield Avenue—a significant upgrade of neighborhood from working class Webster Street. The new locale was distinguished by Trinity College, located just three miles west. Founded in 1823, it was the second-oldest private college in America, next to Yale University.

My fondest memories of Boarding House #2 was the backyard

apple tree, with an inviting low limb, just right for me to climb and hide from Mother. Tucked in my leafy lair, I'd gorge on crunchy apples and survey everything around me: the neighboring cherry tree that no longer bore fruit; the adjacent vegetable garden of cabbage, tomatoes, and corn that Dad tended; and the fertile beds of voluptuous peonies that would always be my favorite flowers.

I remember the house itself as snapshot moments—a deeply shaded front porch, where on hot summer days, I sat on the canvas sofa watching neighbors, strangers, and assorted kids walk along Fairfield Avenue or pass by in cars, buses, and delivery trucks. The interior was designed for separate use: ground floor for family and upstairs for boarders. The entry vestibule opened to a hallway flanked on one side by an over-worked radiator. In cold weather, its noisy heating cycles clanked away under the long, dark metal radiator cover. There, Mother also tried to hide the "boarders no use!" shiny, black rotary telephone. Although many of them wanted to make a surreptitious call, few would risk provoking Mother's notorious temper.

The downstairs belonged to Dad and Mother, Great Dane Brutus, and me, aka "Little Danusia." Our family's rooms were multi-purpose— especially the kitchen. Every day, Mother stood at the big enamel stove, long wooden spoon dipping and stirring unsavory contents in assorted pots. "Is good for you," she'd say as she doled out large servings of "good Polish food" to family or invited others who sat in wait at the linoleum-covered dining table. Between meals, I'd retreat to my childhood desk wedged underneath the kitchen window niche that had an enticing view of the entire back yard. Sometimes I did my homework. More often I drew in my sketchbook, but most often I daydreamed about living somewhere peaceful and beautiful.

The former dining room was converted into Mother's bedroom/ hiding place for "Danusia-no-see" things. The enclosed, but unheated, side porch served as Dad's sleeping room. At the front of the house were two "for company" rooms. On the left was a living room with heavy blue velvet draperies that hung across the doorway. There, Mother's aristocratic past was reflected in her best antique furniture and the ebony upright piano. On the right was a smaller parlor that held a mish-mash of furniture including Dad's well-used chair and a wooden floor lamp. When Dad's relatives visited, they'd sit in the parlor to gab away in Polish while sipping hot tea in tall glass mugs. A small but indispensable downstairs space was the family-only water closet angled tight under the stairway. It was so cramped that we had to squeeze ourselves in for "private business" and barely had room to turn around for cleanup at the petite pedestal sink.

Floors two and three housed the boarders. Whether singles or couples, they paid one week's rent in advance for rooms. All of them had shared use of the enclosed sun porch/Pullman kitchen with its jammed-in Formica dining table. Views from the upstairs windows depended on location, either in front or in back of the house. However, no boarder was permitted to actually sit outside on the front porch or in the back garden. Mother decreed the outdoors was "Nie zezwolenie!"—off limits to boarders. There was, however, a major equalizer at Boarding House #2. The only full bathroom was on the second floor, meaning our family and all the boarders had to compete for bath times. During my fourteen years of living at 360 Fairfield Avenue, not once did I get a relaxing soak in the big enamel bathtub without constant banging on the door from a boarder shouting, "How much longer you in there!"

Despite Mother's rules to separate our family from the boarders, my bedroom was the exception—I slept in a room on the second floor, right next to the boarders. During childhood, I didn't think that was unusual, and I liked my bedroom view of the entire garden and my secret hideout, the backyard apple tree. Also, the stairway was right next to my bedroom door—if I had to pee at night, I could get downstairs to the family toilet real quick.

My parents' oblivion to possible dangers involving their young daughter, alone upstairs at night among strangers, didn't even occur to me until years later when I'd grown up. At any given time, at least a dozen boarders lived with us in the house. Any one of them could've been a thief or worse. But later, I had so many mysteries to contemplate, that sleeping among strangers was a minor detail in the tangled mass of oddities that defined my childhood.

Great Dog Brutus

One of those oddities was that gentle giant Brutus, the family Great Dane, was my designated guardian. Canine Brutus loved ice cream as much as I did. On hot summer days, our favorite place for ice cream was Maple Avenue Drugstore. Walking from Fairfield Avenue down a steep hill was fun and easy: coming back was long and sweaty. Behind the shiny marble counter, busy soda jerks nodded and smiled at me—a chubby little girl who always ordered the same thing. "Two large please ice cream cones, one vanilla and one strawberry."

Mother, Dad, Danusia, and Great Dog Brutus in Hartford, 1946

The vanilla was for me and the strawberry was for Brutus. If any adult patron of the drugstore thought it strange to see a child—I couldn't have been older than four—ordering and paying from a supply of coins in her pocket, they didn't mention it. No one ever asked me where my mother was, or why my only companion was my dog. As for me, all I cared about was getting away from Mother's unpredictable temper and the yucky food that she prepared and I detested.

One blistering hot day, the ice cream was irresistible to greedy me. Sad-eyed Brutus watched me exit Maple Avenue Drugstore, preoccupied by voracious, up-and-down licking of both ice cream cones. Brutus waited for a few minutes until he saw his chance. Then, in one great gulp

he seized his rightful share of the strawberry cone, followed by licking
of my sticky berry-coated fingers. Consumed with outrage, I lunged for
Brutus, grabbed his barrel chest and bit into his Great Dane lip. Like a
wounded soldier howling with pain, Brutus sank to the sidewalk and collapsed his massive torso over the hot cement. Brushing a giant paw across
his bleeding lip, he blinked up at me. I loomed above him—legs-splayed,
gulping in and spitting out hot air. Mere moments later, Brutus lumbered
back up to his full height. Gentle as always, he nudged me away from the
traffic side of the walk and waited for me to grip his leather collar. His
canine strength forged us up the arduous hill—once again, Brutus safely
led me home.

In winter, our routine shifted to the front vestibule, where Brutus'
prostrate body covered nearly every inch of the shabby Oriental rug that
bore endless comings and goings of dirty shoes. On certain days, when
instinct told me that snow was coming, I'd climb over Brutus' supine chest
and position myself in front of the etched glass door panels to watch and
wait. At last, the icy crystals began to fall. My imagination transformed
the snow into delicious layers of melted marshmallow flowing over the
front yard, topping the hedges and covering squares of sidewalk. The entire
world around me had turned into a sugar-coated fairyland.

"Danusia, take letters to mailbox!" Mother commanded from somewhere in the house, piercing my daydreaming and alerting Brutus to lift
up his great bulk. Slowly, he'd pad to the wall of coats and hats hung on
wooden pegs, high for adults, low for me. I'd stretch to reach my red hat
with ear warmer flaps and jammed it over my auburn hair. Then I'd pull
down my snug wool coat and stuff my arms through sleeves blocked by
pesky woolen cords attached to dangling mittens. Puffing with effort, I'd
bend over to pull on my rubber boots and fumble to close two rows of
metal clips.

Wrapped and ready, hanging on to Brutus by his collar, we'd slide
across the icy porch to make our way down snow-covered steps. What
an odd pair we must have been, trekking along the sidewalk to the public mailbox several blocks away. During the early years of my childhood
as I stood on mounds of cold winter snow, I actually believed that the
thoughtful city of Hartford lowered mailboxes in winter so that little

children like me could more easily reach the metal handle of the mail bin, slam it open, and shove important envelopes into the chute. Yet again, if any neighbor saw something strange about a small child and a very large dog undertaking walks together in the middle of winter, I never knew.

Grandma S

In spite of the constant presence of transient boarders, I was a lonely child. No kids my age arrived with the adults who came to live in our house. Perhaps by then, Mother didn't take in boarders with children. Aside from my cousin Theresa, Great Dog Brutus was my sole companion—until Grandma S arrived.

Jennie S, who had no apparent relatives living near to care for her, arrived at Boarding House #2 during my preschool years and found a home with us during her remaining days. Although our time together was brief, I soon called her Grandma S out of love for the only grandma I've ever known.

"I'm ninety-eight years young," Grandma S said, challenging anyone to doubt her piercing blue eyes. "I've lived this long because no morsel of meat has ever passed my lips." A conviction she attributed to being a Seventh-day Adventist.

Mother nodded. "You are first healthy vegetarian person ever stay my house." The deceptive smile on her face told me something devious was on her mind.

Brutus adored Grandma S as much as I did. We followed her around the house and kept her company in her small bedroom. Brutus always took his regular place stretched over the circular cotton rug on the floor. Grandma S would pat the chair seat cushion, too large for her trim bottom, and motion to me. I'd scramble up next to her and watch her fingers, agile and swift despite wrinkles and age spots, guide needles looped with brilliant colored threads. The bouquet of violets emerging within the wooden embroidery hoop mesmerized me.

"Stay close little one," Grandma S murmured. Her affectionate voice, like her slimness, disguised a will of steel. With a thimble-tipped finger, she pointed just below the yellow embroidered bow, a blaze of hundreds of meticulous yellow silk stitches, and said, "Soon I will put your name here."

Never doubting Grandma S, I imagined my name right along with hers. Would it be yellow or another brilliant color?

"Dear child, these flowers wouldn't exist without you by my side," she said. I pressed my chubby body into her leanness. Was the floral scent I inhaled coming from Grandma S or had the embroidered violets come to life?

From day one, Mother loved Grandma S. Unique among boarders, Grandma S was allowed to take her meals with me in Mother's kitchen, where cooking odors seemed embedded in the walls. Even Brutus didn't like the smells. He'd keep his big body turned backward in the corner. Three times a day, we'd wait for what was coming.

Mother shoved a plate heaped with mounds of Polish mystery food in front of me. "Eat!" she threatened with a greasy metal spatula. "Yes, Mamusia," I blurted through a mouthful of yucky mush. When Mother spun away, I raised a paper napkin to my lips and lowered one less mouthful to my lap. Conspiring glances passed between Grandma S and me. And as if he knew and approved, Brutus grunted and farted from the corner.

"Something special for Grandma S," Mother announced at the stove, then turned outstretched hands slick with spillage from the overfilled folk-patterned blue and white bowl. "Is only good Polish vegetables and broth!" As she slid the offering toward Grandma S, I took a suspicious look at the "broth" brimming with solid brown lumps. "No meat for you!" Mother's voice was loud and she averted her eyes. Grandma S kept a serene smile on her face as she reached underneath the table to gently detach my hand from its soggy paper mass and hold it tight.

Grandma S had lived with us only six months when I had the bad dream. I was lost in dense white clouds, searching for someone important who had disappeared. My body temperature spiraled from numbing cold to sweating hot. Suddenly, a small opening compelled me, and I began to step through. A voice commanded, "Get back to earth!" Lightning flashed, everything around me turned black. I was back in my single bed, legs pushed tight against the wall. I twisted around to see pale morning light filtering through the venetian blinds.

It was freezing in my room. Crawling across damp and rumpled sheets, I dropped down to the wooden floor. On my knees, I palmed and circled through layers of dust under the bed, searching for and finally grabbing my worn, corduroy slippers. I found my pink chenille bathrobe draped over a nearby chair, pulled it on, and trussed the belt tight. Shaking with premonition, I raced down the hall to Grandma S's room.

She never locked her door. I pushed it open, desperate to see Grandma S sitting secure and erect in the high-back chair, fingers and silk threads flying in and out of the embroidery hoop in her lap. But not that morning. Grandma S lay still in her single bed, a small mound draped with a pale yellow quilt. I crept close and leaned over. Grandma's eyes were closed, her hair fanned out like a silver halo around her face. She must be tired today, I thought. Maybe last night she stayed up too late reading from her Bible. With tentative fingers I touched her cool, unresponsive cheeks and smoothed away the wisps of silver strands touching her forehead.

"Good morning, my little one," she whispered.

I was relieved to hear her voice. "Grandma S, are you sick today?"

"Oh no, dear child, I feel just fine. Well, maybe a little tired."

"Would you like me to help you get up?"

"No, not just yet, I'll rest a bit more."

"Did you read too long last night?"

"No, I had something else to finish, on the table. Have a look."

On the pine table, next to the high-back chair, rested the wooden embroidery hoop. Its center glowed with the perfectly completed bouquet of purple violets, stems held together by a golden bow. Yellow streamers trailed down to a finely executed inscription: *Made with Love—by Jennie and Danusia.*

Grandma S didn't get out of bed that day, or any other. Her final piece of embroidery complete, she could rest well. No matter how often Mother had pummeled my soul and lashed my body when I disobeyed her, Grandma S soothed my anguish, always ready to embrace and restore me. If only she'd arrived sooner and stayed longer. Soon enough, her little room in Mother's boarding house was occupied by a stranger. Never again would I tiptoe down the hall to push open that bedroom door. Brutus would miss Grandma S as much as I did. At least we had each other for comfort.

In years to come, I would receive another gift from Grandma S— her handsome grandson would teach me a very different lesson about love and loss.

Polish Relatives and Secrets

Our social life revolved around Dad's extended Polish family. Other than occasional Polish boarders and Dad's allegiance to the local Polish newspaper *Novy Swiat*, we didn't mix with the rest of Hartford's immigrant culture. For Dad, Mother, and me, there were no Polish Hall dances, no traditional Pulaski Day parades, no Polish Catholic church.

Mother didn't like sitting around making nice, but she liked free babysitting. Boisterous relatives getting together at someone else's home gave Mother the perfect opportunity to show up just long enough to drop me off. She'd poke at me and announce, "Danusia no make nuisance." Then she'd scoot out the door, head for the Packard, and take off on some mysterious errand.

Hoping to escape attention, I'd snug into a well-worn chair in the corner. No adult relatives suspected that I understood nearly every Polish word of adult conversations. Raised eyebrows and guilty glances signaled that juicy gossip was coming.

"Hania and Juzo—how they live so good, buying them bigger and bigger houses?" Speculation was rampant about my parents' mysterious source of money. They'd owned a house on the Connecticut shore (sold before I was born), Boarding Houses #1 and #2, and the 300-acre Old Glendale Farm, where Dad and I escaped from Mother for days at a time.

Inevitably, one question led to another. "You think Hania and Juzo got plenty secret money from Old World?" Even though I had no idea about the source of any "secret money," such speculation fed my hungry imagination.

Years into the future when those relatives were dead and gone, I yearned to hear them again, gabbing in Polish while dipping and stirring Polish *krusticy*, sugar dusted, fried twists of dough, in glass mugs of hot tea. Such happy memories belonged to times when I believed that grownups had answers to all my questions.

There was one person willing to share the family stories and secrets with me—Aunt Mamie, Dad's sister. She was also the top person on Mother's drop-off babysitter list. Aunt Mamie and Uncle Matthew owned Kazanowski's Delicatessen, where expat Poles came to "taste the homeland" and left with butcher-wrapped kielbasa sausages and squat jars full of pierogies, dough bundles filled with mashed potato, cheese and onions, or sweet fruit preserves.

Mother burst into Kazanowski's with me in tow and thrust me behind the counter toward Aunt Mamie. "Here is Danusia for visit!" With no concession to small talk, Mother whirled back out the door to the Packard that she'd left with the motor running. As always, it was any-one's guess when she'd be back or where she went. I loved Kazanowski's Deli, redolent with tasty Polish treats. And I was in no hurry for Mother to come back and claim me.

Aunt Mamie and unidentified employee in
Kazanowski's Deli, 1947

Gentle Aunt Mamie took my hand. "We go to take-a-rest place," she said, then guided me to the cluttered back room of the deli. Easing into a forgiving leather chair, Aunt Mamie sighed with relief and lifted her swollen legs into the familiar indentations of the poufy leather ottoman. I snuggled next to her and began to ask my questions.

"Ciotka Manya," I said, using the Polish that made her happy, "why do Edith and Carl live in Arizona? Don't they like Hartford?"

Now, the mere mention of Edith's name brings a sense of dark betrayal, but there were early years when I loved and admired my sister. Years when Polish relatives in Hartford extolled Edith as "our free spirit of the desert." She did indeed cross America solo at least once a year in her battered station wagon—journeys that made her mythical reputation as vast as the distances she traveled and as enigmatic as the places we could only imagine.

"Ach, my little Danusia." Aunt Mamie hugged me close to her ample bosom and smoothed back wisps of hair from my damp forehead. I savored how her skin smelled of Ivory Soap. When I pressed my face deep into the folds of her cotton apron, I inhaled scents of Polish ham and dill pickles. "Your mama Hania never talks about how Edith eloped with Carl. So gifted violinist, only nineteen years old when she meet Carl, no-talent baseball player but so-good dancer." Before anyone could stop the "wildness," Carl snatched Edith away to get hitched. "Hania never forgive." Aunt Mamie shook her head at the memory, her blonde braids quivering. "Your mama calls him good-for-nothing Carl."

Aunt Mamie patted my hands as they rose and fell on top of her tummy with the rhythm of her breath. I drew comfort from her warmth and gentle affection. Unlike Mother, Aunt Mamie never yelled or hurt me.

"Edith had so bad sinus trouble," she continued. "Doctors say she must live in hot dry climate. They pack everything in Carl's old junk car and drive thousands miles from rain-and-snow Hartford to who-knows-where Arizona." Aunt Mamie's Slavic complexion glowed with perspiration. It was real hot in that back room, and her plump figure was double-wrapped in a long, crisp white apron that touched her ankles, leaving only a hint of pastel blue dress peeking out at the hem. Aunt Mamie's blue eyes darkened as she returned to her story. "If only they no stop by side of the road. Why Carl go outside somewhere and Edith stay in car? Maybe driver of big truck was crazy drunk when he crash into their car. Edith's body go through the front window. Glass all over, some in her eyes, many broken bones in her shoulders and arms."

A chill ran up my arms. I shuddered at the thought of how much that accident must have hurt Edith. Aunt Mamie lifted up my chin, and her eyes met mine. "You know how her face looks now?" she asked.

I nodded. Edith's face and neck were pockmarked with tiny, indented scars. Even in hot weather, her clothes covered her arms and came right up to her neck. Bright light bothered her eyes so much she wore pink tinted glasses day and night.

"Edith take so long to recover." Aunt Mamie sighed. "Her dreams to be concert violinist shatter like broken glass."

Edith and Carl had a daughter named Reggie. She and I were exactly the same age. My mother was old enough to be my grandmother, Edith was old enough to be my mother, and despite my tender age, I was technically Reggie's aunt. According to family gossip, these were strange flukes and coincidences.

"Where was Reggie born?" I asked.

Aunt Mamie tensed with nervousness and strained to lift herself out of the leather chair. "All I know is they adopt her," she said, avoiding eye contact with me. "Customers waiting." The conversation was over. Aunt Mamie took my small hand in her rough one, and we walked to the front of the store.

That day, I'd learned something only Aunt Mamie would tell me: Reggie was adopted. Edith never talked about anything private. And even though I was young, I knew that there was something forbidden about this conversation—and the word *adoption*. Mother and Dad avoided it like a curse word. During my childhood anything related to adoption was kept dark and secret.

Hunched over my childhood desk under the kitchen window, I retreated into an imaginary world where everything was perfect. In one of the drawers, I kept my treasure chest made from a cigar box, its lid covered with pictures of fashion models torn out of glossy magazines. Inside was my collection of my hand-drawn paper dolls. "Dress like me! Look like

Mother, Dad, Edith, and babies Reggie (L)
and Danusia (R), 1944

me!" they compelled. Every one of my dolls was a fantasy image of me. The cardboard box was so overstuffed with my treasures that I had to patch it together with layers of Scotch tape. None of my paper dolls ever felt lonely or ugly. None of them suffered verbal or physical abuse from an angry mother. In that ideal world, I had a mother who assured me every day, "You are beautiful! You are smart! You are talented!"

I grabbed my box of colored pencils and began to sketch something to make myself feel wonderful—like a pink cashmere sweater with satin bows and pearl buttons.

"Danusia, now!" Mother shouted from the hallway. "Get apples from tree for Ciotka Clarcha."

We never visited Aunt Clara without Mother's idea of a gift, especially if she planned to leave me for an overnight with my cousin Theresa. Aunt Clara was my aunt by marriage; she was married to Dad's cousin Eddy. Although we were several years apart, Theresa and I were as close and complicated as sisters, brought up in very different households, yet Polish customs and relatives linked us together. Throughout our adult years, Theresa and I would forge through family sagas, love and jealousy, laughter and tears. No matter what and where, we were always there for each other.

I scrambled outside to the backyard covered by a bumpy carpet of fallen apples. Furiously, I stuffed oozing, over-ripe fruit complete with stems and leaves into a bulging canvas sack. Mother waited at the wheel of the Packard—motor running, fingers tapping, glaring at me as I ran breathless to the car.

Shoving the bag of apples onto the car floor, I scrambled into the back seat. I had only mere seconds to draw my last calm breath and inhale the smell of rich leather. With a mighty groan, the Packard lurched forward. As a five-year-old vigilante, I knelt at the rear window to report any sightings of highway police. Commando Mother up front braced muscles and quite a bit of fat as she leaned into each swerve of the four-ton Packard careening like a military tank across Hartford traffic. Hapless pedestrians be warned: driver of vehicle does not follow speed limits or roadside warnings! Driver-warrior Mother pushed luck to the limit.

Forty-five tense minutes later, the Packard roared into the driveway of 88 Burlington Avenue in Bristol. Yet again, we'd evaded our enemy, the Connecticut State Highway Patrol. Aunt Clara's white two-story house was my safe harbor after the storm. Its black shutters framed streak-free windows that glistened in the sunlight. Shaky with tension but grateful that we'd arrived, I crawled out of the Packard that seemed to perspire gasoline and ran for the side door to Aunt Clara's kitchen. Mother hoisted the sack of apples onto her shoulder, cradled a large crockery bowl filled with greasy leftovers from last night's dinner in her hands, and puffed along behind.

My Aunt Clara, Connecticut, 1950s

Before I could reach up for the knob, the door swung open. There stood Aunt Clara, stretching welcoming arms toward me. Tall and slim in a pastel pink cotton dress protected by a floral apron, she was the perfect image of the 1950's Polish-American housewife. "*Danusia, moya kohana*," she said. I loved how she called me her "sweet dear." Pressing my short, plump body into her embrace, I breathed in an intoxicating blend of Coty's Lily of the Valley perfume—and Polish apricot bars.

"Hania, again you bring gifts." Aunt Clara rushed to relieve Mother of the heavy burlap sack of apples and placed it upon the polished kitchen counter. She turned to take the crockery bowl from Mother's calloused palms. "Hania, you work too hard," Aunt Clara said gently. "I must rub your dry hands with Jergen's Lotion."

Mother beamed, a young-girl smile on her aging face. Aunt Clara carried the bowl of spoiling contents to the big Frigidaire, opened the door, and cleared a space on the bottom shelf. As she turned her back to us, I saw only the wiggling tail of a fresh tea towel as fastidious Aunt Clara wiped smears of grease from her scrubbed-clean hands.

"Now we take time for tea and fresh Polish apricot bars." Aunt Clara set a copper kettle on the porcelain Hotpoint stove. I spotted my favorite wooden chair leaning against the wall, pushed it up to the red and white checked kitchen tablecloth, and sat down with my elbows bent on the table top, fingers cupping my chin. I inhaled deep, full breaths of contentment. In Aunt Clara's kitchen, I felt safe. Nothing in this house could hurt or disappoint me, especially when Polish apricot bars were waiting.

One cup of milky tea, three sugar cubes and four apricot bars later, Mother was fueled up for the drive back to Hartford. "Tatush waiting I fix good Polish dinner for him," she said. With a cursory wave, Mother sped away. Without me as her backseat vigilante, the stakes favored the Connecticut State Highway Patrol.

With my cousin Theresa at school and Uncle Eddy at work, I had Aunt Clara all to myself. In Aunt Clara's pristine Betty Crocker world, my childhood indoctrination to healthy eating began and ended. Aunt Clara religiously followed the 1950s-era Basic Seven Food Wheel taped to the wall of her tidy pantry: nothing deep fried; plenty of fresh vegetables; measured portions; and no between-meal snacking. I was her avid convert.

In my imagination, dinners at Aunt Clara's house were picture perfect, a typical American family sitting around a table set with matching china, no shouting, Emily Post manners, everyone served heaps of loving from the oven. In reality, we couldn't have been perfect. Maybe Aunt Clara and Uncle Eddy argued sometimes, and maybe my cousin occasionally didn't want to do her chores. But at dinnertime, when I sat across from Theresa, listening to quiet, polite conversation, I felt content and well-fed. And I could actually identify what I was eating—baked chicken, green peas and puffy American white rolls. Bliss!

After dinner, Uncle Eddy typically headed to the adjoining living room and relaxed in his favorite chair to read the paper. Aunt Clara pulled the latest *Good Housekeeping* from a tidy stack of magazines on the coffee table and settled on the sofa without wrinkling her housedress. Theresa—adored by her parents and envied by me because she was older, prettier, and owner of a closet full of pretty clothes and shoes—disappeared upstairs to do homework. This left me alone in the kitchen in front of a heaping dessert plate of Polish apricot bars and a pile of Theresa's dog-eared *Junior Guide* magazines. Life didn't get any better than overnights at Aunt Clara's.

Low voices stirred from the living room, and either Aunt Clara or Uncle Eddy slowly pushed the kitchen door closed. How strange—they weren't reading, they were talking. Tiptoeing to the door, I pressed my ear tight against the smooth wood.

Uncle Eddy repeated a familiar question, one I'd overheard from other relatives, but he also added something new. "How Hania and Juzo afford so fancy house on Webster Street—when those girls were little?"

Those girls? Until that moment I believed my parents had raised only *one girl* besides me—my sister Edith, grown up and gone off to Arizona, long before I was born. What other girls was he talking about?

"Hania found good use for so many bedrooms upstairs on Webster Street," Aunt Clara added.

"Yes, she fill them with boarders," Uncle Eddy said. "Too many poor families in Hartford with too many children. Hania made good business—"

"Until she took in the Holdens," Aunt Clara interrupted. "One day they just showed up, a milkman with his sick wife and four children."

"Clarcha, is no wonder they are poor, with sick wife and four girls to feed and raise. Hard times for them Irish immigrants."

I pictured Uncle Eddy, a quiet man with strong opinions, shaking his head, shaggy with thick, gray hair.

"Juzo has good luck with his mechanic job at Pratt & Whitney. When war come, the factory is crazy busy making airplane parts." He was talking about my dad. My ear pressing so tight against the door began to hurt. I realized that if Aunt Clara were to check on me in the kitchen, there wouldn't be time to scramble back to the table and look innocent. But I couldn't stop listening.

Now Aunt Clara was talking about money. "If you think Hania's money was a mystery, you know nothing!" Her voice, though muffled by the door, turned shrill and grating. "The wife died and the milkman was left alone with four daughters. No mother. No money. Hania and Juzo agreed to keep the Holden girls. Nothing legal—that's how the Irish were."

"So terrible," Uncle Eddy's voice sounded angry, "the father of those Holden girls—he just disappear!"

My head was pounding, sore ear forgotten. Hearing my sweet Aunt Clara sound so blunt and harsh gave me stomach cramps. How could a father walk out on his children? Why did my parents take in four children of total strangers? Almost overnight, Mother suddenly had five children! Everything I'd learned had happened long before I was born. I tried to imagine how I would have felt in Edith's place.

"Hania is tyrant," Uncle Eddy said, describing the same mother I knew—at least that part made sense. "She punish hard and quick."

Aunt Clara finished the story, "Those Holden girls grew up, and one by one, they left. No one in the family ever heard from them again."

Mother showed no compassion for the meager finances of her boarders, and she willingly profited from their distressed circumstances. Yet, the secret I'd overheard behind closed doors in Aunt Clara's house told me that Mother had once saved four young girls from destitution and danger—four girls who apparently felt no need to return and thank her.

In future, I'd again confront the mystery of the Holden girls taken in at Boarding House #1. And I would find evidence—an old photograph of Mother with Edith and four instant sisters—Frances, Mildred, May and the youngest they called "Bunny." Yet, I could only speculate about why Mother had made such an incredible, impulsive decision. Had she rescued others to save something she had once lost and was trying to recover? What had she seen in these motherless girls that perhaps struck a deep chord and warmed her heart? Mother's stories, to be repeated again and again during my childhood, would be clues to her past. As she wove her narratives, I clung to them with obsessive fascination. Were Mother's stories truth, fiction, or a combination of both? And, in the end, would the answer really matter?

Edith (2nd L.) and Mother with the Holden girls, Boarding House #1 in
Hartford, 1930s

Fleeing the Old World

Mother's Lost World

Most days, I didn't know which Mother would show up—unflinching dictator or consummate actress. Would she punish my rare acts of rebellion with a leather belt? Or would she draw me close to her with stories of long lost times in Old World Poland? Would she dictate how I behaved, how I dressed and what I ate? Or would she transform into the pampered young woman of her youth, living in affluence?

I would take my place on a wooden chair in Mother's kitchen strewn about with unwashed dishes and leftover food—to watch a drama I named "Mother's Tragic Destiny." I'd put on imaginary sepia toned glasses that made the past come to life. Mother the actress, whose voice rose and fell with compelling emotion, pulled me into the web of her stories.

Hania Olsezska was the sole daughter among eight children born into a family of notable Polish landowners. Although she never admitted her exact birthdate, I estimated my mother was born around 1900. The Olsezski family (in correct Polish, a woman's surname ends with an "a" and a man's or the plural version with an "i" or "y") lived just outside

Warsaw in a white stone villa surrounded by acres of manicured gardens and a dense, fragrant forest that buffered and disguised its isolation. Unlike boys of Mother's aristocratic class, girls rarely attended public school or university. They were educated at home by tutors. "In Poland," Mother explained with a sad smile, "girls like me learn Catholic religion, painting and embroidery—I was best for watercolor flowers."

Mother never imagined she would have to rear children without a nanny or lift a finger to clean house. And she couldn't have predicted that her elite world of luxury was doomed.

In 1918, the Bolsheviks murdered the Russian Tsar Alexander Nicholas II and his entire family—the last of a long line of autocrats that had ruled Russia since the 1500s. Violent purges followed. Like an avalanche of death, the Bolsheviks eradicated Tsarist sympathizers and rampaged into bordering countries including Poland. All wealthy land-owners were suspected of having links with the Tsar. Unless those links could be manipulated, aristocratic families faced terrible consequences.

To save their seven sons from the Bolsheviks, the Olsezski parents were willing to sacrifice their only daughter, Hania—my mother. They concocted a preposterous plan: to convince Polish society and the Bolshevik spies that all but one member of the Olsezski family opposed the Tsar for his "sins against the people." Her parents fabricated a friendship between the innocent Hania and the Grand Duchess Maria, one of the Tsar's daughters. Hania would be publicly shamed and condemned for betraying her family, the honorable Olsezskis, staunch and loyal supporters of peasants and the common folk of Poland.

"Ach, Danusia, I am rebellious girl always." Mother raised her flaccid arm to the sky. "Eighteen years old, I'm daughter in disgrace."

Hania's parents bribed an artisan papermaker in Warsaw to produce a few sheets of rich vellum paper encrusted with a counterfeit copy of the Royal Seal. Then they convinced Hania's governess to forge a flowery letter in the style of eighteen-year-old Grand Duchess Maria, supposedly written to her secret friend, Hania Olsezska. The final bribe to Warsaw journalists stimulated reported stories affirming the Olsezskis' vehement opposition to Tsarist principles. The fabricated letter that exposed Hania's friendship with Grand Duchess Maria was passed around Warsaw's opulent salons. And gossip flared.

Mother's talent for storytelling was seductive. She lured me into the fictitious friendship between herself and the Grand Duchess Maria. She enticed my imagination with vivid scenes of intrigue and danger facing two reckless young women in a village near Tsarkoye Selo, the Tsar's summer palace. Mother's eyes sparkled with excitement as she described how the Grand Duchess "disguised as servant girl" in the palace kitchens persuaded a peasant farmer delivering fresh vegetables to transport her from the palace to the village. There, her adoring friend Hania waited in an aunt's nearby cottage. A secluded, vine-covered dwelling—"My auntie Mariska, old and deaf, not know what we were talking"—became the friends' perfect hideout.

Mother strutted about, head held high. "I'm remember every word of Grand Duchess Maria in letter," she boasted. "'How I loved pretending we were free,'" she recited. "'Everyone else in the Olsezski family detest Romanovs for royal power over the people. You alone, dear Hania, are my secret friend who does not fear adventure.'"

Beguiled by Mother's fervor, I absorbed the passion of two young women pursuing a forbidden friendship in a world where spies were everywhere. My body tensed when Mother paced around, hand pressed over her heart. As she glided toward the high-back kitchen chair and settled into the seat, I ascribed alluring grace to her and dismissed her thickened body. Her calloused fingers became beautiful and manicured. I even added a tasteful gold ring with a single pearl to her slim finger, my idea of a perfect gift from her parents. My longing for beauty and a respite from the drudgery of boarding house life allowed me to spontaneously transform Mother into the proud and privileged girl of her youth.

Neither Mother nor I would forget the romantic ending to the infamous letter.

"'Write to me as you always have,'" Mother quoted from memory. "'Address your letters to my lady in waiting, Baroness Sophie Buxhoevden, who will guard our secret. Forever your friend, Maria Nikolaevna Romanova.'"

In that long-ago patrician world of Warsaw, young Hania suddenly disappeared. Outsiders assumed that she was cloistered in shame, hidden behind the walls of the Olsezski estate; however, her parents had rushed their only daughter to a covert destination—Gdansk, the Polish seaport city. There they put young Hania aboard an ocean liner bound for America. Not speaking a word of English, she would travel alone.

In Gdansk, Hania cried bitter tears and embraced her parents for the last time. "They tell me, 'You are only hope for us—have courage to save the family!'"

On the departure deck, Hania listened as her parents gave their final orders: on her first night at sea, Hania was to make her way, unobserved, to the aft deck and fling all her identity papers overboard. On her own, she would have to convince American Immigration that she was a political refugee seeking asylum. She'd have not a shred of evidence to link her with the Olsezskis. Her family's very survival depended on her ability to disappear, validating the rumors of her betrayal.

While Hania journeyed toward an unknown future, her parents returned to Warsaw to stage press interviews. Publicly, the Olsezski patriarchs appeared outraged and vehement. Their rebellious daughter had not only betrayed her family, she had fled Poland without their knowledge. "Stories about me in all newspapers," Mother said with a defiant nod as if daring me to contradict her. "I must leave my homeland behind," she said, pausing to cross her hands over her heart—"forever!"

Arriving at the docks of Ellis Island, New York, a teenage Hania summoned up formidable courage. "I'm looking straight into eyes of Immigration mens," she said. "They believe my story of persecution in Poland and welcome me to America! But with new name. No more Hania Olsezska—I'm become Harriet Olse."

When she came to the end of her story, Mother sighed. Her ample bosom rose and fell with subsiding passion. Her eyes fluttered closed. Her cheeks, sagging and badly powdered, were streaked with tears. All traces of her patrician youth and vigor drained away, leaving only an exhausted old woman. She slumped in an ordinary chair and breathed the odors of leftover food in her boarding house kitchen.

Hania in America, 1920s

Was my mother's story incredible? Of course it was. Yet I consumed it like manna for a starving soul. At night, I dreamt of Hania sobbing into bitter cold winds and flinging her identity papers overboard into the vast Atlantic Ocean. And I succumbed to a fantasy that Mother was not entirely betrayed by her parents, that she had left the Old World with tight bundles of jewels sewn into secret pockets of her clothes. How else could Hania and Juzo have purchased "them bigger and bigger houses" in America?

I yearned to give teenage Hania, arriving alone in America, a special gift—English fluency, a secret skill to make her life easier.

Decades later, advanced technology helped me fact check Mother's tales of long ago against historical events. What I learned added layers of incongruities to Mother's accounts of being banished to America. Research confirmed that Hania Olsezska, born in 1892, had arrived in America in 1911 (one year before the ill-fated crossing of the Titanic), when she was age nineteen. Glaring fact affirmed that Tsar Alexander Nicholas II and his family were not executed until 1918—years after Mother actually landed on American soil. Had Mother reinvented her past?

There had been a lot of unrest in Russia before the murders of the Romanovs. Perhaps, given the impending threats to Russia's rigid class system, Mother's parents had anticipated the dire repercussions and dangers to neighboring Polish aristocracy. If so, they might well have deemed young Hania as the most dispensable member of their family and sent her off to America in a preemptive defensive move. I had concocted my own mystique about teenage Hania, with her feisty character and sheltered ignorance of political realities—and my fertile imagination had elaborated on the possibilities. For a calculating family, she would have been a vulnerable candidate, easily persuaded to embellish stories about her friendship with the Romanov princess.

Hania was a passionate young woman imbued with a vital mission and destiny that only she could fulfill by fleeing Poland. I had to rationally weigh the historical information I found against Mother's melodramatic re-enactment that had captivated me during childhood.

However, what I never doubted about young Hania was her formidable courage against adversity. Mother's stories had become real to both of us. With every retelling, we viscerally suffered and mourned the decimation of the entire Olsezski clan. Mother described them rendered like slaughtered animals on political killing fields. Her insistence, that not a single member of her family had survived the Bolsheviks, was supported by evidence. I would never encounter a single member of Mother's family—there were no visits, no letters, no communication of any kind from Poland. According to Mother, the Olsezski estate and gardens, every vestige of abundant wealth was stripped, destroyed or redistributed by the Bolsheviks. The legacy of Olsezski wealth was imbedded in mystery. How else was Mother able to purchase a sequence of large properties in America that provoked the endless gossip among Dad's relatives? Had a fortune of hidden jewels indeed been sent along with young Hania? No matter that my factual research unearthed questions that could never be answered, what I knew for sure was that my mother had been a courageous survivor. Of what, exactly, would remain an unsolved mystery.

•

In America

I had no one to help me understand how young aristocrat Hania from Poland had become the tyrannical boarding house owner in Hartford, Connecticut. Mother refused to join other "foreigners" taking English classes, instead she taught herself a patois of Polish-English. Mother was infamous for bursting out in unexpurgated Polish during fits of anger with boarders. Not surprisingly, I liked to eavesdrop. And I understood Polish very well—a secret I kept until I was nearly six years old.

One day when Dad's relatives were visiting us, sitting and sipping cups of hot tea in the family parlor, Mother suddenly left the room. What had alerted her? Driven by curiosity, I followed.

Lurking outside the kitchen, I spied Mother lambasting a pitiful boarder. Mother shouted, "*Pies krew!*"

I snickered loudly because I knew "dog's blood" was a really bad curse word in Polish. Mother didn't miss anything—when I laughed at her swear word, she knew I understood Polish. Her punishment was swift. Mother marched me back to the parlor and pushed me to the center of the room to face all the relatives.

"Stand straight!" she ordered. "Danusia so smart, she show how good she know Polish." She turned to me. "So, you tell something you know very good in Polish. Loud so they hear!"

No way could I repeat the curse word. I thought of only one thing that might not get me in even more trouble—a tongue twister that I'd memorized from listening to a Polish boarder repeating it again and again. It was a real good one, so difficult to say quickly that even native Polish speakers had trouble: "*Stół z mieszanymi nogami*"—a table with mixed-up legs. The relatives were impressed and tried to repeat the tongue twister. But not a one of them was as good as me. Mother's eyes began to sparkle as she listened to me besting the relatives. I could tell she wasn't angry anymore. Revealing my secret would make it harder to eavesdrop, but it was one of the few times in my young life that Mother showed her approval of me.

Mother was too stubborn to learn how to read and write English. I was stubborn, too. I refused to learn how to read and write Polish, and no matter how fluent I sounded, I remained Polish illiterate. In truth, neither Mother nor I had much tolerance for other people telling us what to do.

I wondered if we had something else in common. As a child, I often felt lonely. Had Mother, too, felt lonely with no one to help her adjust to a new life in America? She'd been pampered and sheltered in her youth—what could have prepared her for future adversity and isolation? I had questions, but getting the truth from Mother was no easy business.

On one of her quiet days, however, I plunged in and asked her, "Mamusia, how did you get from Ellis Island to Hartford?"

She turned her back to me and walked to the stove. No answer.

I tried again. "Did you have a job?"

Mother perked up and turned around with a smile. "I get work in photography studio," she said, her voice filled with pride. "They hire me to paint black and white photographs and make them look like expensive color portraits."

Later on, I'd reflect on Mother's privileged background. How ironic that as a young pampered girl learning something seemingly impractical—like painting flowers in Old World Poland—helped her as an orphaned refugee find work in America.

I pressed on to learn more. "How did you meet Tatush?"

Her eyes softened. "Ach, he is coming to photography studio for making official family picture." She flashed a coquette's smile. "When boss ask if anyone speak Polish, they come to back room where I am painting and send me up front, for make sure customer order most expensive color portrait." Apparently Juzo impressed young Hania with his job as assembly line mechanic at Pratt & Whitney Aircraft Company in East Hartford. "Was good money then, many Polish immigrants want jobs—not many get them."

"Did you fall in love?"

"Few months later, we marry." No details.

I couldn't imagine my parents as a young and tender couple. As a wife, Mother was tyrannical and showed my dad little affection. As a young mother to my sister Edith and the mysterious Holden Girls, she was harsh and drove them away. Edith was the only one who came back for more, although rarely. Mother's relentless "gifts" of leftover dinners and over-ripe apples were confusing in light of her otherwise miserly affection. Later there would be other gifts to strangers, many of them life-changing.

Dad and Mother as
newlyweds, ca. 1919

Edith, Mother, and Dad, ca. 1923

Schooldays Inspection

My upstairs closet was a lonely wasteland. One metal rod separated two sections into *ugly* and *pretty*. The *ugly* side held wire hangers and my horrid school clothes. The *pretty* side had nice wooden hangers. On one, hung my soft chenille bathrobe that kept me cozy every morning and night. On another, my pink satin dress, size Junior-Large, trimmed with a meager row of lace along the neckline. Even when I had no real place to go, I'd put on that dress, stand in front of my bedroom mirror, and imagine I was a beautiful princess.

Three pairs of shoes didn't take up much room on the closet floor. One pair of scuffed school loafers squatted next to muddy olive rain boots. Behind them sat a tightly closed, chocolate brown shoebox from G. Fox & Company. When I lifted the lid and spread open the tissue paper, a glossy pair of black patent Mary Jane's made me giddy with pleasure. Every week I rubbed a gob of Vaseline over the leather until my

fingers were reflected in the glistening surface. If it hadn't been for the
wedding of one of Dad's relatives, I never would have gotten the dress
or the shoes. Mother only bought them because she didn't want to be
embarrassed by her daughter dressed in shabby school clothes and dirty
loafers at a fancy wedding. The bad thing was that my feet and my body
were growing too fast, and soon the beautiful Mary Jane shoes and my
princess dress would be too small.

Every school day, my mother stood like a warden at the bottom of
the stairs, ready to inspect me. I'd descend, halt in front of her before rotat-
ing around like a robot. I don't remember ever being sent back upstairs to
change—there was nothing in my closet she hadn't chosen. What I never
forgot was the disgusting odors of Mother's soiled housedress.

Post inspection, she ordered me to the kitchen and planted her
overflowing bottom on a high-back chair. I squirmed on a small
wooden stool in front of her. "No move nothing!" Her hand waved a
pig bristle brush. Unlike the bobbed style copied by all the "in girls" at
school, my auburn hair had never been cut. When loose, it fell below
my waist.

My sweaty, pudgy fingers gripped the edge of the stool. If we had
fifteen minutes, Mother might do "donuts"—two coils of braids tightly
wound into circles above my ears, anchored by hairpins stabbing into my
scalp. If time was tight, she either twisted my thick hair into one fat braid
tapering into a rubber-banded stump, its wayward ends fanning out. Or
she yanked my hair into two ruler-straight braids measuring from my
ears to below my shoulders.

In school, I tried to act as if being different and looking different
didn't matter to me. But that was a cover up, because my classmates' stares
and taunts shaped a daily gauntlet I had to pass though.

"Mamusia, I hate my old-fashioned clothes and hair—they make
me look like an immigrant!"

Mother's face turned red like a boiling beet. Her pale blue eyes
darkened, and she began to scream in Polish (I'm embarrassed to translate). Furious, Mother stomped out of the kitchen. I didn't move from
the stool, even though I knew what was coming. Behind her bedroom
door, The Warden grabbed the hanging leather belt, wrapped the buckle

end around her hand, and marched back to teach me a lesson that I hadn't learned the last time.

Her hands never touched me. Instead, she lashed the belt wildly at my bottom and my back where bruises wouldn't show. Her outbursts were predictable. It was impossible to know what would bring them on. And that was what frightened me the most about my mother.

The big kitchen clock got The Warden's attention. "Now time go to school!"

Passing the hall mirror next to the front door, I couldn't stand looking at myself. I fumbled with the heavy lock, sighed deeply, and began the thirty-minute walk to school. My bottom still smarting from the morning's punishment, I consoled myself with the memory of gentle Brutus and wished he were still alive and by my side.

Mother's influence over me would last a lifetime. As a wife and a mother, I would ask myself again and again: How had I allowed Mother to insidiously shape my expectations, weaken my self-confidence, and expose my vulnerabilities? Why couldn't I see her as a fractured role model and trust that I deserved unconditional love? Her character, formed by adversity, would weave itself deep into my psyche. Years later, I would finally be able to reconcile that despite the angst, fear, and rebellion that she had provoked in me, she'd also inspired my fortitude, courage, and resilience.

Dad and the Farm

Juzo, aka "Joseph," Sosinski, resembled a bald-headed Ike Eisenhower in khaki casuals, as he drove the 1950s Packard sedan with silent intensity. Beside him in the passenger seat, I stretched up my eight-year-old body and craned my head left and right, like a vigilant bird that couldn't risk missing a critical opportunity. Dad said our journey was to check on things at the farm. But we both knew the real purpose was to escape from Mother who, for mysterious reasons, avoided going to the farm.

Carefree times were rare, and I savored them. For me, the farm was a place of refuge and wonderment. For Dad, the farm offered freedom—to eat simple meals, to enjoy nature, and to withdraw into silence. I felt my presence at the farm was almost irrelevant to him.

Old Glendale Farm was located in the township of Hebron, some eighteen miles from downtown Hartford. During my childhood, the farm was prime rural property—300 acres of fertile pastures, rambling hills, meandering streams, and secret caves. Driving there took us through Connecticut tobacco country, where miles of low-rising, voluminous canopies flapped ever so slightly in the breeze, not tall enough to be tents, yet appearing endless and ominous to a little girl with a big imagination. "Tatush, what goes on under those long white sheets?" I asked.

He tightened his grip on the polished wood of the steering wheel. "Don't ask foolish questions." Dad didn't want his reverie disturbed. I retreated to my fantasies: Under the white-covered fields, hordes of men with dark skin labored—bent and sweating. They sorted whatever grew in those fields into massive bundles.

Decades later, still curious about those mysterious canopies, I did some research. During the 1940s and early 1950s our route to Old Glendale Farm took us through "shade tobacco" country. The white canopies of my childhood fantasies were actually meant to increase the humidity around the crop of tobacco designated for manufacture of high-end cigars.

In the 1950s, smokers received no dire health warnings. Advertising genius of that era instead created a mystique about smoking. Adults puffed away guilt free. Gutsy kids hid in the bushes, coughing and smoking like they were grownups. Glamorous Hollywood stars like Ava Gardner, Rita Hayworth, Frank Sinatra, and James Dean smoked to look sexy, savvy, and virile. Magazines and billboards promoted The Marlboro Man as rugged and handsome. Smoke swirling around his Stetson, he gazed out over America's big, bold country, and passersby were hooked. For almost a century, this coveted harvest was Connecticut's number one agricultural export.

Dad slowed the mighty Packard as we approached the rural village of Hebron and passed a cluster of stone houses, momentary interruptions to the surrounding farmland. In those years Hebron had no enticing farm stalls with fresh produce for sale, no country store serving hand-churned ice cream—what it did have was lots and lots of stone. Centuries before, Yankee ancestors had tilled up more stones than soil and used them to build boundary fences so solid they would last hundreds of years.

Soon the road narrowed into a single country lane, where distance between the roadside mailboxes suggested the size of a property. Anyone wandering by would think Old Glendale Farm was modest, if they judged it by the ordinary stone farmhouse. The two-story structure was built on a slight rise set back about fifty feet from the road. The Packard bumped onto the rocky driveway alongside the house. The farmhouse's façade seemed to have been crafted by quilters working in fieldstones. A quirky wood balcony, too small for a human occupant, jutted over the front door. I never could come up with a practical purpose for it. Across the front yard, wildflowers danced on uncut grass, no sign of a human gardener working a lawn mower. The ramshackle toolshed behind the house had no visitors. On the opposite side of the road, the derelict gray barn loomed. Who else, besides me, could hear the ghostly mooing and jostling of past dairy cows waiting for farm hands to milk them?

Unable to contain my excitement, I leaped out of my seat as soon as the motor stopped and scrambled up the stone steps to the concrete veranda that wrapped around the house. From all sides, the views were glorious. I breathed in the fragrance of the land—a heady mix of field pollen, rotting apples fallen from the trees, and seedlings sprouting in the vegetable garden. Dad planted seeds on impulse. Given the randomness of our visits to the farm, we never knew what had survived for us to eat. Eyes squeezed shut, I plopped down on the cement and began my counting game: "One, two, three, four, how many things do I remember—"

"Danusia," Dad called. "Come help." He stood by the Packard with all its doors wide open. Mother wouldn't let us leave the house in Hartford until she'd stuffed the back seat of the car full of chipped bowls filled with food we'd never eat: oozing leftover ham, mounds of over-mashed potatoes, and dollops of cooked cabbage layered with solidified grease. Loaves of sliced pumpernickel and rye bread got harder by the minute in their paper envelopes wedged between the ubiquitous squat jars of Polish dills and pickled red beets. On the car floor sat stacks of *Popular Mechanics* magazine and a week's backlog of *The Hartford Courant* and *Novy Swiat* that fed Dad's insatiable need to know what was happening in the world. Upright next to the periodicals, a large brown paper bag held my stuff: my pull-on rubber boots, pink chenille bathrobe, flannel pajamas, and finally, my treasured collection of paper dolls in the flip-top cigar box. Folded on top was my yellow raincoat for storms that came without warning and the scratchy wool sweater that I hated but wore anyway when it turned cold.

We loaded up and made our way to the back door, only to drop everything on the cement while Dad fumbled with the rusted lock that never got oiled. Door unlatched, we reloaded and staggered into the farmhouse kitchen, looking for empty space on the long wood table. No luck—it was overrun with crockery from our last trip to the farm, of Mother's cooking long discarded. I don't think disorganized Mother kept track of her diminished supply of dishes in Hartford. Maybe she just kept buying more Polish blue and white pottery as a way to remember her heritage.

We piled all our stuff wherever we found room—Dad and I had no sense of keeping things neat or clean. At the farm, we usually gobbled what we couldn't have in Hartford: fresh eggs from our neighbor's coop; canned Campbell's soup disparaged by Mother; and varieties of pears and apples untouched by insecticides. Oblivious to disorder and disrepair at the farm, Dad and I heeded only Mother Nature and the Emerson radio's weather reports.

The entire second floor was mine to explore. I raced up a flight of creaky stairs, combing my way through the cobwebbed hallway connecting too many bedrooms to remember. Except for mine—the best and the oddest shape, as if it had been sliced away from the bigger room next door. Inside was everything I needed: an iron bed frame hugging a single mattress; one rickety chest of drawers; a drop-leaf table inscribed with old graffiti; and a petite chair, the seat unraveling into raffia puddles on the floor. No closet—wooden pegs along the wall were more than enough for my meager wardrobe. The casement windows begged, "Fling us open!" And I did.

My childhood fantasies reinvented Mother Nature as my beautiful companion at the farm. With every change of season, I cast Mother Nature as a beneficent queen with transformational powers. In spring, she coaxed the abundant trees to bud in yellow and pink so that they appeared to me as billowing ball gowns. In summer, she covered ponds with green algae and cast a dancing net of flying insects over them. When fall came, she dipped her paintbrush into earthy shades of umber, flashes of coral and hues of brown. In winter she became the arrogant Ice Queen, freezing every surface into sparkling diamonds, gleaming platinum and shimmering gold. My little room at Old Glendale Farm became a fantasy setting that Goldilocks herself would've loved.

Dad slept downstairs. His bedroom at the farm was a converted storage closet near the kitchen—its' walls made of thin wood siding were an inadequate shield against the harsh outdoor temperatures, meaning inside was cold and drafty all year. But Dad was used to sleeping cold, and alone. At home in Hartford, he spent his nights in the enclosed and unheated sleeping porch that was beneath the boarders' second-floor kitchen. As a child, I never saw him enter Mother's bedroom. And as an adult, I reflected back on the emotional barriers and striking contrasts between my parents. Mother was a woman who unleashed drama and temperamental outbursts that kept the many boarders and me on guard and in line. Dad, on the other hand, was a man of silence and emotional detachment, seemingly oblivious to boarding house turmoil and Mother's volatility.

Tranquil days at the farm could have brought my dad and me closer together. Yet even there, we remained separate and undisturbed. Nearly every morning, I'd scrounge up odd bits of bread and apples for breakfast and listen to the weather report. If the forecast was good, I'd shove a small flashlight into my burlap sack and take off on yet another solo expedition to rediscover hidden caves I called "my secret places." For hours, managing to beam the flashlight, I'd forage in their damp and dark interiors for ancient arrowheads and exposed bits of what must have been Indian pottery. On my way home, I'd sing out my childish glee, accompanied by the rattling burlap bag of oddities.

On days when the weather was iffy, I'd stay closer to home, most likely sitting on the edge of the cement veranda and dangling my short legs over the scratchy cement foundation. I'd watch Dad in the distance driving high upon the antiquated tractor. Never did he hoist bags of

seeds or hitch a plow to the tractor. As I tracked his upright image across
the fields, I too understood the liberated joy of being far away from
Mother commanding, "Do this! Do that!"

Dad seldom revealed clues to his inner life or personal turmoil. I'd
assumed that his quiet withdrawn personality was a reaction to Mother's
persistent drama. But one day, when the rains were so heavy that even
my yellow slicker and mud boots couldn't tempt me to go outside, Dad
opened up and told me an extraordinary story.

Tired of playing in my bedroom with my paper dolls, I clomped
downstairs to the front room. Dad was settled in his favorite chair, the
shabby high-back, a reading lamp over his shoulder directing the light
to his issue of *Popular Mechanics*. I gravitated to a low stool next to him.
Somehow, that day, I managed to ask the right question at the right time.

"Tatush, will you tell me why you left Poland to come to America?"

Dad lifted his eyes and closed the magazine to set it aside. His glance
was affectionate, as if he was pleased by my interest. "So, Danusia, you
don't know my story." Removing his wire-rimmed reading glasses, he
leaned back into the chair. "Perhaps is time I tell you. When I was young
man, Tsar's police make extreme danger for my family." His voice was
low and steady as he spoke.

"We were hard-working farmers." He nodded as if for emphasis.
"Polish farmers, whose lands on northern border by Lithuania were ruled
by Tsar Alexander Nicholas II, the Russian who named himself King of
Poland and claimed our lands as Russian territories." Dad's expression
turned grim. "Speaking Polish language, reading Polish books was absolute forbidden. Tsar's police roam the land like vultures looking for Polish
prey." Dad leaned forward and bent his bald head toward me.

"One day they arrive to our farm," he said. "I was working in
fields. They tear everything, search everything. And they find our Polish
books—banned books. Tsar's police threaten to take my father to prison."
Reaching into his pocket he withdrew his handkerchief and blew his
nose several times. "Your aunt Mamie was little girl then, like you. She
come running to the field, to warn about the Tsar's police. I drop everything and rush to house. Must save my father!"

I could hardly imagine my aunt Mamie, now grown heavy and tired from serving customers at Kazanowski's Deli, as once being a small girl and Dad's little sister of long ago and far away. I tried hard to imagine my old and silent dad as a vigorous young man working the fields, instead of driving around in a rusty tractor at Old Glendale Farm.

"What did you do, Tatush?" I asked, even though I was afraid to know the answer.

"I tell Tsar's police, 'Books are mine, not my father's. He is man who never learn to read. Take me, not him.' Police agree. I say good-bye. Whole family crying. They see me leave surrounded by guards."

I was shocked to learn that my aged dad had once been a courageous young man who saved his own father from an unjust fate. Yet he was the same man who never protected me from Mother's wild and unpredictable lashings.

Suddenly, Dad stood and walked toward the living room window. He gazed out at the front lawn and barn beyond and no longer seemed to be present in the room, where I sat on a little stool by his empty chair.

"In those days I was strong," he said, looking out at the rain, "very good runner. When we reach fields, I begin to run. For miles. Tsar's police chase behind. I lead them into forest where I know all secret places. And then—I disappear."

I watched my dad's back as he took a deep breath and slowly let it out. He'd never shown me his emotions before. My brain felt as if it would explode. I wanted to know so much more.

"Did you run all the way to America?"

Dad turned and smiled, then began to laugh. I started to giggle. We were laughing together—it felt wonderful. I didn't want that to stop. *Maybe now Dad and I will stay close, like this.*

"Silly girl, America is across very big ocean. First, I go to Germany, work there few years, make enough money to bring whole family by ship to America—parents, two brothers and two sisters, all leave Poland. Never again we fear Tsar's police."

"Where did you meet Mamusia?"

"Ach, your mother, she was beautiful Polish girl, strong and brave," Dad said. His blue eyes began to sparkle. "Has she already told you how she escaped the Bolsheviks, come to America, alone—no family, no nothing?"

I nodded. Rising from my little stool, I moved toward my dad, hoping he would draw me into his arms and hug me close. Instead, he reached into his pocket for his handkerchief. With deliberate care, he rubbed the lenses of his glasses. I waited, arms limp at my sides. Dad slid the glasses into his trouser pocket, turned away from me, and walked out of the room.

Dad's Polish Family in America, early 1900s

Discoveries, Secrets, and Deception

Art, Mermaids, and Music

At Eleanor B. Kennelly Elementary School, the "in girls" wore one of two hairstyles—flipped up or rolled under, not a strand touching a shoulder. They dressed in pastel pink, yellow or blue sweater sets and skirts over puffed petticoats. During lunch, they clustered together like a flock of geese. If one looked up, they all looked up. I sat alone at the next table, dressed in old-fashioned clothes, hair in braids. They all stared and snickered at "Immigrant Girl."

Blocking out everyone else in my fourth grade classroom, I was hunched over the black-and-white exercise book braced open by my elbow, my right arm in constant motion until the pile of colored pencils wore down to stubs. Miss Quail, standing over me, knew I wasn't working on our class assignment, The Ancient World. My notebook overflowed not with words, but with drawings of daily life along the Nile. I imagined slaves hoisting terra cotta water vessels; women with flowing black hair bound with different colored ribbons, scrubbing clothes in the river; children playing in the water; babies' heads peeking from woven baskets lined up along the riverbank.

Miss Quail was like her namesake bird. I had looked it up in the school's Britannica: *Quail (bird)—small, plump and handsome of figure; moves with rapid bursts of energy and is quick to settle when interrupted.* In the classroom, Miss Quail behaved like her avian twin.

"What do you have there?" Her voice was curious, not scolding. I looked up. Were her green eyes interested in me or my drawing? When the class began to study The Ancient World, my imagination had decided to stay there. Miss Quail made a decision that would change my life. She excused me from daily study period and Thursday art class, and she liberated me to work on my own. For the rest of fourth grade, I could dream by night and paint by day.

On 1950's extra-wide rolls of butcher paper, my imagination recreated daily life in ancient Egypt, Rome, and Mesopotamia. At first, I showed my work only to Miss Quail. Until she went public with my art. My paper murals stretched across all four walls of our classroom. Fourth grade suddenly got a lot of visitors—kids, teachers, and parents. Sometimes they came over to talk to me at my desk. "Immigrant girl" had suddenly become "class artist." If I wanted to, I could sit with the gaggle of "in girls" during lunch—they had short memories. Not me.

Miss Quail's nurturing was like a mother bird teaching her young how to leave the nest. She knew how to inspire me to believe in myself and fly with confidence. For the rest of that year, I could see that being "different" wasn't bad; it was about learning to fly strong.

After fourth grade, whenever my confidence dropped, I turned to my sketchbook. On a blank page, I'd draw a beautiful Q shape over and over and think about Miss Quail. And I'd put over each Q a golden halo, the same color Grandma S used in her embroidery. Both Grandma S and Miss Quail made me feel worthy and nurtured my love of beauty. Making something beautiful always made me feel secure and strong.

Fourth grade had been a time of transformation. Fifth grade would be the year of acceptance and celebration. Lotte came from Copenhagen, Denmark with her single mom to live in Hartford, Connecticut for one year. On the first day of school, we each headed for the same vacant table in the cafeteria. True to habit, the flip-ups at the next table all turned to stare at her.

Lotte's slim figure in a simple robin's egg blue jumper and crisp yellow linen blouse gave her an air of quiet modesty. Unless she was provoked by sarcasm or stupidity.

"Denmark," one of the flip-ups asked. "Isn't that where all the icebergs are?"

"No, we haven't got any icebergs in Denmark, we have mermaids."

I loved Lotte's humor—like Danish butter, smooth and delicious.

It turned out we also took the same route home after school. Our houses were only a few blocks from each other. The porch of Lotte's red brick, two-story house was clean and tidy, no clutter of dusty outdoor furniture, just two sculptured terra cotta planters overflowing with freshly watered red geraniums that flanked both sides of the front door. I could see a willowy version of Lotte standing in the doorway. "You must meet my momma," Lotte insisted. Her momma gave me a passionate embrace laced with the heady scent of Shalimar. Right away, I knew Danish mothers were different from other mothers, especially mine.

That year in Hartford it stayed hot and muggy right through September. The second week of school, Lotte invited me to spend Saturday afternoon at her house. Asking her to mine would take a lot longer.

Walking up the porch steps, I heard waves of feminine laughter through the open windows. Lilting words in a language I didn't understand somehow told me a lot of fun was going on inside.

Several times I pressed the doorbell. No one came. I tried the door. It wasn't locked. Mother always locked our front door. *Danish people must not worry about criminals.* I let myself in and followed the laughter through the entryway into the living room. Two shiny metal fans whirring at high speed on opposite sides of the room did little to cool it down. But, it wasn't the heat that shocked me.

Four bare-breasted women hooting with laughter were clustered around a card table. None of them had a stitch of clothing on their top parts. Each woman held a glass of sparkling liquid in one hand, and in the other, a fan of playing cards. Every card they slapped down or picked up from piles in the center of the table came with another burst of laughter. I'd never seen a group of women having so much fun together—definitely not four bare-breasted women! One of them twisted around to a tiered, metal stand and helped herself to mini-triangle sandwiches and yummy-looking cookies.

"Oh, my sweet new daughter is here!" Lotte's mother said. I recognized her face, but not her two rosy breasts. Her joyous smile and knowing blue eyes took in my awkwardness. "Little one, come meet my girlfriends. They won't bite you!"

"So, this is Lotte's new friend," winked a robust, blonde owner of another distinctive pair of breasts. "How lovely you are! Your braids remind me of our Danish girls at home."

A third Danish woman, her bosoms so abundant that I didn't even notice her face, held out her arms. "Come, let me hug this pretty young friend."

I stood, transfixed, unable to move. Yet another woman stood up, placed her drink on the table and, two perky breasts bobbing, walked over to embrace me. "Don't be shy, we're only girls here having fun." She smelled sweet and pungent. Her skin was silky, warm, and glowing with perspiration.

Lotte, meanwhile, was hopping around from behind one pair of bare shoulders to another, reaching for another unattended glass on the table. One sip here, one sip there, Lotte closed her eyes each time. The contentment on her face told me the lemonade in those glasses tasted really good.

During that sultry afternoon, four Danish women shared with me their joy, affection, and celebration of each other. One year of immersion in Lotte's friendship transformed me from being isolated and different to feeling included and loved. Where Miss Quail had taught me to fly strong, Lotte, her mother, and the Danish women taught me to celebrate womanhood, friendship, and cultural identity. When Lotte and her mother returned to Denmark, I thought my heart would break. "Pen pals forever" was all we could promise.

Without Lotte, I had to face sixth grade alone. It was a dark year for me—a time of loneliness, humiliation, and betrayal. Starting with Miss

Boyle, aka "The Boyle," my sixth grade music teacher. She patrolled up and down the aisles of the classroom. Her piercing eyes missed nothing; her wrinkled apricot ears heard everything.

In the school library, *Webster's 1950 Giant Illustrated Approved Dictionary* listed "Boyle" under Boyle's Law—Physics. *The volume of a gas at constant temperature varies inversely with the pressure exerted on it.* The Boyle was full of gas and pressure. And she was obsessed with the color blue, wore it every day—a squared-off navy jacket over a light blue blouse that varied only in collar shape and a navy blue skirt that hung mid-calf or longer. Chunky-heeled navy pumps anchored her thin legs wrapped in baggy blue stockings.

Vocal Music with The Boyle met every Wednesday before lunch. Herds of boisterous students streamed into the music room and filed past the front podium, where The Boyle loomed like a dark bird of prey with a wooden baton gripped in her claws.

Thinking she couldn't see or hear me in the middle of a circle of girls, I got a little cocky. "I sing pretty well," popped out of my mouth, "but how awful that we have Miss Boyle."

The Boyle rapped the baton so violently I thought it would crack. An ominous pall settled over the class. No one dared to make a sound. The Boyle, like a menacing guard with calculating eyes, surveyed the class and picked her victim.

"It has come to my attention," she spat, "that a student among you has a special talent for singing." Eyes gleaming, she continued, "Today she will have the chance to entertain us." She smirked. "That person is Donna."

Heads turned in unison, pairs of bullet eyes riveted on me.

"Come to the front of the room. Bring Workbook #5 with you."

I sat paralyzed, my bottom cemented to the chair. The Boyle glared, arms crossed against her flat chest. Silence stretched into eerie silence.

"I've changed my mind," she sneered. "Don't bother to bring the workbook." She oozed contempt. "Donna is probably better than any of us. So, come up here, Donna, and lead the class."

Everyone in the room watched to see what I would do. Nothing could make me follow The Boyle's order. For an eternity of silence, I sat in my chair and watched her face contort with meanness as she decided my fate. The Boyle used silence as a weapon.

Finally she spoke. "I see that Donna has no desire to demonstrate her special talent." Her eyes narrowed with vengeance. "By next class, she will memorize all the songs in the workbook. I will pick one. And Donna will sing for all of us."

That time never came. I skipped the next four Wednesdays of Vocal Music class by hiding in the girls' restroom. When I returned weeks later and slipped into the back row, The Boyle treated me as if I were invisible for the rest of the semester. In January, report cards came out. I received the only "F" of all my school days, written in bold black, next to Vocal Music, initialed *HB* ("Horrible Boyle").

For years, The Boyle's legacy stayed with me. I avoided the spotlight and never sang if anyone could hear me. But at home, in front of the bathroom mirror, I howled along with Patti Page:

How much is that doggie in the window?
The one with the waggely tail.
How much is that doggie in the window?
I do hope that doggie's for sale.

Mother had her own idea about my music education. "Danusia, is time you take piano lessons," she announced. "Wednesday after school, Mr. Catlin will teach!"

Had The Boyle told Mother I'd skipped Vocal Music? Or had Mother seen me sneak through the blue velvet draperies into the living room and slide onto the bench of the upright piano? Though I never touched the keys, only wiggled my fingers above them, pretending I was a child prodigy.

The first Wednesday at 4:00 p.m. the doorbell rang. I was already seated at the piano bench, waiting. The velvet draperies parted. In came Mother, followed by a rotund man wearing a brown suit and a stained yellow necktie. I stared at his puffy lips capped by a mustache that bristled.

"Danusia, here is Mr. Catlin, piano teacher of good student, Jadzia Bokovska." She was also the obnoxious show-off daughter of our next-door neighbor. Mother pointed at Mr. Catlin. "You are paid after," she announced and disappeared through the draperies.

Mr. Catlin flung his bulky briefcase on the ornate coffee table that Mother always warned, "Never touch! Delicate!" Plunging his hand into the depths of the briefcase, he pulled out a wooden box about the height of the kitchen's giant peppershaker. "Meet Captain Metronome, on duty for every practice and every lesson." Mr. Catlin positioned the little dictator on the left side of the piano, right above the keyboard.

Again he dug into the briefcase and brought out a worn red and white booklet, *John Thompson Series, Book 1, Level 1, For Beginners*. Mr. Catlin opened its earmarked pages and shoved the book against the music ledge. One more time he reached into the briefcase. This time, he ceremoniously withdrew a cigar box as if it were a rare treasure. On its cover was a sexy dark-haired woman with big bosoms. Above her head, bold black letters spelled out *Havana Delights, Made By Hand*. In smaller script at the bottom, *Genuine Cuban Cigars made in Venezuela*.

With gusto, Mr. Catlin flipped open the lid and surveyed the contents. His thick fingers fluttered over the cigars as if they were waiting piano keys. He selected one and raised it up to his nose. He held it between his teeth, reached into his pocket, and withdrew a gadget that clip-clipped the tip of the cigar. Then Mr. Catlin lit up the first cigar I'd ever smelled and would never forget.

Even my big imagination couldn't have invented the way Mr. Catlin transformed into Maestro of Doom. He loomed over me, shouting drills, spewing billows of cigar smoke into a toxic fog that enveloped the Maestro, the piano, and me.

The precise moment the grandfather clock struck 5:00 p.m., Maestro of Doom roared at me, "By next Wednesday—practice, practice, practice!" while he carefully packed away his beloved cigar box. He snapped shut his bulky briefcase and yanked it across Mother's precious antique table. Then, puffing his cigar, Maestro of Doom disappeared between the blue draperies. As soon as I heard the front door slam, I flung open the heavy drapes. Like a flapping penguin, I ran around the living room, trying to force the toxic residue into the hallway. My head ached, my eyes watered, and I dropped to the carpet and gulped in what I hoped was cleaner air.

On practice days when the living room was completely smoke free, the piano exercises were easy for me, and my career as a concert pianist seemed possible. I even relished telling Mother, "I'm on my way to practice the piano!"

"Finally you do something useful, instead of you silly drawing all time." If Mother ever gave encouragement, she cloaked it in criticism.

Week after week, Maestro of Doom and his cloud of smoke came on Wednesday afternoon, for one hour. I took shallow breaths and tried not to cough. But my chest tightened, my head throbbed, and my throat burned. I was getting sicker and sicker. Finally the day came when the Maestro went too far. The grandfather clock struck 5:00 p.m., and he flicked ashes across Mother's oriental carpet as he exited.

That did it! Holding my nose, grabbing my stomach, and ready to vomit, I staggered into the kitchen. "Mamusia, you must—" I faked a coughing fit.

Mother's attention shifted from me back to the massive pot of *kapusta* with *kartofle*.

"Mamusia, you must listen to me!" I shouted out between coughs. "It's Mr. Catlin. His awful cigar smoke is making me sick—really sick." Moaning with desperation, I shifted tactics. "I love playing the piano—and I'm good at it." Then I plopped myself into a chair, forced tears flowing down my cheeks, and positioned my hands into fervent prayer mode. "Please, Mamusia, will you find another piano teacher for me? "

Dead silence from Mother.

Even though I was bent over, scrutinizing the floor, I had to check Mother's mood. Things looked bad, very bad. She stirred like mad, long wooden spoon circling so fast I thought it would jump right out of the pot.

"No! What is good for Jadzia Bokovska is good for you."

The next day I had such a bad sore throat that I went to the school nurse. She sent me home, where Mother immediately shoved me into the Packard. "We go to Doctor Jacobski!"

The doctor poked and swabbed, took my temperature, and shook his head at Mother, who was sitting in the examination room. "Donna must stay home from school," he said. "She needs complete bed rest for one full week. Nothing else."

As ordered, I stayed home. My raw throat was so sore I couldn't possibly swallow Mother's lumpy cooking. For a week I ate only ice cream, and I recovered.

Maestro of Doom never returned. No other piano teacher replaced him. My dreams of becoming a classical concert pianist evaporated. But there was one happy thing—shoving Captain Metronome into the trash barrel.

Pretty Things

After Maestro of Doom left, The Imposter arrived. One day I came home from school, shut the front door, and heard sounds of a Polish shouting match coming from the kitchen. Instead of running upstairs to shed my ugly school clothes, I headed to the kitchen. On the table sat an enticing plate of Kazanowski's fresh *babka*, my favorite Polish coffee cake filled with raisins and glazed with sugar. But the kitchen was clouded with cigarette smoke. Horror had descended upon 360 Fairfield Avenue!

"Danusia, I want you give big hug Auntie Geynia," Mother ordered. "Nice surprise, she is come from Poland to stay our house."

No way she was a genuine aunt, because none of Mother's true family had survived the Bolsheviks. Auntie Geynia, The Imposter, was one of the Polish immigrant women Mother impulsively absorbed into our lives. Right away I didn't like this wire thin, fake auntie whose arms moved like wooden sticks.

Reeking of cigarette smoke and settled in like she already belonged, Auntie Geynia grabbed and hugged me. "You must come to Poland," she thrust up a skinny arm for emphasis, "to learn best Polish accent from daughter Krystyna." She puffed up with pride when she bragged about her daughter back in Poland being "*bardzo ladna.*"

I didn't care if her daughter was a "very pretty" person or not—precious Krystyna was of zero interest to me.

Overnight I became servant-to-Auntie-Geynia. As soon as I got home from school, Auntie Geynia's commands started. "Danusia kohana, come here!" she said. I cringed each time she called me her "dear."

"Danusia kohana, you find pillows for my aching back." "Danusia kohana, turn on Polish radio station." "Danusia kohana, find my cigarettes."

I handed her matches. I followed her with ashtrays as she walked through the house flicking a trail behind her. I ran for the Hoover and vacuumed like mad, trying to clean the stinky residue before I went into a smoke spasm.

On weekends, I ran errands for her. She even sent me out to buy a second copy of *Novy Swiat* because Dad was too slow reading our home-delivered copy. I expected she would eventually give me a nice compliment—it never happened.

During the eternity of the three months she stayed with us, Auntie Geynia never missed a chance to criticize America. "You are eating corn in this country? In Poland, corn is for pigs only," she insisted. While all along, she kept putting on fat from eating so many big portions of American food. "Hartford, ach! Where is kultura here? A city only for . . . How you say? . . . too many insurancing peoples."

To build up a stash of American dollars, Auntie Geynia took any job: cleaning lady, waitress, leaflet-passer. And she stole my babysitting jobs. When I was upstairs doing homework, Auntie Geyna would dash to answer the "boarders no use" telephone. In butchered English she'd filter the calls. If it was someone calling me to babysit, she'd lie, "Danusia no home, but I very good to come."

One day, Mother told me that Auntie Geynia was going back to Poland. The Impostor's last day was going to be one of my happiest. So I thought. The morning of her departure I gave her a good-bye hug that made her eyes tear up. After school, I came in the front door ready to whoop it up, knowing Auntie Geynia was finally gone. But when I started up the stairs to my room, a sick feeling began in the pit of my stomach. My bedroom door wasn't closed like I always left it. The closet door was wide open. Hanging on the nearly empty rail were only my dingy school clothes. My pink chenille bathrobe that kept me cozy every morning and night? Gone! My Cinderella dream dress? Gone! My glossy black Mary Jane party shoes and the chocolate brown shoebox from G. Fox & Company? Gone! Filled with rage I stumbled down the stairs. My heart pounded as I ran to the kitchen.

"Mamusia," I shrieked, "where are my clothes?"

Mother stood, legs splayed, facing the white enamel stove. She had one hand on her hip as she stirred something thick in a large aluminum pot. I grimaced from the smelly mystery food that sputtered over the rim.

"Ach, the clothes." Mother didn't even turn to look at me. "I decide Auntie Geynia take them to daughter Krystyna in Poland. Good girl deserve few nice tinks."

The Cinderella dress and patent leather shoes were too small for me now. I'd grown. But they were still the few "nice tinks" that hung in my closet. And they were mine! When Mother gave them to Auntie Geynia to take back to Krystyna in Poland, she gave away more than just my clothes. She stole the only things that made me feel beautiful. I never forgot her betrayal.

A New Pair of Loafers

My cousin Theresa was so pretty and popular that she could've been on *Dick Clark's American Bandstand*. Her dark hair was short, sculpted, and fashionable. She wore pink lipstick. A strand of pearls circled her neck and her pastel cashmere sweater stretched over her nice, full bosoms. Because Theresa was a teenager and I was still in sixth grade, I always hoped some of her perfection would rub off on me.

Theresa in high school, 1950s

Early fall on a Saturday morning, I was in the kitchen at my desk, trying to sketch the backyard apple tree in vivid autumn colors when Mother marched past me and grabbed her canvas shopping bag from the pantry. "Theresa and Ciotka Clarcha coming for visit today." Across the kitchen, down the back stairs she stomped. I watched her cross the yard and enter the garage where the Packard was parked. No telling where Mother was headed or when she'd be back.

A couple of hours later, I heard her come in the front door and go directly down the hall to her bedroom—odd. I decided to snoop. The bedroom door stood open just enough to reveal Mother's back and the canvas shopping bag she'd tossed on the cluttered floor. I tried to get a better look. All I saw was a chocolate brown shoebox from G. Fox & Company peeking out of the bag. Spying on Mother was dangerous business. I hustled up the stairs to my bedroom. Soon I heard a door slam—that told me Mother was heading for the kitchen, probably to get ready for our guests. I envisioned how she'd poke into the large tin on top of the Frigidaire for *krusticy*. Mother bought them in bulk from Kazanowski's, and I never saw her throw any stale ones away. I had fun watching guests try to soften rock hard *krusticy* by dunking them in their glass mugs of hot tea.

In my bedroom I paced and wondered what was in that chocolate brown box. Had Mother decided to buy me a new pair of shoes to make up for the wardrobe she'd stolen from me to give to "good girl" Krystyna in Poland?

Cheerful voices rising from downstairs interrupted my guesses. I raced down the stairs to fling myself at Aunt Clara and Theresa. Polish-English bounced between Mother and Aunt Clara. Theresa didn't have to learn Polish. She spoke American English only.

"How's school going so far?" Theresa wrapped a sisterly arm around my waist.

"Just great," I lied. This wasn't quite the moment to tell her about The Boyle. I flashed Theresa the EFP (escape-to-the-front-porch) hand signal. In seconds we were out the door, heading for the porch glider. The seats stank of mold and who knows what else. We each pinched our nose with one hand and with the other brushed off dust clearance for our bottoms. Plopping down, we enjoyed the breeze wafting across the porch. Theresa's green eyes brightened when she talked about the latest boy with a crush on her. "I wonder if he'll ask me to the fall sock hop?"

I'm sure my eyes didn't sparkle when I described the boring reading list for English class. They probably lit up when I talked about my latest art project, then teared up when I launched into being under siege from the devil in blue.

Theresa squeezed my hand. "Things will get better, you'll see."

I doubted that.

"Danusia, Theresa—come inside now!" Mother's voice could penetrate even a closed door. We popped up and marched inside and headed for the kitchen. "Ciotka Clarcha is going now to grocery shopping," Mother said. "She wants make dinner for us!"

I felt bad that Aunt Clara had to buy her own ingredients. She was the disciple of healthy eating, and Mother was the atheist. Mother's food was either fried greasy or boiled tasteless, and the only jam allowed on the breakfast table was strawberry. I vowed when I grew up, not one bite of Polish food would enter my mouth. Never ever again would I eat strawberry jam!

We'd just said good-bye to Aunt Clara when Mother announced, "Theresa, I show you something. Both wait here!" Mother sped down the hall to her bedroom. Theresa and I sat rigid in the wood chairs at the kitchen table, grimacing at the smells of food-encrusted dishes piled high in the nearby porcelain sink. Desperately I wanted Aunt Clara to walk into the kitchen laden with grocery bags of fresh food. But instead, Mother burst in, face beaming, hands clutching the chocolate brown box.

With calculated slowness, she looked back and forth from Theresa to me. Then she sat down—in front of Theresa. "I want you see what I buy!" Mother slid the shoebox at Theresa, whose quick reflexes stopped it from flying off the table. "Go ahead, open!"

With delicate fingers, Theresa lifted the lid, parted the layers of tissue paper and drew out a shiny new pair of cordovan penny loafers. The label on the box read Size 6-Medium.

"You like?" Mother demanded.

Theresa stole a quick glance at me. I aimed back a glare. We both knew that she was already wearing a new pair of penny loafers with two glowing copper pennies tucked into the leather slots, right where they belonged.

Mother's right foot tapped. "What you think?"

"Well . . . um . . . ," Theresa threw me a hopeful look. "Auntie Hania . . . these are really nice loafers. Any girl would like them."

Mother loved praise. "What size you wear, Theresa?"

"Um . . . I'm a size six, Auntie Hania." Now, Theresa looked nervous. Mother looked happy. And I must have looked incensed. I bit my tongue until I tasted blood. With Mother, I had learned that showing her my tears and pain only gave her more control over me.

"Danusia size five and half." Mother's chin wobbled as she nodded. "New loafers too big for her—perfect for you!" She snatched the loafers out of Theresa's hands, jammed them into the tissue paper, forced the lid back on, and thrust the box at Theresa. "You take. Is gift!"

No one refused Mother—not even Theresa.

Enraged, I wanted to dash to my room, make a fat, ugly paper doll of Mother, and shred her to pieces. After that, to draw a beautiful Theresa in my sketchbook and smear thick brown and red poster paint over every part of her. Instead I stayed silent and brooding in the kitchen.

After Theresa and Aunt Clara left, I went upstairs and got my treasured box of paper dolls, its battered lid still covered with pictures of fashion models from glossy magazines. It was stuffed with handmade paper dolls I'd been crafting for years. But I couldn't depend on those dolls anymore. The time had come to let go of my little girl illusions. I carried the cardboard box out to the back yard, flipped open the lid, and watched the layers of bright paper dolls flutter away, carried off by the wind.

Eventually, Theresa would make things right—we were more like sisters than cousins, too close not to forgive, but too close not to forget.

Adoption and Secrets

Horrible sixth grade was finally over and hot summer had arrived. Mother left me at Aunt Clara's, to spend the day with Theresa at nearby

Lake Compounce. Because Theresa and I didn't like the crowds on the beach, the offshore floating swim platform beckoned. Early birds got the prime spots, but it took a 200-yard swim to get there. Theresa was fast in the water, and I was slow. Anyone watching us climb up the platform ladder would notice her nice lean body and my short chubby one. We grabbed the last two spots at the platform's edge and settled down, dipping our toes in the water and leaving the rest of our exposed skin to roast in the sun—the more rays the better.

Theresa's shapely limbs got plenty of attention from gawking boys on the swim platform. As if she didn't notice them watching her, Theresa decided to tell me a big secret.

"I'm adopted . . . did you know that?"

Her question stunned me. If ever the word "adoption" slipped out in family conversation or gossip, everyone instantly hushed up. The topic was taboo. Didn't Theresa know that? I stared down at my feet and started splashing them so loud that the neighboring boys switched their attention from Theresa to me.

"You're adopted too," Theresa's voice rose over the splashing, "Did you know *that*?"

Shock and confusion filled my whole body. Stumbling to my feet, unable to speak or look at Theresa, I gulped in air at the platform edge and leaned forward until gravity pulled me into the murky water. I paddle-swam back to shore, then staggered out of the water and collapsed on the sand. Feeling sick to my stomach, I swallowed bile and stared out at the swim platform.

Eventually, Theresa stood up and dove into the lake. Within minutes, she surfaced right in front of me. Without saying a word to each other, we leaped over umpteen legs and bodies looking for our trampled beach towels. When we found them, we shook them out vigorously, scrunching our eyes shut to avoid the sandy debris and angry glares from kids who didn't like sand showers.

Theresa in the lead, we headed toward the second most popular place at Lake Compounce: a cluster of buildings housing the snack bar, changing rooms, and the public phone booth. Theresa disappeared inside. Assuming she was phoning Aunt Clara to come and get us, I waited outside. A few minutes later Theresa came out, wearing crisp Bermuda shorts and a clean blouse. Wrapping my gritty wet towel around my too-tight bathing suit, I plodded after her. On a long wood bench next to the parking lot, we sat and pretended that the passing cars packed with noisy kids were fascinating. No eye contact, no talking between us for thirty minutes was record breaking. Eventually, Aunt Clara pulled up in her Chevy; Theresa climbed in front, and I sat in back. Aunt Clara drove two pouty, silent girls back to Bristol, probably thinking we were pooped from too much sun and swimming.

Back at Aunt Clara's house, Theresa and I sat in the kitchen and demolished a stack of tuna fish sandwiches washed down with cold glasses of milk—until the roar of the mighty Packard sounded in the driveway. Mother burst into the kitchen. "Danusia, come, we go home!"

Giving a big warm hug to Aunt Clara, I didn't mumble even a "good-bye" to Theresa. Slumped in the back seat all the way to Hartford, I hardly cringed from Mother's wild driving. *Could Theresa be right?* Was I adopted? What came to mind were two vintage images: a photograph of Mother's family when she was about my age, and a beautiful painting of Mother as a teenager. Both were compelling reminders of Mother's lost world and the family legacy we shared.

No one ever said I looked like Mother, not that I'd asked anyone. But my secret wish was that I would grow up to be just as beautiful as she'd been as a teenager. When I was little, viewing the photograph of Mother's family meant sneaking into her bedroom, standing on the upholstered chair next to her high dresser, and stretching up to reach the photograph. Its tarnished silver frame was jammed between a clutter of Mother's hair-clogged brushes and boxes of face powder. Grabbing the frame, I'd sink into the chair below, sigh with contentment, and stare at the photograph from Mother's lost world, the family I'd always yearned to know.

Sepia-toned, about the size of my small sketchbook, the scene was the Olszeski clan gathered in the garden of their Warsaw estate. Mother was in the center, a young girl dressed in a lacy pinafore over a flouncy white dress, pale stockings, and high-buttoned shoes. Gathered around her were her seven brothers—my uncles—ranging from strapping boys to handsome young men. In the second row stood my grandparents, proud and confident as if assuring the viewer that all was secure. An impressive figure stood to the far right: the family priest wearing a triangular black hat and voluminous dark robe. According to Mother, "Every rich Polish family having own priest—for when needed."

A second portrait hung in the family parlor of 360 Fairfield Avenue. It was a gilt-framed oil painting, positioned so every visitor could see it. "I was painted by best artist in Warsaw," Mother boasted.

To my child's eyes, the young woman in the painting seemed life-size. She was a teenage beauty dressed in an elegant, ankle-length lace dress the color of rich cream. Her abundant hair flowed like dark honey over her shoulders. She wore a broad-brimmed, straw hat with streams of rose satin ribbons around the crown. One slender hand rested on the handle of a ruffled green parasol. The other grazed the head of the family dog, a Russian Borzoi. Such a serene and confident girl could easily have walked in the gardens of the Tsar.

Gazing at the painting always made me curious about daily life in Mother's wealthy family. What fancy dishes were they served for their meals? How did Mother behave with the servants? Had she ever fallen in love? And what young men in her aristocratic circle would have been her eligible suitors? My soul yearned to be transported into that beautiful world, where Mother had lived—before it all disappeared.

That night, doubt planted by Theresa at Lake Compounce took hold of my dreams. The next morning, I awoke disoriented but determined to know the truth. Hunting for Mother, I found her outside at the backyard clothesline, bottom up and head down to a mountain of just-washed sheets—a sign of boarders having moved on. Not interested in talking to Mother's rear end, I waited for her to stand up.

"Mamusia, I need to ask you something really important."

"If important, you wait!" Hanging big sheets took priority.

Tired and grumpy, I stood for as long as I could and watched Mother bobbing up and down, sopping sweat from her face with a wet tail end of the nearest sheet. Eventually I slumped down to the top step of the laundry stoop, stretched my arms over my knees, and fell sound asleep. Until Mother, blocked from getting past, bent over to poke at me.

"Wake up!" she said, her voice irritated. "Yesterday too much swimming with Theresa—no good."

"Mamusia, is it true that I'm adopted?"

"Ach," she said dismissively and turned away from me to pick up the empty laundry basket on the stoop. "Who is telling you stupid stuff?"

"Theresa. She says I'm adopted. We're both adopted."

"Theresa is foolish girl, knows nothing. Why you listen?"

Back and forth we went—Mother defending and accusing, me persisting and demanding. Until Mother finally agreed to answer my questions. Before, I'd had only snippets of gossip that I'd translated from relatives gabbing in Polish and Aunt Mamie's somewhat reliable but also mysterious answers to my questions. What I was about to hear from Mother was a completely different version.

So began her "absolute true" story.

That she had borne her other daughter, my sister Edith, when she and Dad were young and newly married. She claimed being pregnant with me, "Late in life and too old. Family would give shame only." Mother looked convincing as she continued, "I'm decide to hide and have baby at farm."

But Mother hates going to the farm. Why would she go there?

According to Mother, Edith was the attending nurse for my birth at the farm on February 2, 1943. Afterward, she and Edith returned to Hartford with a newborn baby they called Danusia. If she was hiding her pregnancy at the farm, how did they explain an instant baby to the boarders and relatives?

As an adult, I checked the *Farmer's Almanac*. The winter of 1943 was the coldest on record in Connecticut. An *unheated* farmhouse, that frigid February, would have been a risky place even for a young, healthy mother to have a homebirth. And a preposterous place for an older mother. As a child, I didn't connect Mother's illogical stories to her unpredictable behavior. Later as an adult, I identified certain common elements had always been there: drama, deception, and willfulness. They had shaped who Mother was and the stories she told.

The mystery of adoption and the truth about my birth would stay buried for another decade. At age twenty-four, I would return to Arizona as a bride-to-be with joyful news. Instead of celebrating my happiness, my parents would choose that visit to tell me yet another incredible version. Would it finally be the real, true confession about my birth?

Exodus to Arizona

Remembering

In the 1950s, Americans avidly read newspapers and listened to the radio; nearly everyone watched popular TV shows. In 1956 the United States Supreme Court ruled illegal segregated busing in Montgomery, Alabama, and the SS Andrea Doria sank off the coast of Nantucket. The NY Yankees won the World Series, and Marilyn Monroe married Arthur Miller. Elvis Presley appeared on the Ed Sullivan Show, and his hit single "Don't Be Cruel/Hound Dog" made number one on America's music charts. Also notable that year, I graduated from E.B. Kennelly public school in Hartford as salutatorian of my eighth grade class. June 1956, how did a girl who feared the spotlight manage to deliver a graduation speech about patriotism to hundreds of people staring at her from the audience? She pulled it together, gave the speech, and the rest was a blur.

Although my transition to Bulkeley High School must have been challenging, I forgot most of the details, except for one event—the summer of 1957—that changed my life.

•

Don't Trust the Mythmaker

"Yoo-hoo, it's me!" Edith, waving both arms in the air, stood next to her 1950s Ford wagon at the bottom of the driveway. "Is anyone there?" she hooted. Edith didn't believe in giving advance notice about when she'd show up in Hartford. That year, she auspiciously arrived at the beginning of the summer.

Poking my head out the kitchen window, I shouted back, "It's just me here!"

Edith switched from dramatically waving to aggressive pointing at the wagon.

"Okay, okay . . . hold your horses," I mumbled, trekking across the kitchen, down the stairs to the back door and across the lawn to greet my sister. Edith's visits irritated me because they generally meant I'd be at her beck and call. She behaved like "Free Spirit of the Desert," a nickname she was given by Hartford relatives who'd never seen the desert but fantasized about it. She dressed like a not-so-young Hopi maiden in ankle-length, pleated broom skirts or long-sleeved buckskin dresses, arms and chest draped with Old Pawn—antique Indian turquoise and silver jewelry. Around her waist she wore a heavy silver *concha* belt.

Edith, "Free Spirit of the Desert," 1958

Edith's turquoise skirted bottom was sticking out the wagon's open tailgate. "Help unload!" came a muffled order that I pretended not to hear. The car's exterior was encrusted with the grit of 2,500 miles of Southwest desert sands, Rocky Mountain red dust, prairie rainstorms and New England mud. I peered through the grimy side window. Usually the wagon arrived fully packed. This time, there were no stacks of *Arizona Highways* magazines or boxes full of prickly pear cactus jellies. Just Edith's leather suitcase and her thin bedroll wrapped around a sleeping pillow wedged behind the front seats. The back seat, down flat, was littered with empty paper bags—nothing new about that. At rest stops and parking lots, Edith typically fed herself from sacks of canned food and dehydrated meals packed at start-up, and she took her naps in the wagon. Free Spirit didn't believe in wasting money on motels or buying meals at roadhouse restaurants.

"Time to hose down the wagon." Edith's bottom emerged and the rest of her stood upright. I'd learn that Edith took better care of that car than she did the people in her life. Gathering up the accordion hem of the broom skirt, she tied it into a fat knot high on her hip, a way to proudly show off the long legs that, unlike much of her body, had not been scarred in that accident years ago.

Edith handed me a big sponge. "Scrub it good," she ordered and pointed to a stack of frayed towels on the floor below the passenger seat. "Use them all!"

While I scrubbed and sweated, Edith poured cool water from the hose over her legs as if she had nothing else on her mind. We were mismatched in age, looks, and behavior. Edith and I didn't have much in common. Until—

"Donna, you're fourteen years old now, pretty grown up." Edith suddenly stopped hosing. "Isn't it time to cut off your long hair?" That got my attention. "If you come back to live with me in Arizona, you can have a whole new life."

I couldn't see Edith's eyes, hidden behind the tinted glasses that she wore day and night.

"Think about it—freedom and independence!" Edith untied the broom skirt and let it cascade over her damp legs. "You can be *a star* at Sunnyslope High with Reggie!"

How did the sister I saw only once a year, with whom I'd never shared personal stuff, know that I secretly yearned to be a free-spirited woman?

Edith and I teamed up for a brilliant sales pitch to Mother and Dad. Edith made eye contact with Mother and jabbed at me. "Donna will finally learn how to take care of herself!" She assured our parents that, under her guidance, I'd make a healthy adjustment to desert life and enter my sophomore year at Sunnyslope High School with my cousin Reggie. Remarkably, they agreed to everything. I'd leave Hartford and drive with Edith to Arizona.

That night in my bedroom, I thought about what I knew and what I didn't know. Reggie had red hair and lots of freckles. We were the same age. Hartford relatives gossiped about our ages being a "strange coincidence?" But what was coincidental about that? I wondered about the car accident that ended Edith's future as a concert violinist. What did it do to Edith's mind? Carl, according to Aunt Mamie, was a "real good dancer." In their desert home, did he and Edith twirl around in their house doing fancy dance steps? If I went to live with them, would I truly become liberated and turn into the free-spirited woman I longed to be?

Mid-June 1957, the wagon was packed and the back seat flipped down to receive our supplies. Mother shoved an insulated aluminum chest into the car. It was filled with Polish dill pickles, ham sandwiches, potato salad, and thick slices of poppy seed cake. "Eat good for couple days," she said.

Wedged next to the cooler was Edith's large, leather suitcase that held her Hopi style wardrobe. My much smaller Samsonite was only half full, Edith having culled my Connecticut clothes. "We'll get you all new outfits in Arizona," she promised. By special concession, I was allowed to take my plastic bin of art supplies and one square cardboard box filled with my drawing notebooks. The so-called free space in the wagon was only sufficient for two sets of rolled up bedding. Little did I suspect that most nights we'd be sleeping crunched up like stowaways in the wagon.

On the awning-shaded porch, Mother and Dad stood together and watched their two daughters leave them. From the passenger side,

I waved and attempted to stop the unexpected tears that blurred my vision. Hania and Juzo were holding hands, something I'd never seen them do before. In the driver's seat, Edith backed the wagon out of the driveway and shot up a cursory wave. She made a sharp turn, and the wagon lurched onto the street. The figures of our parents grew smaller and smaller as 360 Fairfield Avenue disappeared from view. Not until much later did I acknowledge the conflicting emotions I felt that day: resignation that I would never again walk through the glass-paneled front door of Boarding House #2; and anticipation about my liberated future.

How many days and nights did it take road warrior Edith at the wheel of the wagon and me in the passenger seat to drive 2,500 miles across America? I had no idea. My assignment from Edith was to learn how to read US roadmaps so that I could track all the tourist attractions—so that she could bypass every single one.

Carl and Reggie were left to wait and guess when we'd arrive. They got only erratic reports from Edith shouting in public phone booths next to highway gas stations. On impulse, she'd call home and come clean— about where we were, that is. Only once, when we began to smell really bad, did Edith rent a room so we could take showers.

"Almost there!" Edith poked at me slumped and snoozing in the passenger seat. I sat up to views of flat and arid landscape, interrupted by Saguaro cacti, clusters of other desert plants and distant surrounding mountains. Driving past isolated homesteads, there were no boundary fences. Who owned what land was revealed by painted family names on hand-hewn mailboxes atop wood or metal posts along the road. Desert craftsmen apparently got inspiration from local lore. Giant scorpion bodies, tubular Saguaro cactus, Hopi rain fetishes and cowboy paraphernalia decorated wacky mailboxes big enough to hold family mail, daily newspapers, and bulky Sears Catalogues. During my year in the desert with Edith, I'd meet desert folks who were as quirky as their mailboxes.

Suddenly the wagon swerved off the road, bumped down a rocky driveway and halted. Flinging open the passenger door, I staggered out. Heat of at least 115 degrees blasted me like a wide-open furnace. Edith was immune to heat. Maybe dressing like a Hopi maiden in long-sleeved buckskin served both as mythical allure and as sun protection. Leaning on the horn, Edith sent obscene hoots into the desert silence.

Within seconds, Carl and Reggie rushed from the house, he as tall and skinny as she was short and plump. At most I'd seen Reggie four times in my life on the rare visits when Edith "tolerated" her company for a trans-America road trip. Having stolen Edith three decades before, Carl never returned to face Mother in Hartford. Not that I blamed him. We met, for the first time, in that desert driveway.

"Glad you're home." Carl's quiet voice held little emotion. "We've been waiting."

Reggie ran to the driver's side window. "Mom, it's good to see you."

Edith pushed open the door, extended her long legs and stood up with no apparent effort or physical strain from the long drive. "You can help unload the wagon," she said giving Reggie a brief hug. She didn't bother with Carl and marched into the house, leaving the three of us behind to unload and scrub down the wagon.

My first impression of Carl would turn out to be accurate. He was patient, tolerant, and submissive to Edith as boss of everyone. Like mother, like daughter.

Reggie and I would be sharing the guesthouse over the garage, a space she'd previously had to herself.

"Take the back room, you'll get a closet that way," she said to me, leaving out a few details. The front room had a picture window with panoramic views of the desert and a direct-entry staircase. The back room overlooking the driveway had a window so small I could barely poke my head out, and the closet was merely a concave wall niche with no door.

In coming days as I adjusted to my new home, Reggie's habit of tossing her wild mop of carrot red hair and grinning mysteriously made me wonder what was going on inside that head. I was about three inches taller than Reggie. She was stocky, and by then, I'd lost my baby fat. She liked to wear electric colors, tight Capri pants, and her blouse tied in a knot over her fleshy waist. My to-be-determined style would depend on Edith, who was my only source of money. As it turned out, she was in no hurry to fork any over. Meanwhile, I had to forage through my meager stash of Connecticut clothes, which was too oppressive for desert heat, and wonder how bad my sweaty body smelled.

But in my sketchbook, I designed a perfect wardrobe for desert life, as if modeled by Sandra Dee, "1950's Queen of Teens": flouncy sundresses in brilliant colors, soft cotton slacks paired with adorable rainbow plaid blouses and stylish leather strappy sandals. In spite of all the beautiful clothes I drew in my sketchbook while sitting in the triple digit heat of my room over the garage, my closet with no door had nothing pretty, airy, or cool hanging inside.

During that summer's heat, Edith, Carl, Reggie, and I slept outdoors on Army cots, the only way to catch rare nighttime breezes. Toilet trips to the house were life threatening if we didn't first use our flashlights to expose any scorpions lurking about in the dark. At sunrise, when Edith shouted, "Wake up!" Reggie and I would groan and roll over, grope for our slippers and slap them hard against a wooden leg of the cot. If anything crawled out, we'd grin maliciously and send another creepy-crawler to its doom.

On cool nights—below 100 degrees—Edith and Carl retreated indoors to their sleep alcove with no door. The main house was a maze of unskilled carpentry and no insulation against desert heat. "Rooms" were created by partitioned spaces that served different functions—kitchen, dining, living area, and office. Walls stopped short of the ceiling; there was no soundproofing, no doors, and no privacy. Except for one communal bathroom, where the roof sloped low to meet the walls, and the only interior door in the house could be closed and locked by looping a bent nail into a mounted hook. Inside there was a toilet, a pedestal sink, and a cavernous walk-in shower lined with gray pockmarked tiles. Strictly-rationed water (the only kind of water in the desert) meant the gigantic shower was limited to a five-minute flow. When Reggie and I merited rare shower time, Edith stood guard outside with a stopwatch.

Over the garage, Reggie and I did have fleeting privacy from Edith and Carl. But at night if I had to use the restroom, I had to creep through Reggie's room, trek down the rickety stairs in the dark, and take the chance of waking up Edith and Carl. I paid a heavy price—my constipation that began in "Desert Paradise" held me hostage for years.

The Haircut

Reggie pressured, "Do you know how to bleach out freckles?" She had them all over. I had no clue about stuff like that. What obsessed me was getting my inaugural haircut—a lure dangled by Edith, who didn't deliver. But Reggie did—when she soon introduced me to Jean, a somewhat nearby neighbor who cut hair at a "high-fashion place."

On the phone, Jean's raspy voice told us she might be willing to restyle my hair for free. "Well, depending on how long it is."

"It's fourteen years long, never been cut."

"Any coloring?"

"Are you kidding?" There was no coloring hair in my mother's world. The only things that changed color were the red beets she cooked that turned pink in Polish soups.

"Okay, okay. You can have a free haircut . . . if you give me everything left over. It might make a nice hairpiece," Jean's voice dropped low, "for someone who needs one."

"You mean like a charity case?"

"Not exactly, they'll have to pay a little something for it."

"It's a deal, but I have to have it now."

"Sure. I'll do it today, at my house, all for free, no salon fees."

Ten minutes later Reggie and I arrived at the front door of Jean's funky house built right into the mountainside.

"Come in girls," Jean cooed, a smoldering cigarette drooping between her scarlet tipped fingers while she directed us toward a short hallway. "I've set us up in the kitchen."

I followed Reggie, and Jean followed me, her fingers fondling strands of my pristine waist-length hair. When we entered the kitchen, Jean nudged me toward a high, swivel-type barstool next to a chipped Formica counter littered with assorted scissors, none-too-clean hairbrushes, and a square plastic basin. "Plant yourself down and get comfy," she said.

I couldn't scramble into that chair quick enough—the most important transformation of my life was about to happen.

Jean twirled me around. I studied her desert tan face that blended right into the mustard brown color of her stringy hair. *This woman really could use a good hairpiece*, I thought. Two glossy lips puffed out smoke reminding me of the dreaded Maestro of Doom. Bile rose in my throat. *Stop it!* I told myself. *Jean is your liberator, not your enemy.*

"Time to get beautiful." Jean took the plastic basin from the counter, placed it on the floor, and draped my shoulders with a giant pink plastic smock. Each scissor snip sent another long auburn swirl into the basin. With every lock, I shed vestiges of Immigrant Girl.

"Up to the sink and bend over." Jean's fingers massaged globs of shampoo into my scalp for blissful moments and poured hot, precious desert tap water in triple rinses over my hair.

"Back to the chair." Jean plucked pink plastic curlers from a cardboard box, wrapped shortened strands of hair around each tube, and lined them tight against my scalp. "Now thirty minutes under the dryer!"

My head, full of bumpy, prickly plastic curlers, was pushed into a giant shower-cap attached to a fat snake of plastic hose. Jean flicked the command switch and hot air immediately puffed up my head to triple size. During the next half hour of drying and waiting, my chest expanded and contracted with so much tension I thought I was having a teenage heart attack. Not until the timer went off, the cap deflated, and Jean unraveled the curlers did my panic subside and my breathing get normal.

"Now the best part—comb out and deep tease." Jean grunting, me inhaling, we got a rhythm going. "You have the thickest hair I've ever handled," Jean said. When she ripped off the plastic smock, her scarlet lips broke into an enormous grin. Jean shoved an almost smear-free, plastic mirror into my hands. "Voila!"

Staring back at me was a shocked teenage face surrounded by glorious, glistening auburn hair, ends flicked up and sassy, not a strand touching my shoulders. Immigrant Girl was gone forever! The teenage face looking at me was so pretty that I gave her a big wink.

From Reggie, I got briefed on her mother's life among the Hopi. Apparently, the Indian community gave Edith, their sometime-resident practical nurse, a coveted adobe house. Not that she had a legitimate diploma or certificate. As far as I knew, Edith had no formal nurses training. Hopi patients paid her in Old Pawn jewelry. Off-reservation collectors of such prized antiques were willing to pay plenty of dollars for them.

One night over the garage, we sat on Reggie's bed drinking Cokes snatched from the downstairs fridge. Reggie felt like talking about things she'd kept inside for a long time. "I was real little when Mom started to leave me alone to look after Dad . . . a lot." Her green eyes blinked back tears. Her stubby fingers twirled carrot colored strands of hair as she finished her thought. "She'd leave us to go back to her Hopis."

Apparently, Edith also had left severe emotional scars on Reggie. Even as a young girl, Reggie was expected to take care of herself and Carl, a security watchman who worked nights. It was strange how Reggie didn't complain about being lonely. Instead, she'd give a wry smile and say, "There's always a lot of guys around who like my company."

Reggie and I had parental neglect in common—we just handled it differently. We were same-age-opposites in background, academics, and our relationships with boys. During the year we lived together, Reggie and I were two lonely girls yearning for some kind of sisterhood, who became caring companions, until adults interfered. And they did.

Summer Camp—Edith's Version

After allowing me two weeks to settle into desert life in Sunnyslope, Edith decided that I was ready for more. No matter what I needed to experience she didn't include Reggie. Edith and our mother had something in common—neglecting their daughters while nurturing outsiders.

"Donna, you're going with me to the Hopi reservation," Edith said. "Get your stuff together!"

"What will I need to bring?" I had no idea how long we'd stay or where the reservation was located.

"The Hopis don't care what you wear." Edith shrugged. "It gets cold there at night—bring a sweater."

Over the garage, I threw random items of clothes into a canvas bag. Reggie sat on my bed and watched in silence, as if she already knew why only I was packing. Even though I wondered why Edith chose to take me and not Reggie, I wasn't compassionate enough to ask Reggie how she felt about being left behind. I was afraid to confront my sister Edith, who again like our Mother, issued orders freely and got no opposition.

Atop the Hopi high desert mesa, I learned how arduous daily life was up there. Water for every use had to be carried from a stream below. Women and girls lugged it up in heavy buckets. Toilet function for women and children was over a communal ditch, no modesty shown. Hopi men had their own place, I don't know where. My scanty memory of Hopi foods was that their fried bread tasted greasy and delicious, and that they took their main meal (a stew of mysterious ingredients) communally in a so-called Longhouse.

I sat in the corner of Edith's designated adobe dwelling, a silent observer of the long line of Hopis waiting to be summoned in by Edith. Each one told her what ailed them. Despite any lack of formal credentials, Edith responded as if she were a fully licensed doctor/dentist/midwife. She doled out advice and treatment for minor injuries, dental problems, pregnancy, and (I think) its prevention. Although Edith attended no actual birth while I was there, I heard tell from Hopi women that my sister was much admired as a midwife.

Before supper, Edith interviewed a different audience—Hopi youth newly accepted for fall attendance at the Phoenix Indian School. Edith selected a few among those kids to stay at her home in Sunnyslope for some sort of pre-entry counseling. She promised to also prep them about "off-res" relationships and rigorous academics awaiting them. I used to wonder if anyone had ever counseled Edith in the same way she had prepared Hopi youth for their upcoming challenges in life.

The Phoenix Indian School, or Phoenix Indian High School in its later years, was operated by the Bureau of Indian Affairs (BIA). During its existence, it was the only non-reservation BIA school in Arizona. From 1891 until it closed in 1990, Native American students from elementary through high school received off-reservation formal education paid for by the US Federal government.

As soon as we got back to Sunnyslope, I reveled in having a five-minute shower and sitting on a proper potty in the cavernous bathroom. But my leisure was short-lived. At the end of June, Edith issued my next assignment.

"We're going to Yellowstone—" she announced one morning. "Just think, you'll be working on a dude ranch!"

"What! I don't even know how to ride a horse. What will I do there?"

"We'll be there for a month. You'll be cleaning cabins," Edith said confidently. "I'll be in charge of the laundry—maybe you can work yourself up to something more interesting. " Her smirk wasn't assuring.

Again, Reggie was left behind.

The opulent beauty of Yellowstone National Park was almost surreal in contrast to the simplicity of Flagg Ranch. There, hard-working horses had to carry riders of all ages on trail rides guided by cowboys in jeans, boots, and sweat-stained felt hats. During that auspicious month, I fell in love with one of those cowboys, whose name has ridden away with him into the long-ago Wyoming sunset. Every teenage girl at the ranch was obsessed with being "in love." We all fantasized about those manly cowboys whose easy laughter and knowing eyes lured our attention across wooden tables in the employee dining room. When cowboy booted steps faded into the night, we'd sigh and sensuously inhale lingering smells of pungent horses, the great outdoors, and habitually chewed tobacco.

Yellowstone summer jobs were coveted and filled mostly by college kids. At Flagg Ranch, I was probably the youngest employee since I was still in high school. Edith was senior (in age, not status). Landing a job at the nearby elegant Old Faithful Lodge was top of the heap. Flagg Ranch in comparison was nothing to boast about. Late night steaming parties at hot mineral springs, enthusiastically attended by summer staff from all the surrounding lodges, were hot spots for socializing and gossiping about pay, perks, and bathing suits. I scraped bottom on all three.

It turned out Edith was right and wrong about Flagg Ranch. She also underestimated me. The entire month of July, Edith stayed put as Laundry Assistant, washing and folding endless sheets and towels. I started out as a cabin cleaner making guest beds with perfect, hospital corners, cleaning yellowing toilets, vacuuming everywhere like mad, and pocketing every cookie and potato chip left by departed guests. Within two weeks, I got promoted to Server /Ice-Cream-Shake-Maker in the employee dining room. Dipping hundreds of scoops of ice cream significantly built up my right arm strength, and I learned firsthand flirting techniques from the other girls competing for sexy winks from "my" cowboy.

Edith taught me lessons I didn't sum up until much later: how to read US roadmaps; no complaining; work, work, work; be grateful for any creature comfort earned from deprivation. When I still lived in Hartford and we exchanged letters, Edith delivered unsolicited grammar lessons. With each letter from her, she included my last one—slashed with red ink corrections. Until time passed, and she couldn't find any mistakes to cross out in red.

Sunnyslope High

One thing Edith couldn't dictate was the school calendar. My sophomore year at Sunnyslope High was about to begin. I had no lightweight clothes to wear—she couldn't postpone our shopping. Edith chose the store, Sears, and every item acquired: two pairs of over-large beige shorts; two ugly gray slacks; four drab neutral blouses; and one yucky yellow dress. The shoes Edith picked out for me were equally ugly: one pair of black penny loafers, one pair of stark white gym shoes, and one pair of old-lady sandals. My entire new wardrobe would be unimaginable to Sandra Dee and detested by me.

The Sunnyslope High student body was a melting pot of backgrounds, skin colors and origins. All of us were immigrants from somewhere else (except for nearby Phoenix Indian School, whose students were the only true natives of the land). However, at Sunnyslope High no one called me Immigrant Girl—there were no "insiders" or "outsiders." In retrospect, "pre-Hippy" probably described the laid back attitude, and my styled-by-Jean haircut could have been called "pre-chic."

During fourteen years of life in Hartford with Mother and Dad, I'd never heard them say a word about moving to Arizona. After Edith snatched me away to Arizona, our parents followed in less than a year.

Now I ask myself if I was a sacrificial pawn in the mind game of Edith vs. Mother and Dad. Had Edith calculated that by taking me to Arizona, they would follow? Was it jealousy, resentment, or revenge that drove Edith? When I was a naïve teenager, I didn't ask such probing questions.

It would take me decades of reflection and writing to recognize the remarkable fortitude of Hania and Juzo leaving Hartford in their senior years. Divesting their possessions and losing the support of Dad's extended family was as courageous as the young immigrants they'd been at the turn of the century, fleeing oppression in the Old World to face an unknown future in America

When my parents sold the house on Fairfield Avenue, along with all the furniture and most of their personal items, they surrendered two items that I never expected to lose—the oil portrait of Mother and the sepia photograph of her entire Old World family. I blamed Mother for surrendering those significant mementos to strangers, and I condemned myself for not telling her how much those visual treasures had meant to me. If she had brought them as her only tangible reminders of an aristocratic legacy, why did she impulsively dispose of them? Were they fabricated by consummate actress Mother as stage settings for her "Tragic Destiny" tales that captivated my childhood imagination? Had she acquired the evocative painting and vintage photograph from a stranger's estate sale? If anyone in the family had disclosed them as fakes, would I have believed them?

I'd also lost Old Glendale Farm, where my fantasies had grown as wild as the untended fields and gardens. When Hania and Juzo quick-sold the "prime rural" farm to a profiteering developer, he'd carved up three hundred acres into high-priced "prime country" lots designed to lure aspiring buyers. My childhood fantasy views of springtime trees budding in yellow and pink—gone. Vistas of summer's ponds laced with green algae—gone. Imaginary portraits of winter's diamond landscapes—gone. Instead, I was left with the legacy of family gossip—"Hania and Juzo sold hundred acres for what they pay twenty years before!"

Few would have considered Hania and Juzo a compatible couple. I never saw them treat other with kindness. Perhaps that was a consequence of their conflicting background—she'd been raised aristocratic and he came from a hardworking farming family—or maybe it was simply growing older and more vulnerable that caused my parents' ongoing alienation. However, in 1958, when they migrated to Arizona, Mother and Dad finally found a way to make peace together—they chose to live in separate houses. I was shocked by that decision. The only person who knew more than I did was my sister Edith, and she was the last person to whom I could turn for the truth.

Mother purchased, in a somewhat shabby downtown neighborhood of Phoenix, a two-story seven-bedroom house with two full bathrooms and a long front porch. She even managed to find forest green awnings reminiscent of those at Fairfield Avenue. And she negotiated good prices for old furniture from classified ads and secondhand furniture shops. With a sweep of flabby arms, Mother parted the sheer curtains of a downstairs window. In the far left corner, she placed the same wood-framed sign she'd been using for decades. Large black letters easily read by passers-by offered Rooms for Rent. Boarding House #3 was open for business!

Dad acquired a single-story ranch-style house, newly constructed in a former citrus grove on the boundary line of Phoenix and Sunnyslope, far enough from Mother downtown and Edith in the desert. He boasted, "Now I'm having fresh-picked oranges and grapefruit every day." With the exception of our time at Old Glendale Farm, this would be the first time in over forty-five years that there would be no tyrannical woman living with Dad and bossing him around. His freedom would last a decade, until his health failed and Edith would step in and take over. Like Mother, like daughter.

Dad and Mother in Dad's citrus grove,
Arizona, 1959

•

Sunnyslope High as "Home of the Vikings," was either odd or creative, considering their athletes competed in the desert. For sure, I was a sports ignoramus. What I instead found at Sunnyslope High was a haven of no-stress learning. Thanks to the academic rigors of 1950s Connecticut public schools and being a straight-A student my freshman year at Bulkeley High School, I didn't have to work hard to get top grades at Sunnyslope High. For the first time ever, I had incentive to participate in extracurricular activities, such as being elected to The National Honor Society, being voted Optimist Girl of the Year and campaigning for Student Body President. Losing by a few votes taught me the foibles of political leadership. Never again did I have any political ambition.

Reggie hung out with a different crowd at Bob's Big Boy Drive-In, "original double deck hamburger!" Her group drank their Cokes with Seagram's Seven. From a slick-haired, muscle-ripped boyfriend called Petey Powers (my pseudonym), Reggie learned about car repair, drag racing, and sex in his hot rod Chevy.

Edith and Carl didn't get to meet Petey until one day, when all hell broke loose at the end of sophomore year. Edith just happened to be off reservation and at home in Sunnyslope when the phone call came from Sunnyslope High's school counselor. Reggie and Petey had been arrested for shoplifting auto parts from the local Texaco station. Edith and Carl had to bail out Reggie at the Sunnyslope police headquarters. Whether Petey had to spend some time in jail, I'd never know.

Holed up in my room over the garage, I was probably doing homework when I heard the wagon pull in below, followed by doors slamming and angry voices shouting words I couldn't decipher. Minutes later, I heard the wooden stairs rattle with violent stomping. Edith barreled through Reggie's room and raged into my room.

"*You* are responsible for what happened to Reggie!" Edith shrieked. Her body was shaking. She lunged around the room with such fury that her tinted glasses fell off. Terrified, I stood staring. Her eyes were tinged with inhuman yellow around the irises. My out of control sister grabbed my arm, dug her fingers deep into my flesh, dragged me up from my chair, and slammed me against the wall.

"You knew what was going on with Reggie!" she screamed. "Why didn't you tell me?" Edith was so close that the pockmark scars on her face were magnified in ugly detail.

Childhood memories of Mother's abuse coursed through me. But this time was different. Now I wasn't a scared little girl, I was a teenager enraged by injustice. The sister I'd trusted, who promised me a new, healthy life had not taken good care of her own daughter. And outrageously, she was blaming me for her own sins.

"You're her mother!" I shouted in disgust. "You deserted Reggie to be with Hopi kids. She was left alone a lot. No wonder she got into trouble."

Edith gasped and struck me full force, across my face.

I stumbled backward. My fingers trembled as I covered my blistering cheek, and I traveled backward in time. Was Mother looming over me, the whipping belt wrapped around her fist? No, this was her daughter Edith. We faced each other in the middle of the room, our eyes assessing, tension escalating like desert heat rising.

Edith jerked herself around. I could see the heavy streams of sweat down the back of her traditional Hopi blouse. Her long legs, the ones she was so proud to shown off, propelled Edith out of my room and across Reggie's room.

At the exit door leading to the stairs, she halted—had she forgotten something?

I watched and waited.

"You don't belong here!" she screamed at me. "Get out!"

Over the garage, I packed up my worldly possessions. Being expelled from "Desert Paradise" meant I had to find a new place to live. How would I be able to continue at Sunnyslope High School for my junior year? I never knew where Reggie was that night. Maybe she hid out in the cavernous bathroom, behind the only door that could be closed and locked. Surreptitiously, I crept downstairs, entered the house, and prayed the coast was clear. Luck was with me—no Edith, no Carl, no Reggie in sight. In the corner of the living room, I reached for the black desk phone. My hands shook as I dialed.

"Jean, it's me, Donna, I need another huge favor. Tomorrow morning, can you drive me to Phoenix?"

"No hair trim, just a ride?"

"Yes, only a lift downtown, to my mother's place. Maybe some folks there will need their hair cut."

"Kiddo, I've got plenty of clients at the salon tomorrow. If you can be ready to go at seven, I'll pick you up."

Reggie and I never saw each other again. Edith and Carl sent her off to reform school—or so I heard—to be "rehabilitated" from her bad habits. I couldn't blame Reggie for anything that had happened. Edith had betrayed us both. She was like The Boyle of my childhood, who took insidious pleasure from demoralizing vulnerable victims. Years into the future, I'd hear news of Reggie, via the Hartford family grapevine that trailed across miles. The gossip was that Reggie had given birth to an illegitimate baby, but eventually married the child's father. I'd always wonder if his name was Petey Powers.

Coming of Age

Mary Jane

Jean drove her clunker car reeking of cigarette smoke from Sunnyslope to Phoenix. I tried to inhale fresh air from the open passenger side window and clear my thoughts. How was I going to explain to Mother why Edith had kicked me out?

We pulled up to Boarding House #3, unloaded my two suitcases and three large boxes, and lugged them up to the front door. I reached for Jean. "You've rescued me again." I hugged her. "If anyone needs a haircut, I'll send them straight to you."

"Do that, kiddo, and we're even." Jean's cerise polished fingers, lit cigarette dangling between them, rested gently on my shoulders.

Baggage piled around me, I waved good-bye to my generous friend, rang the bell, and waited.

Mother came to the door and shoved it wide open. "Why you here?" Angry face. "Not with Edith?"

"Reggie's in trouble. Edith blamed me and kicked me out." After that, I tried to fill in details that I didn't even understand myself.

Mother and I sat together in the kitchen and talked. My junior year

81

was coming up. Where could I live and not have to change high schools? The boarding house was twenty miles away from Sunnyslope High. Dad's place was on the wrong side of the Sunnyslope-Phoenix boundary line. I knew that selling off everything in Connecticut had funded my parents' two separate houses in Arizona, and that morning I learned something else—unpredictable Mother had acquired a third place. "I buy for good rent income." Mother gave a rare explanation of her motives. Apparently, she had a small, furnished cottage, empty and waiting for a tenant. And by amazing circumstance—or Mother's savvy instincts—it was located in the town of Sunnyslope.

Mary Jane Hart, a single mother from Whitehall, Montana, had long been searching. Her young daughter, Lisa, born with severe handicaps, needed residential care. When Lisa was five years old, a special needs school in Phoenix had an opening. Lisa's care in the new city would cost a lot. Mary Jane needed a new job, and she found one. Beginning the first day of summer, 1958, Mary Jane Hart would be Greater Phoenix Youth Recreational Director, responsible for hundreds of teens from multi-ethnic neighborhoods in a city nothing like Whitehall, Montana.

Mary Jane had spent her first day in Phoenix enrolling Lisa at the residential school. Late that night, driving through a downtown neighborhood, she noted *Rooms for Rent* in the window of an otherwise unremarkable two-story house. Hoping for something she could afford, Mary Jane rang the bell. Mother, who stayed up late, had opened the door.

"I need a room," Mary Jane pleaded.

Without knowing anything about her, Mother instantly vetted Mary Jane as "good person" and gave her the last vacant room. Her gut instinct would pay off with Mary Jane Hart.

After I'd been kicked out of Edith's house, Mother knocked hard on the door of Mary Jane's room. As soon as Mary Jane opened it a crack, Mother barged in. "I'm having little house in Sunnyslope-not-far," Mother announced. "For very low rent, is yours—if you are looking after daughter Danusia, no-trouble-go-all-day-Sunnyslope-High-School."

Mary Jane, warm-hearted woman on a tight budget, agreed on the spot. That afternoon we moved into the Sunnyslope cottage.

Living with Mary Jane turned out to be better than any paradise I could've imagined. Five days a week, the Sunnyslope High school bus dropped me two blocks away from the cottage, where the door was never locked. I'd find Mary Jane doing what she loved best—sitting on the living room floor, her athletic tan legs crossed flat against the floor, yoga style. Her head, covered with short, curly brown hair, bobbed up and down as she poked fun around a circle of teenagers howling with laughter. No matter age or skin color, everyone got her special attention. The year with Mary Jane was filled with affection, warm bodies, and irresistible rock and roll music.

"Hey girl, get down here!" one of the kids would say. "We got all kinda snacks. Tell us 'bout your day."

I'd toss my book bag into the corner and slide into the circle, confident that I belonged there. We called ourselves "Mary Jane's Kids." The size of the group expanded and contracted depending on who needed a place to stay. Parents showed up at different times to claim their teenagers at Mary Jane's place.

Nicknaming became a competitive sport. "Runnin' Rosie," for her rapid-fire Spanglish; "Watchin' Ramon," who loved only one thing as much as he loved Rosie—making us double up with laughter by mimicking our quirks. "Amazin' Amon," astonishing athlete who could twist into dance positions none of us could pull off, no matter how hard we tried or how compelling the music. I was "The Fixer" of burned out light bulbs, dropped clothes, clearing off the table before dessert. More than five decades later, I've kept the compulsion but lost the nickname.

The music! A vintage kitchen radio wasn't loud enough. So, Mary Jane bought a secondhand record player, and kids brought their own rock and roll vinyls. We'd shout-sing along with Dick Clark's American Bandstand and dance like crazy on the makeshift dance floor, a one-degree-cooler screened in porch. Mary Jane charmed everyone, including the neighbors who adored her, and no one ever complained about our racket.

I didn't know the name of the illness that ravaged little Lisa, only that she suffered from severe mental and physical handicaps. Every morning before work and every single weekend, Mary Jane went to visit Lisa. Until the morning of May 15, one week before the end of my junior year, when little Lisa died in her mother's arms.

I entered an ominous and silent cottage. Mary Jane was alone, no boisterous teens around her. Wrapping her arm around my shoulders, she led me to the living room and sat me down next to her on the sagging sofa. I studied Mary Jane's face for clues. The sparkle in her blue-gray eyes was gone, her animated lips were pursed tight.

"Lisa's in a special place now," Mary Jane whispered, "where all sweet, innocent children can play their hearts out, free from any pain." Her breaths became anguished gasps. Our tears flowed, and we hugged. Mary Jane reached down, grasped my hands tight.

"With Lisa gone, I must return to Montana, to grieve with my family." Her words filled my heart with dread. How was I going to manage my life without Mary Jane in it?

"There's still a way for us." Mary Jane's voice sounded almost normal. "You can fill the void in my heart. If you come with me to Montana, my people will love you as much as I do."

My hopes surged. Would Mother let me go to Montana? Everyone loved and trusted Mary Jane.

Fueled by love more powerful than our fears, Mary Jane and I went to face Mother. At Boarding House #3, we three gathered around the kitchen table: Mother sat on one of the hardwood ladder-back chairs, her heavy body shifting constantly to find a comfortable position. Mary Jane sat opposite Mother, hands clenching and unclenching. I sat between them, hunched forward, scrutinizing the two most important women in my life. Mother's gaze wandered from me, to Mary Jane, and to the half-filled mug of milky tea and bits of mysterious crumbs in front of her on the plastic tablecloth.

Mary Jane made a passionate plea—I would be nurtured, loved, and safe in Montana; the high school there was a really good one. I would fit right in. Spending my senior year in the embrace of her welcoming family, Mary Jane promised, would be better for me than changing to a new high school in Phoenix and living who knows where or with whom.

No rational person could read Mother's mind. If she had one consistency, it was unpredictability. Under the table, my fingers crossed so tightly they went numb. I was sure Mother could hear my pounding heart. Minutes seemed like hours. I was horrible at waiting.

Mother raised her mug, took a deep swallow, and spoke. "Now Edith no good. Juzo's place not in Sunnyslope . . . In Phoenix with me, only bad high school for you." Mother and I made eye contact. "Danusia, I'm let you go to Montana. You be better there—with Mary Jane."

I hugged Mother. Mary Jane hugged Mother and me. Three bodies clung to each other as if merged into one.

But there was a remaining detail—telling Dad. Mother said she would do it. "I'm drive to his house. We talk."

Mary Jane and I returned to the Sunnyslope cottage filled with hope. Dad had always done what Mother wanted. Why would this time be any different?

The next morning, the phone rang in the cottage. Mary Jane picked it up. "It's your mother," she said smiling, her hand over the receiver. As she listened to Mother's voice, Mary Jane's face fell. Her eyes shifted away from me, her body tensed.

"Yes, I understand." Mary Jane's voice was barely audible. "I'll tell Donna." With infinite care, she replaced the phone in its cradle. "Your father won't agree to let you go. Your mother agrees with him now." She reached out and held my hand in hers for silent moments.

What could I do? Should I go see Dad, try to convince him to let me go? Mother had always ruled at home, yet my passive dad had picked this one time to oppose her. His "No" was astonishing. But when had I ever understood the actions of my parents? Picking up the phone, I called Mother.

"Manusia, you let me go with Edith and she's a mess!" I wailed.

"Is true, Edith no good for you—or for Reggie." That was a striking admission coming from Mother. "Juzo is right. We don't let you go . . . to strangers."

I felt like a child again, trying to convince Mother to save me from someone like the Maestro of Doom and his stinky cigars. Mother hadn't changed—she wasn't moved by my suffering. And she refused to budge.

In the memory-filled kitchen of Sunnyslope cottage, Mary Jane and I turned up the volume on the little radio, preset to Top Fifties Hits. The Everly Brothers were singing their hearts out. Mary Jane reached for my hand, gave it a long, gentle squeeze and said, "My dear, sweet girl, I shall always love you no matter how many miles we're apart." Then we listened to the song:

> Bye, Bye love.
> Bye, Bye happiness.
> Hello loneliness. I think I'm gonna cry.

Like an oasis in the desert, Mary Jane appeared in my life when I needed to be saved. She gave me love and sustenance in a home filled with kids who adored her and each other. Finally, I'd found a place of *belonging*. My year with Mary Jane taught me how to trust and open my heart, and I learned something that would stay planted in my psyche—that every relationship happens for a reason. Some last for a short time, some stay longer. I wondered if I was meant to be with someone I loved for a really long time.

It Will Be Wonderful

The beginning of summer 1959, I was holed up in an airless room on the second floor of Boarding House #3 in downtown Phoenix. Heat wrapped me like a straitjacket, and my head throbbed. For one year I'd been safe and adored as one of Mary Jane's Kids. But I'd lost my tribe. Never again would we dance together to rock and roll music that shook the walls and stirred our souls. How was I going to get through the summer? Even if Sunnyslope High would allow a straight-A student living outside the school district to graduate with her class, where was I going to live?

While I agonized about my future, Mother was plotting a way to distract me. Unfathomable as always, she suddenly chose to remember Jennie, the woman I'd called "Grandma S." For a brief time during my childhood, we'd cared for the waif-thin Seventh-day Adventist as if she was a member of our family. She'd spent the final months of her ninety-eighth year with us in Hartford. The day my only grandma died had been the saddest of my childhood.

After Grandma's death, Mother had sorted through Jennie's meager possessions until she found her heavily worn Bible. On a back page titled Family Members, the list included "Jennie S, born 1849." Mother had used a leaky ballpoint and scribbled in her erratic penmanship next to Jennie's name, "Died March 15, 1947." She didn't think it was right to list our address as Jennie's residence. According to her Bible, Jennie was the oldest member of the family's clan in Los Angeles, California.

Mother re-examined the old evidence in Jennie's Bible. "Here is address for them—is good." It was as if Mother had known to keep the Bible, because she'd need it twelve years later.

Somehow she convinced a long-distance telephone operator to surrender an unlisted telephone number for Joseph S Sr. of Los Angeles. Within twenty-four hours, Mother had made contact with the family. I'd never know what motivated Mother to suddenly call up an unpaid debt. Did she feel guilty about promising me I could leave Phoenix with Mary Jane? Was Mother sorry that she'd given in to Dad's decision, acquiesced to his judgment, perhaps for the first time ever, as being better for me than her own?

Mother phoned the S family in California, and they hadn't forgotten who'd cared for Grandma S at the end of her life. I pictured Mother's powers of persuasion working Mrs. Joe S Sr. over the phone. How else would she have elicited the incredible invitation for me to be guest of the S family in California for two weeks, including a round-trip plane ticket? Though Mother casually shrugged off their generosity, saying, "Is no problem for rich people."

My very first flight aboard a silver clipper, passengers around me focused on the clinking bottles and icy concoctions offered by the stewardess pushing a cocktail cart down the aisle. Tucked away in my seat by the porthole window, I stared at white nothingness as we flew through a world of billowy clouds. Suddenly, atop a white cloud cliff, Grandma S appeared, proud and erect in her favorite high-back chair, silver hair crowned by an elegant chignon. Ever so slowly, she turned to face me and spoke words only I could hear. "You'll see—it will be wonderful!" A surge of throttled engines sent tremors through the aircraft, rattled the drinks cart, and diverted my attention from the window to the nervous and fidgeting passengers around me. When things settled down, I turned back to the window. But Grandma S had disappeared.

For the rest of the flight, my nerves irritated my bladder and sent me out of my seat to the restroom so often that a vigilant stewardess stopped me at the rear galley. "My dear," her arm wrapped gently around my shoulders, "is there anything you need?"

"No thank you." I tried to look sophisticated. "Really, I'm prepared . . . for everything."

Yet, in the massive arrival hall of Los Angeles International Airport, I wasn't prepared at all—for the gorgeous guy with sparkling green eyes, dressed in knife-pleated beige chinos and a chocolate brown corduroy jacket. Instinctively, he seemed to recognize me in the crowd of disembarking passengers. He walked straight to me, carrying a bouquet of yellow roses tied with satin streamers.

"You must be Donna," he said, his voice low and compelling as he extended the bouquet. "I'm Joe S, Jennie's grandson. My family can't thank you enough for taking care of her."

"What beautiful flowers." My eyes grew moist. "I was just a little girl then, and I loved your grandma like she was my own." Tears began to creep down my cheeks. "I think she knew we would meet one day." I sniffled but had no tissues.

Joe reached into his jacket pocket and produced a crisp white handkerchief that he pressed into my palm. When his long fingers brushed against my forearm, prickles of warmth trickled across my skin.

"Come, let's get your suitcase," he said. "I hope you brought a scarf to wrap that auburn hair. My car's a convertible."

I'd never even stepped into a convertible, let alone a sexy red MG that sighed and purred in sync with Joe's nimble gear shifting. I didn't own even one pretty scarf, but I pretended to search through my borrowed tote bag. "It seems I forgot to pack one of my scarves," I said, my voice deliberately low. "It's a good thing I'm used to the wind."

"Well, we'll have to go shopping." Joe smiled. "I'll choose one to go with your hair."

In the sleek convertible, wind blowing through my hair, cruising through balmy Southern California, I lost track of time. Until crunching sounds under the MG brought me back—we'd left the highway. I blinked at the scene ahead. A long, gravel drive led to the most romantic Mediterranean villa I'd ever seen—in movies. It was like a beautiful landscape painting where whitewashed walls gleamed, scarlet bougainvillea clustered, and dancing shapes of sun and shade filtered through the canopy of trees. Joe drove the MG to end of the drive, flicked the ignition switch off, and leaped out of the car. With a flourish, he opened the passenger door and stretched out his hand to receive my palm.

"This is it, pretty one—my family's place," Joe said.

Trying to look alluring while easing out of a low convertible was not easy, but I did my best. "Let's go inside," Joe pressed my hand, "the folks are anxious to meet you." A portrait flashed into my mind, the one of Mother when she was young and beautiful and could have easily walked in the gardens of the Tsar.

Now I can't remember how Susan and Joe Sr. actually looked or what they wore. But I never forgot how intimidated I felt by their sophistication and lifestyle. It was a world beyond anything I could've imagined in my sketchbook, a world seemingly designed by MGM studios—pure 1950s Beverly Hills. The legendary domain of movie stars and moguls: Rodeo Drive boutiques where women matched their wardrobe to their lofty aspirations; trendy restaurants where the right table and "being seen" surpassed any temptations on the menu. I imagined myself as the lead in a Hollywood movie—*Scene One: provincial teenage girl budding with nascent sensuality and lust for adventure, awaits seduction. Her fantasies about a handsome hero are about to come true.*

Each morning at the S family villa on a shaded breakfast terrace overhung with perfumed, flowering vines, invisible servant hands arranged a table-for-two draped with ivory linen. Buttery French croissants, fresh-squeezed orange juice, and a silver carafe of chicory-laced coffee awaited. I soon realized that only Joe and I were expected for breakfast—no one else ever joined us.

With each unstructured day, it also became clear that our only agenda was lounging by the kidney shaped pool. Wearing a Sandra Dee pink bikini, I stretched out on a lime green terrycloth covered chaise. Joe couldn't know that the swimsuit and most everything else in my suit-case were borrowed from Jadzia, a well-endowed Polish nursing student staying at Mother's boarding house. If Joe suggested a dip in the water, I wouldn't be able to hide the wads of tissues I'd stuffed into the oversized bra top. Turned out that he had zero interest in swimming, and I would have more compelling things to figure out.

"You have gorgeous skin." Joe's sensitive fingers tracing along my thighs made me tingle with pleasure. He made fingertip circles around my lips. "Be sure to take good care of these lips, keep them moist like they are now." His instinct for the right words was incorrigible. "Donna ... you are so beautiful and sweet smelling ... soft in all the right places."

My tumescent dreams were never this good. Now there were real kisses in places never kissed before. "Joe, I've never felt like this with any-one else."

His magnetic touch sent heat waves through my body. Our leisurely days together encouraged Joe to talk and me to listen. "I want to tell you everything about me." Having graduated from Harvard-Westlake, an elite prep school that sent affluent young Californians "back East," he'd been accepted pre-med at Duke University, to start in the fall. "I've always wanted to be a doctor. To help and heal is my destiny." His words stim-ulated my starry eyed imagination. How easily I imaged myself as the adoring wife or Joe S, eminent MD.

Just as Grandma S had promised, it was wonderful. A miracle did happen when her grandson came into my life. He was a gorgeous, con-fident man who made me feel adored, pampered, and safe. Right up to our last moment together.

At Los Angeles International, Joe and I clung to each other. "When I take my flight back east to Duke, I'll stop over for a few days in Phoenix," he said, his emerald green eyes smoldering with desire. "We'll be together there. And after that, Homecoming at Duke will be perfect." My soul stirred with passion. "Will you come to me ..." his moist lips nibbling my ear.

"My Joe," I swooned, "of course I'll be with you."

Like Cinderella whose golden evening evaporated at midnight when she returned to her dismal scullery, a penniless high school girl from

Phoenix, Arizona returned to her dingy room at her mother's boarding house. For the rest of the summer, I escaped into my sublime fantasies. Handsome, sophisticated, and college-bound Joe was meant for me. Hadn't Destiny and Grandma S willed us to be together?

Reality wrote a different ending. I composed passionate love letters to Joe, but never mailed a single one. And no letter from Joe ever reached me. When the time came for him to leave for Duke, he didn't stop in Arizona. I invented reasons why: Joe's parents forbid any change of plans. He was forced to travel non-stop from LA to Durham, North Carolina. He had no other choice. Joe and I never had our reunion in Phoenix, or anywhere else.

A year later, the mailman delivered to Mother's boarding house, a heavy parchment envelope, creamy bisque in color with double postage for its extra weight. Addressed solely to Mother, it contained an even thicker card enveloped in a sleeve of fine tissue paper. The engraved message announced that Mr. & Mrs. Joseph S, Jr. had been married on June 5th, 1960 in the Duke University Chapel. The marriage date coincided with what I calculated to be the end of Joe's freshman year at Duke.

Joe had been totally irresistible to naïve and lonely me. I couldn't keep myself from yearning for someone to finally love and protect me. Joe was a self-obsessed Adonis, virile yet gentle. I saw him as my perfect Prince Charming who would sweep me away into a world of luxury, beauty, and safety. It would take me many more decades to realize I could only reach such a place of security by empowering myself.

Dad's Dark Side

My dad had a dark and different lesson to teach me. It took place during my last year at Sunnyslope High School. Administration agreed to bend rules and allow me to graduate with my class—if I lived somewhere near the district. Dad's address would qualify. I moved into the back bedroom of his house, where I had a side view of the citrus grove, a spacious closet (with a door), and my very own bathroom. The comfort of this quiet home was a deception. Violence lurked there.

Well into my senior year, I finally had a date. I don't remember his name, only that he was a skinny guy with curly red hair who played clarinet in the Sunnyslope High band. He picked me up in a car borrowed from his brother, took me to a concert at school, and drove me home before my 10:00 p.m. curfew. We sat chatting in the car for a few minutes, no kissing, not even handholding, sharing only our shyness.

Walking up the driveway to the house, I turned and waved goodbye. At the entry door side window, I could see lights glowing inside. *Dad must still be up, probably asleep in his favorite chair,* I thought. I used my key and slowly pushed the door open to the vestibule.

An ominous figure was waiting—his face was boiling red, his blue eyes riveted on me. His sour odor was terrible. How could this wild looking man be my senior citizen dad? A powerful shove hit my chest, flung me back against the front door.

"You whore! Dirty whore with that boy right outside in that car?" A hand rough from gardening came flying at my face and struck like burning sandpaper across my cheek, lips, and jaw. "You disgusting whore. My daughter the whore!" Fury and spittle poured from his mouth.

Never in my life had my withdrawn and placid dad, old enough to be my grandfather when I was born, even raised his voice to me. But neither had he defended me during my childhood when violence triggered Mother into rampages through the house, chasing me with the hated leather belt coiled around her hand. My dad had abandoned me then. And now he'd unleashed his own inner demons against me.

I fled to my bedroom, slammed shut the door without locking it, and crawled into my bed. Tears streamed down my bruised cheek that stung like fire. No episode of Mother's abuses had demolished me like Dad's singular outburst. His transformation had shaken me to my core. Finally, sleep enveloped me like a coma.

In the morning I awoke fully clothed, stretched like a log across the single bed. Leaning on my elbow, I bent my legs, pushed them over the bed to the floor, and staggered to the bathroom. I wondered, *Did I have a terrible nightmare?*

The mirror over the sink gave a wretched answer. My puffed-up lids squeezed my eyes into slits. The sides of my face looked like they belonged to two different people. One side appeared normal; the other side was like a semi-inflated, crimson balloon. A long purple bruise jagged to my chin and spread into a bumpy rash from neck to collarbone. No nightmare had caused this ugly face.

A few minutes later, I made my way toward the kitchen. I could hear Dad at the back door, preparing to come into the house from the garden. Preoccupied with a basket of fresh picked grapefruit, he didn't notice me watching him. He looked like a harmless old man—so different from the night before. Yet, I was still afraid of him. Smiling at his collection, he gently set the basket on the cement floor leading to the kitchen and lowered himself to a stool by the door. With effort, he bent to remove rubber garden boots caked with mud and mush. It was Saturday, the day after irrigation, when a thin flood of water over the yard had receded, leaving its slimy brown residue. Dad kept the boots side by side on the shabby rug by the back door, and never hosed them off. "Waste of time," he used to say. "Only get dirty again."

When Dad entered the kitchen, he couldn't avoid seeing me at the counter, reaching up to the cupboard for a plate. Yet, he walked right past, said not a word. On other days his silence wouldn't have been unusual. However, that day my dad didn't pass for normal. He never apologized for his shocking eruption and violence. Although he never again lashed out at me, I never stopped fearing that he would.

Was there a link of festering violence in my mother, my sister, and my dad? Had anger taken root in our family and clung to them like poisonous vines? What about me had provoked in them the need to punish someone innocent? Mother, as a young woman, had been cast out by her parents in a doomed attempt to save seven sons and themselves from the terrorist Bolshevik onslaught. Such betrayal could well have planted toxic seeds in Mother's psyche, later to poison her mental stability. Edith had been raised as an only child until the sudden invasion of the Holden girls, who she had to accept as four instant "sisters." As an adult, Edith manifested Mother's worst characteristics when she dismissed the needs of her own daughter and violently punished me, the young sister she'd pledged to nurture.

As for Dad, I had overheard plenty of family gossip about "Juzo's other women." When I was a naïve child, I thought that referred to his domestic realm of women—Mother, Edith, the Holden girls, and me decades later. Mother and Dad hadn't shared the same bedroom in our home on Fairfield Avenue. But not until his physical attack and sexual obscenities lashed against me as a teenager did I realize my dad was a misogynist. "Other women" had somehow fostered Dad's depravity— yet I'd never know why or how.

Only through later sessions of personal therapy would I finally be able to soothe the neglected girl of my childhood and vow to heal my own wounds. I was determined to put an end to the cycle in my fam- ily—of damaged adults passing on their dysfunction to their children.

The Secret Benefactor

The Sunnyslope High School Class of 1960 couldn't wait for graduation a month away. There were parties every weekend, but I was in no mood to celebrate. When a senior asked "Where 'ya going?" it meant to which college. I hadn't applied anywhere. According to Mother, "You have nothing but silly drawing—no talent to deserve expensive education." Apparently she had forgotten that when she'd first arrived to America, it was her artistic ability to retouch photographs and make them look like portraits that had given Mother her only livelihood.

At Sunnyslope High Awards Night, they called out my name as "Outstanding Business Student" of my graduating class. Everyone knew this was a hyped up award for best grades in shorthand and typing. However, those practical skills would enable my escape from my family in Arizona and open doors for me in decades to come.

One of my habits, reading newspaper want ads in *The Phoenix Republic*, gave me a fertile idea. The US Department of State adver- tised secretarial positions open to qualified applicants willing to work overseas. I phoned for an application. It didn't matter where they sent me—I'd go anywhere!

When paperwork arrived a few days later, I used my best typing skills to list my National Honor Society grades, my high school business teachers as references, and my official residence as my dad's house. Adding extra stamps on the envelope, I mailed it. Every day, when I checked the mailbox and found there was nothing for me, my anxiety grew. Two long weeks had passed when old Mrs. Dewhurst from next door (she and Dad exchanged grapefruits for oranges) stopped me in the driveway. "Donna, who are the men asking questions about you?" Mrs. Dewhurst was almost deaf—her answers must have given the FBI investigators an earful.

But after two more weeks, a fat manila enveloped marked US Department of State appeared in the mailbox. Grabbing it up, I raced to the kitchen, sat down at the table and pulled out the contents. The letterhead was impressive, royal blue ink embellished with a red, white, and blue official crest. My breathing got faster and faster, my hands shook as I read:

```
You have been accepted for employment by the United
States Department of State.
Assignment—Junior Level Secretary
Location—KABUL, AFGHANISTAN
```

I was astounded. Without that letter in front of me, I wouldn't have known how to spell Kabul, Afghanistan. Until I located the city and country in The World Atlas, I'd no idea they even existed.

The next morning in the kitchen, I was buttering my toast when the phone rang. Sunnyslope High School Counseling Office needed to see me immediately. I wondered, *Is there a problem with my graduation records?* From the window, I could see my dad working in the garden, so I decided to borrow the car and make a quick trip to campus.

A solo counselor in the office sat at a desk piled high with papers and files. "Donna, good to see you . . . better sit down." He pointed to a folding chair next to his desk and pulled out a file from the messy stack. "Young lady, it seems you have an anonymous benefactor."

I was stunned to learn that I'd been awarded a full-tuition, four-year merit scholarship to attend Arizona State University. My own mother thought I was a girl without talent, except for "foolish drawing," who didn't deserve an expensive education. How was it possible that a total stranger would want to pay for my college education?

ASU was in Tempe, no need to check the atlas. The campus was only thirteen miles from Dad's house. Suddenly I had two choices— ASU or Afghanistan? Both were intimidating, and I had to make a critical decision. Either one would change my life.

Times-A-Changing

I never learned the identity of my anonymous benefactor. More than five decades later, I still speculate about the life-changing decision I had to make at age seventeen. What would have been my future if I'd taken the job in Afghanistan instead of accepting the scholarship at Arizona State University?

During the first few weeks of freshman year, there were far easier choices to make—which classes to take, when to study, and where to live. Coeds with charisma, image, and the right legacy would choose to go through Sorority Rush Week. Those who passed the gauntlet would be invited to live in campus sorority houses. For former Immigrant Girl, being judged by others was enemy territory. If anyone asked me whether I'd be going through "rush," I'd shrug dismissively and answer, "Not interested."

"Welcome to ASU's dorm for nerdy gals," voiced a tall girl with shiny braces as she checked me into South Hall, my campus home.

Quickly, I unpacked my minimal wardrobe: assorted drawing supplies, double sets of bed linens, and a zipper bag of toiletries. Later, the unoccupied floor space on my side of the closet would serve a unique purpose. Judy, my red-haired roommate from Durango, Colorado arrived with extra everything, including a super-generous heart. During freshman year, Judy became my precious friend and willing foil against surprise invasions by Mother.

Right after I moved into the dorm at ASU, Mother started something new—she began to drive from Phoenix to Tempe. Without any prior notice and at random times of day or night, Mother would arrive on campus. In spite of her broken English, she managed to acquire the dorm entry code for South Hall. Only the mind-boggling layout of the ASU campus prevented her from also finding the Registrar's Office and getting a copy of my class schedule. Using her stolen code, she'd slip into South Hall, head for the stairway to the second floor, turn right and count down four identical doors. She was infallible about finding my room. Soon, gossip was rampant at South Hall about the strange woman, grey-brown hair flying and corpulent body bursting the seams of her housedress, carrying overflowing crockery food bowls to "Donna's room." No one had to ask me who she was—they knew.

Although I got used to the gossip about Mother's invasions, I never stopped fearing her unpredictability. What was coming next? Why the sudden urge to take care of me? Was she driven by guilt for the years of neglecting me while running the Hartford boarding house? Or was she trying to make amends for entrusting me to Edith, who had proven to be an irresponsible mother to Reggie and a vengeful sister to me? Because I had no hope of second-guessing Mother's motives, I decided to invent what I desperately longed to believe—that Mother actually loved me. That her tribute bowls of "good healthy" Polish food were gestures of love she felt, but otherwise couldn't express.

But I lacked courage to test that perception by asking Mother face to face. Instead I avoided her in every way possible. My scholarship didn't cover room and board, so I worked twenty hours a week as secretary to the Dean of the Foreign Language Department, and I carried a heavy course load in my dual major of English and Business. Mostly Judy was there in our dorm room when furious banging on the door signaled Mother's arrival. If the door wasn't locked, she'd barge right in.

When Mother showed up during the day and I was out, Judy would greet Mother with a beatific smile. "So sorry, Donna's at class." If Mother showed up after dark, Judy would explain, "Donna's at the library—she studies a lot." Mother would shove a dripping bowl of Polish leftovers at Judy. "I'll be sure Donna knows this is waiting for her." Judy would promise in her soothing voice. Mother never lingered. As soon as her heavy footsteps faded away down the hall, Judy would head for the "residents only" back stairs to the dorm kitchen, where she'd scrape the bowl's contents into a garbage pail. Back in our room, she'd add another chipped crockery bowl to the growing stack of sticky, smelly dishes on my side of the closet floor. I nicknamed my roomie "Saint Judy."

Whenever I returned to the dorm and entered our room, I'd sing out, "Saint Judy—has she been here?"

Judy would answer, "Count the bowls, sweetheart." And we'd both giggle.

Donna at ASU, 1960   Roommate Judy at ASU, 1960

Return of the Mermaid

One day, hungry and late for my English Lit class, I rushed through the main lounge hoping to snatch a stray bowl of popcorn for lunch. No such luck, only the TV was blaring in the deserted lounge.

Walt Disney's voice wouldn't normally have caught my attention, but a fleeting image of The Muse of Copenhagen, aka The Little Mermaid, sure did. Walt was talking about his travel series. "Tell me, Lotte, why do you think this lovely mermaid is symbolic of your city?"

I stared at the television, where my best friend of long ago, who once had worn a crisp blue jumper and possessed humor smooth and delicious as butter, was looking out at me from that TV screen. Even though Lotte was grown up and dressed in a trim suit and silk blouse, I would have recognized her anywhere. "We Danes love our Mermaid," she said. "Because she swims with strength and beauty, and her spirit of independence inspires us to be proud and true to ourselves."

From thousands of miles away, for a few fleeting moments, Lotte returned to me. And like the symbolic Little Mermaid, Lotte assured me that her Danish spirit was still there, encouraging as always. Never would I forget Lotte's message.

By the end of freshman year, I had sobering facts to face: ASU wasn't far enough from Mother; I needed to put at least 1,000 miles between us; Kabul was a long-gone option; and I had zero extra money for a survival fund. At ASU's Financial Aid office, I pleaded "serious financial problems" to a compassionate staff person. After listening to my story and decision to work full-time, but hopefully attend ASU part-time, she reassigned my merit scholarship money to cover as many night courses as I could manage.

But where to get a full-time job with a real salary? My boss, the Dean of the Foreign Language Department, came to my rescue. He phoned an executive friend at General Electric's Computer Division headquartered in Phoenix. "Donna is the best secretary I've ever had," he said. "She needs a full-time job, and I'm sure you have one." One brief interview later, I had landed the job of secretary to the GE Manager of Programming.

Building a nest egg wasn't easy. If I moved back in with my dad, I could save the cost of room and board, but I'd have to leave my dear friend Judy. Sophomore year, Judy pledged a sorority and went to live with sorority sisters. They were the lucky ones.

•

During my year at GE, I carried nine hours of night courses at ASU. My off-campus boss gave me an outstanding job rating. "You have great potential." He wanted to nominate me for training as a GE computer programmer. That might have been a good career, but it was the wrong time and the wrong place. My burning obsession was to escape from everyone and everything in Arizona.

On February 2nd, also my nineteenth birthday, I picked up my last check from GE and cashed it, giving me a total survival fund of $4,000. But where would I go next? The answer came to me in a dream—I was walking past buckets of enormous red apples lined up in a never-ending row. I awoke with clarity. Those bright apples were waiting for me to pick the biggest one, and bite it right down to the core. I was meant to consume that big apple—in New York City.

When the time came to tell my parents that I was leaving Arizona, I should've known they'd be unpredictable. Deciding to tell Dad first, I found him in the living room, sitting in his favorite upholstered chair, reading the Phoenix newspaper.

"Tatush, I have something important to tell you," I'm sure my voice sounded confident. "I'm going to start a new life—in New York City."

Dad removed his wire-rimmed glasses, rubbed them with his hand-kerchief and replaced them on the bridge of his nose. I watched him walk to his desk in the corner of the living room, sit down, and pull open the top drawer where he kept his ledger checkbook. He began to write.

"You will need this." Dad tore out a check, handed it to me, and took off his glasses. "New York is expensive place." The check was for $1,000—the largest amount of money he had ever given me. Perhaps it was a late act of contrition for his violence against me two years before. I'll never know his actual reason, only that I felt grateful for his money. It seemed to mean he approved of my leaving Arizona. However, the dark memory of Dad's cruel side would never leave me. Years into the future, he would give me another $1,000—tainted by death and betrayal.

After telling Dad, I headed over to Boarding House #3. Mother was waiting for me in the kitchen. She sat at the same Formica table where, three years earlier, Mary Jane and I had pleaded for her to allow me to leave Arizona. However, this time I didn't need Mother's permission, and my heart wasn't filled with dread or fear. My hands stayed tranquil and folded on the table. Mother's once abusive hands lay quiet on the table next to mine, and her blue eyes looked clear. Mostly, she listened to what I had to say.

"Mamusia, I'm going away soon," I said, my tone resolute, "to be on my own. I'm moving to New York City."

For once Mother looked me directly in the eyes. She was calm and attentive. "Danusia, is right time for you now." Her voice was reassuring, almost tender. "New York will be good place."

We hugged with a fervor we'd never before shown or likely felt for each other. It was as if I had melded into my mother and she had absorbed my youth. My leaving could have been a re-enactment of young Hania leaving the known world for her unpredictable future.

In the future, I would come to realize how adversity had shaped both Mother and me. She had met formidable challenges in her life with courage and resilience. My path was to be convoluted. Like hers, my choices would be lonely and difficult. Mother's strength and determination were her legacy passed on to me. They would serve me well.

New York City

It was 1962—The Big Apple was bobbing in all directions. And I was a nineteen year-old woman hungry for bites of that spectacular city. In a bank near the Phebe Warren House for women at 35 East 68th Street in Manhattan, I deposited my $4,000 survival fund and Dad's check for $1,000.

At Phebe Warren, I met two gals with the same mission—to find a New York City apartment. Blonde and comely Sue, from Atlanta, Georgia, was a student at Parsons School of Design. Brunette and statuesque Libby, from Canada, was at Traphagen School of Fashion. I admired Libby's straightforward personality, and we hit it off right away. With savvy scanning of the real estate ads we located a fifth-floor walk-up in the fashionable neighborhood of 81st Street off Madison Avenue. Students Libby and Sue, and I on a secretary's salary, agreed to split the $150 per month rent plus utilities—high rent for a 1960s New York City walk-up and tiny one-bedroom apartment. Unless we shared costs, none of us could afford the rent.

After the school year, Sue returned to Atlanta for the summer, and Libby and I needed a temporary roommate. We invited Nita, also at Traphagen with Libby, to move in for the summer. Nita was a beautiful woman, inside and out. We loved her talent, gracious personality, and her world-traveled Air Force family based just outside New York City. Her father was a US Air Force Major. At the end of the summer, because we expected Sue would be returning, Nita moved out.

Instead, Sue gave Libby and me our inaugural lesson in racial bigotry. Her father was a prominent Atlanta physician, and her mother was a woman of pure Southern upbringing. After they learned (from Sue) that our summer roommate Nita was African-American, Sue's parents decided that Libby and I were no longer suitable roommates for their daughter. They arranged for for Sue to live with "untainted" acceptable roommates. Libby and I never saw Sue again.

We hoped Nita would move back in, but she'd already found other roommates. We missed her greatly. Somehow we managed to divide the rent by two and keep our apartment on 81st Street for a couple of years, until Libby got married and moved to another apartment with her new husband. After that, I settled in and out of several residences including four shared places, a brief no-share, and a group summer rental house in the Hamptons. During my five years in New York City, I had a total of fifteen different roommates. Among all of them, Libby and I would remain friends for life.

During my early years in NYC, contact with my parents consisted of superficial phone calls of "I'm good. How are you?" Mother didn't like long talks—not in Polish, not in English. Until my parents insisted that I handle their finances and pay their bills long distance. "We no trust Edith with money," Mother said. Her voice over the phone was

Libby in New York City, 1960s

resolute. Not only was I poorly qualified for such a task, but also I'd deliberately put long distance between my family and me for sheer survival reasons. Despite what had happened between Edith and me when she cast me out of her house, after I moved to NYC I advocated for Edith. "She's right there—I'm far away. She's your daughter too. Let Edith help you."

After a year of late payment warnings from utility companies ready to shut off services at Mother and Dad's homes, we had to confront reality. Soon, a certified letter arrived from Phoenix. It was official notice that Edith had been appointed Legal Guardian of our parents' finances and personal care. I actually felt relieved. But my conscience told me how irresponsible and selfish I was to relinquish sole care of our parents to Edith—a warning I disregarded and would always regret.

My work career in New York City had begun with an uninspiring stint as secretary to a woman banker on Wall Street. Fired up and restless, I soon moved on to Booz Allen & Hamilton Inc., management consultants. Booz Allen occupied the entire 20th floor of 380 Madison Avenue. Its mid-century modern decor was an elite style for an elite firm. Every workday I'd be the first "girl" to arrive. Passing the entry foyer mirror, I'd flash myself a "You're looking good!" smile.

Strolling down the row of empty executive recruiting offices (the men came in late and stayed late), I saw no other secretaries at their desks. Tossing my damp London Fog raincoat on a peg of the wooden coat rack, I stashed my real-leather handbag in the bottom drawer. My boss, Elmer Van Horn, was head of the Executive Recruiting Department. For top-of-the-heap Booz Allen clients, our department searched out cream-of-the-crop executives. Mr. VH handled key negotiations and vetted top candidates: every college degree verified; credit records scrutinized; employment gaps and suspicious performance reports duly investigated. Finalists bore Ivy League degrees with top honors, established non-stop career progress, and provided impeccable references. No female executive candidate ever made the final cut during my time at Booz Allen—not only was this New York City in the sixties, it was Madison Avenue during the real life era of Mad Men, an era that would be brought to life for millions of TV viewers decades later.

I looked and behaved like the quintessential classy secretary of the time—feminine and stylish, not overtly sexy, charismatic and constantly smiling. Above all, I learned a woman's place in a man's world. Booz Allen was my workshop to quick-study competitive men destined to lead the corporate world. Within five years, I would marry just such a man.

After I'd been at Booz Allen for two years, an amazing coincidence happened. Brenda and I had been "Hi there" acquaintances on the campus of ASU. When Brenda moved with her husband Jim to the Big Apple, among millions of job possibilities, she incredibly chose Booz Allen and was hired. Not just in any department—Brenda walked straight down the hall to work in Executive Recruiting. Our desks were next to each other, and we would become lifelong friends.

Through walnut paneled doors, I entered Mr. VH's corner office and began my daily routine by organizing his day: sorting the messy stacks of legal size folders into impeccable order; cross checking each folder against the precisely timed interview schedule; and placing the folders into the discrete top drawer of the partner's massive desk.

Mr. VH officiated from a custom leather desk chair. He swiveled right to the intercom that summoned me to take dictation or escort a visitor, swiveled left to absorb the panoramic views, or positioned himself straight ahead, with a smiling welcome on his face for an important client, or his piercing intimidation of a nervous candidate. Whether traveling in the US or overseas, or at home in the NY Office, Mr. VH kept a set routine. If I heard "Book me lunch" over the intercom, it meant The Rainbow Room, top floor of the RCA Building.

Sorting files was boring, but for a compulsive daydreamer like me, views from the corner office were alluring. One particular morning the heavy mist played its tricks on me. Shapes and hues of skyscrapers became the ebony and ivory piano keys of my childhood piano lessons. The enveloping fog swirled like smoke from the Maestro of Doom's cigar, so thick I gasped for fresh air.

My body went into fantasy flight. I soared up and away from the boring stack of file folders. Then straight out the 20th floor picture window of Mr. VH's office, across Madison, quick-turned at Park Avenue, zoomed south, and halted at a towering fortress spanning the intersection of Park Avenue and 42nd Street. No one could mistake the dramatic Pan Am Building. Its international style and awesome height made it distinct among 1960s New York City architecture.

I zoomed up fifty floors to the top of the building. Like a bird of prey, I circled the expanse of black tarmac below. A Pan Am helicopter awaited boarding—a few businessmen in predictable beige trench coats, holding traditional briefcases, and one fur-bedecked blonde swinging a fancy handbag and no briefcase. A loud departure announcement pierced the air. Everyone was aboard the helicopter, except me. My entire week's salary wouldn't cover the cost of even one Pan Am helicopter flight from Midtown to JFK International Airport. Some strange force compelled me to the edge of the Pan Am building. As I peered down fifty stories, the dizzying sea of swirling ground traffic and rising toxic fumes made me nauseous.

I turned around. The helicopter was gone. In its place, a magnificent silver and blue Pan Am clipper ship rose majestically into the clouds, a glistening silver stairway was lowered to the tarmac.

Beckoning from the entry door above, a mysterious figure summoned me. The moment I placed my foot on the bottom step, my daydream evaporated. Suddenly, I was back in Mr. VH's office staring at the still-waiting messy stack of files. Everything around me looked familiar, but I was a woman with a new mission—I was meant to fly the world with Pan American Airways!

Two mornings later, in our shared apartment, I sorted through the collection of clothes we often shared and assembled what I thought would be perfect for the momentous day ahead: a gray gabardine suit that clung gently yet emphatically to my figure, a crisp blouse showing pristine points of white at collar and cuffs, and a pair of glossy black pumps. In the full-length mirror behind the apartment's bathroom door, I envisioned myself as a Pan Am stewardess with a beautiful smile.

At Booz Allen I took an extra-long lunch break "for a dentist appointment." At 11:45 a.m., I arrived at the personnel office of Pan Am. It took me sixty minutes to fill out application forms and pose for photos—"front, side, and full views, please." And fifteen minutes for a personal interview with a thirty-something guy in Brooks Brothers pinstripes. While he shook my hand with just the right pressure, he scrutinized every inch of me and still managed to look friendly.

"I speak fluent Polish and college French," I piped up. These were my best qualifications, or so I thought. He jotted cryptic notes in the corner of my application form. "And I'm passionate about foreign cultures—"

"Excellent. Now if you don't mind stepping on the scale there in the corner. No need to remove your shoes."

Since I thought my weight was fine, I didn't mind one bit.

"Ah, seven pounds over the Pan Am weight limit for your height." He circled a bold #7 at the top of my application form. "If the pounds go, you'd be an excellent candidate for Pan Am."

"Oh, that won't take me long." I sent him one of Mother's do-not-doubt-me looks. Wouldn't any candidate lose weight to get the job she wanted? Brooks Brothers Guy ushered me to the door.

"If you do manage to lose those extra pounds, we'll have you back for another interview," he said.

I flashed him a big, bright smile.

During my fifteen-minute trot back to Booz Allen, typical me strategized a plan: give Booz Allen the required two-week's notice; move out to the Hamptons (I'd just signed up with five other gals for our summer rental there); exercise like crazy and drop the pounds; be accepted for training in Miami by fall; graduate as a new Pan Am stewardess by year-end 1966 ready to fly the world. That very afternoon I submitted my resignation at Booz Allen.

For the next two weeks, I didn't daydream even once. On my last day of work, Mr. VH took me to lunch at The Rainbow Room.

My friend Brenda was promoted to fill my job as secretary to Mr. VH. She likely got a modest raise. My one regret leaving Booz Allen was not being able to visit with Brenda every workday.

Summer of '66

At the apartment on 81st Street, I culled my worldly goods and selected seven wash-and-wear outfits, five pairs of shoes (a challenge for my shoe obsession), essential cosmetics (according to Super Model Veruschka), and one vintage set of electric hair curlers. I stuffed everything into two battered suitcases and a Bloomingdale's Big Brown Bag. No space wasted, I also crammed in six paperbacks: *Madame Bovary*, four gothic romance novels, and one dog-eared erotica paperback sandwiched between back issues of *Cosmo* featuring inspiring, wispy Twiggy and willowy Penelope Tree.

My destination was the Hamptons, Long Island, a desirable enclave of picturesque villages, waterfront estates, and income-producing rental houses that offered allure to New York City singles, silver spooners, and blue-blooded oldies. Five socially motivated New York City career women and one unemployed daydreamer seven extra pounds overweight had pooled enough money to rent, sight-unseen, a modest yet over-priced cottage in the quaint Hamptons town of Quogue.

On summer weekends, schlepping heavy bags aboard jam-packed LIRR trains at Grand Central Station was a nightmare, but early Monday morning the Hampton Local was nearly empty. Loaded down with all my worldly possessions, I climbed aboard, daydreamed for an hour or so, and disembarked at Quogue. I staggered to the taxi queue, where a burly Italian driver with a friendly smile and a glossy mustache looked susceptible to my charms. At the cottage he didn't flinch once at the driveway being far from the front porch. How easily his muscular arms hefted my two suitcases and the bulging Bloomie's bag. His devious fingers even managed to tweak my bottom once as we climbed up two flights of stairs. Italian fortitude!

On weekends, my housemates and our assorted boyfriends filled the little cottage to bursting. We nicknamed the house "Roseland" because every room was covered with rose themed wallpaper that was peeling, mottled, and musty. The whole house had a chronic moldy smell. Our cure for that nasal overload was alcoholic drinks, in steady doses, served all weekend.

By Sunday evening, the mass exodus left me the solo resident of Roseland Camp for Overweight Girls. I set strict rules for myself. Kelloggs-in-a-box diet: Shredded Wheat for breakfast; Rice Krispies for lunch; and Raisin Bran for dinner. Daily exercise: walking or bike riding everywhere. Weekly weigh-ins: judged by Trusty Rusty, the bathroom scale. Activities: the Hamptons social scene.

I cycled my way to a travel agency and fibbed that I was a school teacher hoping international posters on the walls would inspire my students to be future world travelers. A gullible agent handed me a dozen glossy illustrations of Pan Am destinations in Europe and South America. He rolled them up in a fat mailing tube, and I strapped it on my bike. Back at Roseland, I smiled and taped glossy posters across peeling wallpaper in the living room, kitchen, dining room, and the bedroom I shared with three other gals.

What I'd left out of my all-encompassing plan for that summer was something I never dreamed would happen—falling in love with Bob Wilhelm.

Taking Flight

Meeting Bob

If someone asked, "How'd you two meet?" Bob and I hand-signaled which of us would answer. Bob's version was precisely like his mindset; my version was peppered with creative details.

His story was that we were properly introduced by my friends Alice and Ron, members of the Sandbar Beach Club. "Donna and I had both been invited to the official start of summer, Sandbar's Memorial Weekend Party."

My version began with how I pedaled my bike to a popular singles bar in South Hampton and worked my way through a lot of uninteresting single men who'd arrived early for happy hour. As I was leaving, Bob came in and blocked the rustic oak door.

"Why are you leaving?" he asked. "This could be the start of an unforgettable friendship."

I noticed his dimpled chin and wide-spaced blue eyes. "Possibly," I said with my most provocative smile. "But I turn into a pumpkin soon."

We had a quick drink and a rushed "Bye-bye. See you at the beach." No way did I want to risk pedaling home in the dark considering the drinking habits of Hampton drivers.

That same weekend, we stood across from each other at the buffet at Sandbar. I couldn't keep my eyes off the guy in rumpled, plaid Bermuda shorts with a mismatched shirt and squared, black-rimmed glasses. My favorite memory of the weekend we met is one I've seldom shared: how he reached across the laden buffet and grabbed up a huge turkey leg. Gnawing on a greasy turkey leg took dedication and didn't flatter the chewer. I sensed this man wasn't about superficial chatting or looking good. And I would learn there was nothing simple about Bob Wilhelm.

Most ambitious New York City bachelors fired off the same typical questions—"Where is it you went to college?" "Which sorority?" "So you grew up in Connecticut?" "Westport or Greenwich?" "What company does your dad work for?" "You worked at Booz Allen—so does my buddy X from Harvard Business School, how's he doing there?" Those opportunistic questions raised immediate red flags for a gal trained in quick assessment at Booz Allen.

Although superbly talented, educated, and poised for success, Bob was a man without pretension—that earned my immediate respect. Sunset that night seemed to last for hours as we sat by the bonfire on the beach. Our conversations covered the Vietnam War, the state of the economy, what was hot on Broadway, and (more than I wanted to know about) season projections for the Pittsburgh Steelers and the Pittsburg Pirates. His relentless ability to spew encyclopedic facts on any subject was brilliant, and intimidating. Bob's early politics made him an avid campaigner for John Lindsay, the charismatic Liberal Republican candidate for New York City mayor. As Bob climbed up the corporate ladder, he would evolve into a staunch R-Conservative.

If Bob had been interviewing at Booz Allen, he would have been a cream-of-the-crop candidate: top academic achievements (B.S. Physics, High Distinction MIT, Harvard Business School Baker Scholar); ambition to be a top frog in a major pond; strategic career path with Standard Oil of New Jersey (SONJ). Top offer made, candidate accepted. (Just as SONJ would become the mighty Exxon, Bob Wilhelm would become the corporate Golden Boy for decades—until his platinum blond hair turned silver and he was no longer the youngest man in the boardroom).

•

Labor Day weekend signaled that the memorable summer of 1966 was over. Our lease at Roseland ended. Any time with Bob was on countdown. Trusty Rusty had confirmed my ten-pound weight loss (three pounds extra for good luck). An official letter from Pan Am announced that I'd been accepted for training in Miami, second week of September. The night before my departure, Bob and I exchanged passionate kisses and promised to phone each other.

Pan Am Boot Camp

Training Week One—I settled into the Miami Springs location with other excited Pan Am trainees. Total immersion in the making of a 1960s Pan Am stewardess began. We learned what to say, how to say it, and how to look when we said it.

Training Week Two—an official Pan Am blue envelope, my name in all caps, appeared in my cubby mailbox. Hands shaking, heart pumping, I pulled out a single sheet of PAA letterhead:

> You are cited for having a bad attitude.
> If this continues, you will not be eligible to graduate.

Was it my sullen expression in response to what the trainer said? "A passenger with bad manners must be treated with full respect!" Did I look incredulous when the trainer read the rule, "Any weight gain over two pounds is a weight check violation and means for grounding—without pay"? Hadn't I smiled when the same trainer criticized my slightly imperfect caviar service? Was my lipstick the wrong shade of pink? Had my hair grown more than the maximum two inches below the chin line?

Weeks Three and Four—never before, or after, have I been as smiling, willing, and delightful as I was those last two weeks of Pan Am Boot Camp. Unlike four devastated women who didn't graduate with our class, I survived the gauntlet. Sixteen new Pan Am stewardesses, impeccable in

our tailored uniforms, lined up according to height for the group photo
of our diploma, matted in Pan Am Blue.

More than a half century later, the graduation photo hangs on the
wall of my office. If a visitor asks, "You were a Pan Am stewardess?"
I nod. And if I hear "Wow! That's you, second from right, front row!" I
flash a big, bright Pan Am smile.

We behaved like a herd of bustling sheep in the hall outside the trainer's
office, waiting for our initial base assignments. No individual requests or
preferences were allowed.

"Oh God, please let me be based here in Miami where my boyfriend is."

"I'll just die if I get sent to San Juan. They can't do that to me!"

"San Fran means I'll be on the Asia route, please, please let me fly
Europe instead!"

My white-gloved fingers wandered up to my right shoulder. "Where
I'm assigned isn't important," I said, buffing up the shine on my new Pan
Am wings. "I'll go anywhere."

My remark got dubious smirks from the others. Survivors of Pan
Am Boot Camp thought they knew a lie when they heard one, but
they didn't know that I'd almost moved to Kabul, Afghanistan. When I
was summoned into the office for the verdict, I walked out cocky and
excited.

My inaugural Pan Am assignment was New York City.

Before I could fly as a Pan Am stewardess, I needed a United States
passport. To get one, I had to produce my birth certificate. Naturally,
I thought it would be filed in Hebron, Connecticut, where I con-
tacted their records office. However, Hebron had absolutely no record
of my birth. Speculating that urban sprawl had likely annexed Hebron
into Hartford, I persevered with the Hartford Department of Health
and got lucky— Hartford, Connecticut sent me an official copy of
my birth certificate. Indeed, Harriet and Joseph Sosinski were listed as
Parents to Child, Donna Mona Sosinski, born February 2, 1943. Mother
listed her residence as Boarding House #1 and her mailing address as

Donna, Pan Am stewardess, 1966

Boarding House #2. Edith was named as nurse and witness to the birth. Most curious, however, was that the document was filed on October 10, 1943, seven months after my birth, and that my birth was listed as having taken place at Hartford Hospital. I was thrilled to finally secure my birth certificate, and I dismissed the discrepancy of Mother's story during my childhood, that I was born at Old Glendale Farm in Hebron. I'd become a brand new Pan Am stewardess—I would be living my daydream.

Bliss, Break-up, Back Together

For two months, Bob and I had it all: blissful infatuation, naïve overconfidence, and youthful optimism. I moved into his one bedroom walk-up in a Sutton Place brownstone. He chose the neighborhood, not for its old-guard prestige, but because he could easily walk from there to Standard Oil at 30 Rockefeller Center in twenty-five minutes. For my Pan Am flights to Europe and the Caribbean, I took a cab from Sutton Place to the East Side Terminal, boarded a bus, and traveled forty-five minutes to JFK Airport.

Contentment settled over me like a security blanket. Nights and weekends with Bob convinced me that we were truly in love. For only the second time in my life (the other being my year with Mary Jane), I felt as if I really belonged with someone. Unlike my romance with Joe S, Bob was unpretentious, fully educated, and primed for professional success— a grown man whom I had come to admire and trust. Until the bomb-shell exploded.

We sat in a neighborhood Irish bar on First Avenue. I've forgotten the name of the bar, but not the argument. Maybe we'd had too many drinks, and I felt compelled to know our commitment to each other. It was dark and also smoke-filled, adding some breathing anxiety. My nervous fingers gripped the side of a wobbly table. I leaned forward. "Bob, how do you feel about having me in your life?" I tried to steady my voice. "Where do you think we're going together?" After the mutual intimacy we'd developed, I never expected the answer he gave me.

"I depend on one person—myself." Bob's voice was firm.

Even in the dim light, I could discern that his wide-spaced eyes were unflinching.

"I don't need anyone else to help me, and I never will." His tone was dispassionate. Bob the pragmatic scientist added, "I'm not responsible for the inadequacy of others. Competence takes proof."

The insecure woman I was in my twenties interpreted Bob's response to mean I hadn't earned his trust and didn't deserve his confidence. His message whipped at my unhealed wounds from childhood, when Mother and Dad disparaged and dismissed me as undeserving and unworthy. Later, I would come to realize that Bob had revealed his own insecurities. He likely wasn't criticizing me. And definitely, he had evaded answering my question.

Overcome by rejection, I ran out from the bar onto First Avenue and went on a wild search for the nearest public phone booth. Along the way, I lambasted myself for my vulnerability and entrusting Bob with my heart. A phone booth appeared—I flung myself inside and called Libby, my ex-roommate and dearest friend. Her husband Ben, an interior designer, had been drafted for Vietnam (Bob, who worked in the "vital interest" energy business, was draft exempt). Libby offered me a precious niche of space in her small apartment. I rushed back to Bob's brownstone apartment, shoved my clothes, makeup, and scattered possessions into my two worn Samsonite suitcases. I deposited my key on the kitchen counter and marched out the door—for the last time. "Good riddance to you, arrogant Bob," I shouted at him in absentia. "Face your self-sufficient future without me!"

Soon enough, Bob began to bombard me with apologies and pleas to make things right again. And I gave in during a few unremarkable dinner dates. Yet I couldn't stop how much my heart hurt. And I couldn't silence what my brain ordered—"*Stay true to your mission!*"

About a month later, Bob was promoted to become Manager of Economics and Planning for Esso Colombiana, one of SONJ's affiliates in Latin America. It was a formidable career leap for a 26-year-old employee. Bob didn't ask for my help in packing for Bogotá, Colombia, and I didn't volunteer.

Pan Am had opened a new base in Washington, D.C., where I saw an open window of opportunity. I put in for a transfer to D.C., checked out to be upgraded to Purser and passed. My bumped up salary covered new responsibilities: supervise the cabin crew; assign on-board cabin duties; deliver the bilingual announcements; and complete the copious flight and passenger paperwork. Lugging a heavy documents briefcase didn't bother me one bit.

Home in D.C. was the elite Georgetown neighborhood and a charming townhouse shared with four other Pan Am stews from around the world—Chris from Seattle, Lieke from Holland, Beth from London, and Kristine from Munich. All of us were ecstatic about our new base and Pan Am routes to London, Paris, Frankfurt and other key European cities. When we moved in, we huddled and toasted each other with champagne—"To the good life! Sisterhood! Youth and Beauty!" I didn't fathom that my glamorous Pan Am career would last only nine months.

After each flight, I'd come home and check the mailbox, where a stack of letters and picturesque postcards from Bob in the Andes awaited.

> *Missing you. Bogotá is amazing. Come see it!*
> *Missing you every day. WHEN can you get here?*
> *Really missing you. Use those Pan Am flight passes. YOU WON'T BE SORRY!*

Bob pursued with bulldog tenacity. The Baker Scholar at Harvard Business School excelled at case study analysis, and he applied that method to me: e.g. *Case: Convince an achievement obsessed woman with intellectual curiosity about exotic places; entice her with an international lifestyle; challenge her vulnerabilities and lower her defenses. Confirm your success.* Bob's goal was to get me to Bogotá and propose marriage.

Yet only a few months before in a dark New York City bar, he'd refused to express his love and commitment. My past experience with men like my dad and Joe S, my first love, had revealed their deception. The self-absorbed and opportunistic men I'd met in New York City before Bob were driven by fierce ambition. I flew to Bogotá for what I thought would be an exotic adventure, nothing more.

The awesome beauty of the Andes Mountains captured my soul and enticed my imagination. And Bob surprised me. Instead of rejecting commitment, he made fervent offerings of eternal devotion. From childhood, I'd been yearning to belong with someone. I'd also learned to love my independence. I wanted to feel safe and cherished, yet I also craved excitement and challenges. How could I overcome the battle between my mind and heart? Based on past times of joy together, I knew that Bob and I shared intellectual curiosity, similar value systems, and high achievement. During the few days and nights we were together in Bogotá, I painted an idyllic virtual image—Bob and I building a brilliant future—together for life. I agreed to marry him.

However, the episode of Bob telling me he needed and trusted no one would stay buried in my psyche. During our future years, Bob would never disappoint me in matters of the head. But I would grievously disappoint him in matters of the heart.

Return to Arizona

Five years before, I shed my past as if it were a desiccated snakeskin and left it behind in the Arizona desert. I flew away to New York City, a destination I'd only dreamed about. When I couldn't keep my feet on the ground in the Big Apple, I took to the air with Pan Am. Now I had news that wouldn't keep. In two months, I'd be a married woman making a new life in South America. Before taking my wedding vows, I had to break another promise I'd made—never to return to Arizona.

Even in my fantasies, I couldn't have envisioned what happened that weekend. News of my getting married would be minor compared to what my parents had to tell me—a secret they'd hidden from me for twenty-four years.

I arrived in Phoenix on a Friday afternoon in July of 1967, the peak of summer heat. Air conditioning wasn't standard in rental cars then, and the manual shift, two-door sedan had two ways to cool off—push the fan to max, or roll down all the windows. Driving from Sky Harbor airport to Dad's house, the air whistling through the tunnels of my sweat-drenched, sleeveless blouse would be the only relief I'd feel that weekend.

Smells of decaying citrus wafting into the rental car told me I was close. It was irrigation day. Muddy water poured over the neighborhood lawns and had lapped right up to the cement driveway of Dad's house. Mother's Buick sedan, the same one she bought eight years back when she set up Boarding House #3, was parked askew and blocked any other car from getting around it. I had to park the rental at the soggy far end near the roadside. When I opened the car door, I sighed. My white Bernardo sandals weren't going to stay that way in the muddy goo below. Gripping my blue Pan Am carry-on bag, I scraped my feet along the pitted cement driveway that couldn't clean my sandals or erase old memories.

Return to Phoenix, Dad's house on
irrigation day, 1967

I peered through the glass panels of the front door and into the living room beyond. There they were. Mother sat on the old beige sofa, her short legs dangling inches above the worn carpeting. Dad slumped in the same shabby chair. No talking, no TV or radio. Just two old people silently waiting.

When I rang the bell, they shoved at each other to get to me first. Both babbled welcomes in Polish-English. Dad gave me an awkward hug while Mother pawed at my arms. How old and frail they looked after only five years under Edith's care. I was alarmed.

"Mamusia, Tatush," how easy it was to slip back to childhood Polish, "let's sit and get comfortable. I have so much to tell you."

"*Tak, tak, Danusia.*" Mother sighed. "Also we have tinks to tell you—many tinks." Mother rocked back and forth on the ancient sofa. She nodded her head, wispy silver hair unraveling from two unmatched plastic combs. Dad, who'd always looked comfortable in his favorite chair, leaned forward as if his back was hurting. Removing his metal-rimmed glasses, he wiped his bald head and sweaty face with a soggy handkerchief. The living room was stifling hot. In the corner, a solitary floor fan rotated uselessly, back and forth, bringing no relief.

"I'm getting married and moving to Bogotá, Colombia," I said. "You would be impressed by the man I'm going to marry. He went to the finest schools—the Massachusetts Institute of Technology and Harvard Business School. He's a golden boy with brilliant potential." I felt so proud, as if I were absorbing his achievements as my own. "He's working in South America for the world's most important oil company. Our ceremony will be in two months. But he has so many responsibilities we can only take a one-week honeymoon."

Mother and Dad stared at me, then at each other.

"What kind of place you go, this Bogotá, Colombia?" Mother shrugged. "I'm no understand." Her eyes, clouded by cataracts, no longer flickered with anger. The toll of years seemed to have subdued her demons.

"Is high up in the mountains?" Dad was better at geography. "Like Switzerland?"

"Bogotá is 8,600 feet in the Andes Mountains," I tried to simplify, "but Colombia will be nothing like Switzerland. They don't call it a 'developing' country for nothing."

"Ach. Danusia, you will enjoy the mountains. Always nice and cool." Dad wiped beads of sweat from his forehead. "How long you stay?"

"We don't know. The company could keep us there a long time," my voice faltered, "or a short time. When they want to move Bob, it could be to anywhere in the world."

At the age of twenty-four, I was a bride-to-be in love with fantasy about the future. Nothing on my radar warned me about the reality of the powers of future Mother Exxon, dictator of where we would live, when we would move, and how long we would stay.

"*Tak, tak, rozumiem.*" Dad said he understood, but neither he nor Mother asked for details. I interpreted their tacit nods and heavy sighs as old age and fatigue.

Restless and hoping to ease the cloying heat of the living room, I walked to the fan in the corner and let the tepid air dry my sweaty face. Moments later when I turned around, I saw my mother crumpled on the sofa, sobbing like a frightened child.

"No good keep secret so long time." Swabbing at tears running down her cheeks, she said, "Is time I tell you what is true."

Diabolic Wedding Gift

Late December, 1942, in Hartford, Connecticut, the bell rang at Boarding House #2. Mother opened the door to a woman who introduced herself as Irma Lettrich. "I'm remember so beautiful red hair, eyes color hazel, and how afraid she was." Irma was young, alone, and pregnant. She saw the *Rooms for Rent* sign and begged the landlady for one of them.

"After I give good Polish food, she was better." Mother, typically apathetic about her boarders, mopped her tear-stained cheeks this time. "Irma was poor Irish immigrant girl. Who do you-know-what with son of rich family from Pennsylvania."

Apparently Irma's boyfriend told his family he planned to marry a wonderful woman from poor circumstances. What he didn't tell them was that she was pregnant. The family response was immediate. If he married such a low class woman, they would disown him. Their threat worked—he abandoned Irma.

I stood in the sweltering heat of the living room, alarmed by how much my parents had aged, and that now once-tyrannical Mother was completely unraveled over something that had happened decades ago. Why was she telling me this story now? Didn't she care about my news? Was Mother trying to warn me about men's unreliability? How would I feel if I were alone and pregnant? I was deflated and utterly confused.

"Irma got nothing from him." Mother's face expressed her disgust. "Because of shame, she must leave Pennsylvania, come to Hartford— somehow she find my house. I allow poor woman to stay with me until baby due in February."

Mother suddenly began rocking back and forth. I looked over at Dad to see his reaction. He didn't make eye contact with me. He didn't even glance at Mother. Instead, he was preoccupied with cleaning the lenses of his glasses, over and over, with his soiled handkerchief.

"We move Irma to farm in Hebron," Mother continued, "more pri-vacy there."

Was another baby besides me born at the farm?

Pulling at the soggy tissues in her lap, she went on. "Edith was nurse, she help. Freezing day in February but Irma give birth to healthy baby girl."

Suddenly it dawned on me that *this story had everything to do with me. I was born in February. Irma's baby, born at the farm, was me!*

My thoughts reeled. For twenty-four years, Mother had lied that I was her birth daughter.

"Irma very healthy, and she recover quick." Mother affirmed.

I couldn't take my eyes away from Mother as she spoke. She sat hunched over the soggy tissues now shredded in her lap. She continued to describe how she and Edith hustled Irma and the swaddled newborn me into the back seat of the Packard, and that Mother drove everyone from the farm in Hebron back to Boarding House #2 in Hartford.

Mother raised her head to look at me, as if needing to be under-stood—perhaps even praised. "She give her baby to me—raise as my own." Her tone sounded strangely noble.

More questions raced through my brain. *How had Mother passed off the baby as her own? What did she tell the relatives who, unlike me, were far from naïve. She must have been very convincing. Or did Juzo deal with them?*

I couldn't imagine how Mother would've escaped scrutiny by the boarders, seeing their landlady (overweight yes, but way too old to be pregnant) suddenly caring for a newborn baby. *Wait a minute—no one needed any explanation because they knew the truth. That's why Aunt Mamie dodged my questions all those years ago. That's what Theresa tried to tell me. And of course Edith—she was there for the birth! That's why she has such resentment toward me. Does Reggie also know? She never said she knew anything about my birth.*

This was the big family secret that apparently everyone knew, except me. Hania generated so much power that no one—relatives, boarders, even Edith—dared to stand up to her.

"Irma had people in California. She want make new life there." Apparently Mother drove Irma to the Greyhound station in Hartford. "I put her myself, on bus to California." Mother's voice dropped to a whisper. "After that . . . we never hear from Irma again."

I could hardly absorb what I'd learned. I imagined myself as a fellow passenger on that bus ride across the country, seeing a woman named Irma sobbing and trying to convince herself that she had done the right thing. Somehow, she had to justify surrendering her baby. Perhaps the shock of being abandoned by her boyfriend had convinced young Irma that she was unfit for motherhood. When a seemingly compassionate, older woman running a boarding house had taken the baby, did Irma believe that it was best—for everyone? How did she feel when the door closed and the bus pulled away leaving her baby in the arms of her landlady? But the most unsettling question for me: Wouldn't my birth mother want to know, in the years to follow, how I was doing?

Throughout the telling, Mother and Dad exchanged only furtive occasional glances. Dad stayed silent—how true to form.
Mother shifted her weight to one side and reached into the pocket of her too tight housedress. She pulled out two frayed envelopes and thrust them into my hand. "Here is what I save from Irma."

One was regular size, the other was legal size; both were soiled and yellowed with age. The first letter was addressed in Mother's erratic script to Mrs. Irma McMarkwell in Redondo Beach, California; she'd included her return address: Harriet S., Glendale Farms, Amston, Connecticut. The street address was missing, there was no stamp—the letter had never been mailed. The second envelope was typewritten, addressed to Irma Lettrich at 96 Webster Street (Boarding House #1) in Hartford, sent airmail and registered mail, January 14, 1943 (two weeks before my birthdate). The whole right side was ripped as if it had been opened in frantic haste.

What had that envelope contained?

Unanswered questions plagued me: Why was Mother writing to Irma from the farm, where she hated to go? Was it to make sure no one in Hartford saw her communication with Irma, including myself? After all, I used to go get the mail. Or, was Mother trying to cover up that there was indeed further communication with my birth mother? Or, a third possibility: Mother and Dad decided to move shortly after my birth and set up Boarding House #2 on Fairfield Ave. Was Mother afraid Irma would come back to claim me? Why was Irma Lettrich now known as Mrs. Irma McMarkwell and living in Redondo Beach, California?

Rising from the sofa, clutching the envelopes in my sweaty palm, I staggered from the living room to the entryway, where I'd left my Pan Am flight bag. With care, I inserted the envelopes into the inside pocket and pulled the zipper closed. When I returned to the living room, Mother was slumped on the sofa, head down as if she was napping.

Now I had two mothers—one who'd given me away when I was born, the other who'd lied to me for twenty-four years. I reached out and shook her shoulder—we were not finished.

"Why have you waited all these years to tell me?" I demanded.

Mother raised her head and turned to face me, her eyes wide with fear. "I must try protect you from Edith. She is sister you cannot trust!"

Amazing—Mother had never protected me from my sister in the past.

Everything was turned upside down. I'd come home to my parents to share my joy about a wonderful future. Instead, they had crushed me with secrets and deception. And this outrageous warning—to fear my sister?

"Why do I need protection from Edith?"

"Ach, Danusia, so many tinks you never know about Edith." She coughed and cleared her throat. "Even after you live with her."

Tremors forced Mother's cheeks into puffy mounds that deflated into wrinkled flesh. She began to rock again with agitation. "Edith will never forgive! She stay jealous because I give others what she always want." Mother's voice dropped, her shoulders drooped forward. "Juzo and I are weak, old now," she mumbled, "no strength to fight Edith."

Long, silent moments followed. I was left wondering what it would take to satisfy Edith. What did she really want? Had Mother read Edith better than I could ever have imagined?

Suddenly, Mother shot up from the sofa, staggered forward a few steps, then turned back to face me. Had her old demons returned?

"Edith wants to kill us! She will come after you!" Mother screamed, and her clouded blue eyes showed panic. Before I could stand up and try to calm her, Mother stumbled back to the sofa and fell deep into the cushions. She sat slumped like a lifeless ragdoll. Complete exhaustion enveloped me. For long moments, I rested my head in my hands. When I raised my head to stare vacantly into the room, I listened to the droning of the ancient fan.

What had caused this terrible fear in Mother? Were there depths of darkness in Edith waiting to erupt into vengeance? I'd been warned—but what should I do about it? Was I meant to protect my parents from Edith? Who would protect me, and from what? Mother feared for her life. Was she possessed by old demons that compelled her to cast me into a toxic well of betrayal.

No one I could trust existed in my family. To protect myself, I had to escape from everything they'd told me. Soon, I'd be a married woman living in a faraway country with my husband—*Bob will take care of me! I'll be safe.*

I began to count the hours until Sunday, when I could fly away to safety. Until then I had to spend two nights in Dad's house, alone in my old high school bedroom. Insomnia replayed Mother's dire predictions. Edith was only a short distance away in the desert, but I knew I couldn't summon the will to drive out and confront her.

For the rest of the weekend I existed in a trance. Mother drove her battered Buick back and forth between her place and Dad's. The three of us made pitiful attempts to talk about something innocuous such as the juicy wedges of grapefruit and oranges heaped on a plate that Mother shoved in front of us in the kitchen.

At last, it was Sunday. Mother, Dad, and I stood together in the living room where the pitiful fan oscillated the air of sadness and fear that surrounded us. When I tried to utter words of kindness, they came out as garbled nonsense. Mother gripped me with the desperate strength of a drowning swimmer. Dad's embrace was the longest I could remember.

Slinging my Pan Am blue bag over my shoulder, I walked down the driveway to the rental car. Pausing for a brief remembrance, I glanced back at my parents. They stood under the shade of the carport, leaning on each other for support. I gave a feeble wave and locked away my emotions—no tears on my cheeks. Slipping behind the steering wheel, I flung my tote bag to the passenger seat, turned on the ignition, and backed out to the street. As I drove away, I watched my parents in the rearview mirror—two shrinking figures waving. I didn't realize that this would be our last good-bye.

Safe aboard the silver plane rising into the clouds over Phoenix, the constant droning of the engines lulled me into an eerie sense of detachment. Once again, I'd been flipped upside down by events. Mother's confession had capsized nearly everything I'd believed about my family. The mother and father I thought were my birth parents were not. Edith was their only birth daughter. But apparently Polish Hania had a soft heart for strangers. Long ago, listening at the door of Aunt Clara's house, I'd learned about the Holden girls, whose mother had died and whose father had abandoned them—to be cared for by the owner of a boarding house. We were raised as the daughters of Hania and Juzo—Frances, Mildred, May, Bunny, and now me—but none of us had been legally adopted. The significant difference between the Holden girls and me was that they had been old enough to know what had happened—and why.

I reflected about how complicated it had been to find my birth certificate. First, I'd searched for it in Hebron, but then I found it in

Hartford. The certificate listed my birth at Hartford Hospital. Mother had taken Irma Lettrich's baby and gotten a legal document that listed her and Juzo as my birth parents. What mysterious power did Hania hold over people—in our family and, even stronger, with outsiders?

I'd learned that Edith wasn't the sister I'd thought she was. If Mother's accusations were true, Edith's resentment of her five imposter sisters had been festering for decades. Would rage drive Edith to seek revenge against her parents and me—were we truly in danger?

Unable to process everything that had happened, I needed to find a safe place. Like so many times in my life, I invented a fantastical retreat. Aboard the plane flying through the clouds, I blew up an enormous imaginary balloon with all my confusion and fears hidden inside of it. Then I tapped the balloon over my shoulders, watched it sail through the plane's portal window, and saw it vanish into dense whiteness that could swallow anything. I was also flying away from abandonment by my birth mother and the deceit and betrayal of my parents. A strange sense of relief enveloped me. At least my adoptive parents' dysfunctional genes were not my genes—that realization lifted a heavy burden that otherwise I would have carried for the rest of my life. But a different weight now descended on me —whose genes did I carry?

In the future, wherever Bob and I lived, I stored the evidence of the two white envelopes in a secure place. Not until three decades later would I finally decide to search for my birth mother—Irma Lettrich. By then, it would almost be too late.

Wedding, Wife, and Colombia

Becoming Mr. and Mrs.

I returned to Georgetown, where my Pan Am housemates welcomed me with excited hugs. They asked about my family reunion, but I gave superficial answers. If I opened the floodgate about what really happened, I'd drown in angst. "All I want now is to plan my wedding," I said.

Eventually, I'd share the diabolic wedding gift with Bob, but not until we'd had enough private time together. I don't remember whether I told him during our honeymoon or after we reached our new home in Bogotá. I do remember how he processed the details—in his unflappable manner, so typical of Bob. Never did he condemn or blame me for the hellish behavior of my family.

The frantic weeks leading up to our wedding absorbed me. I had to plan a wedding ceremony, the honeymoon, and everything I thought was needed for my new life in Bogotá. Bob had accrued only enough time off for our wedding and a one-week honeymoon. Almost daily, he sent me letters on airmail stationery, the envelopes affixed with unique Colombian postage stamps. The contents included copies of Bob's passport and a document in Spanish (with English translation) notarized with an official wax seal. The evidence was necessary to prove that I was marrying a legitimate US citizen who was in good health. Bob's letters of that time would be so dear to me that I formed them into a stack wrapped with pink silk ribbon. For all the years to follow, I stored them somewhere safe, to reread when I needed a reminder—that my husband Bob could express his emotion and affection for me, in writing.

At night, I had trouble falling asleep because I felt anxious about the future. I was an independent woman with a promising career. But as a married woman, I wouldn't be allowed to fly for Pan Am—stewardesses had to be single. I tried to imagine married life in a foreign country, but no amount of speculation could prepare me for life as a corporate wife, or for the omnipotent control the corporation would have over where, when, and for how long Bob and I were assigned before another career advancement.

To get a good night's rest, I had to think positive. But I couldn't stop worrying about an impending event—meeting Bob's parents for the first time. Given the wrenching betrayals of my own family, I longed to find a place of belonging within Bob's German-American family. Would they genuinely welcome me into the fold?

One month before the wedding, I flew to Pittsburgh for my inaugural visit with the Wilhelm clan—without Bob. His parents' home was a modest red brick in the Pittsburg suburb of Mt. Lebanon. When I walked in the front door, a group of women of all ages shouted, "Surprise! It's a shower!" Bob's mother had assembled all the female relatives into a group of boisterous celebrants immersed in a bobbing sea of pink and white balloons.

The Wilhelm women appeared friendly and approachable. Just like Bob, they were unpretentious—what I saw was what I got. Cindy and Dottie, Bob's pre-teen sisters were curious about me—their eyes followed me around the room. There was chitchat. But no one asked personal questions, no queries about my career, what I thought about life overseas, let alone how I felt about marrying Bob. Compared to my own bizarre family and growing up in a boarding house, the Wilhelm clan seemed predictable, stable, and incredibly normal—devoted to family, tradition, and their suburban lifestyle. In years to come, my first impression would be confirmed again and again. The Wilhelm clan extended their apparent affection and welcome. However, forging deeper bonds between us in future would require that I behave according to Wilhelm values and that Bob's family accept me as more than "Donna-Bob's-wife."

My parents, debilitated by advanced age and their exhausting confessional in Phoenix, had no intention of coming to my wedding. Probably for the best, I decided. But who would give me away? Mr. VH, my former boss at Booz Allen, had been a father figure to me. But how could I ask him such an intimate favor—to be surrogate father of the bride at my wedding? Hands shaking, heart thumping, I picked up the phone and called Mr. VH in New York. My insecurity vanished when I heard his familiar deep voice that had always given me confidence. I poured out my news, and he was thrilled that I was getting married. Inhaling a deep breath, I asked Mr. VH to give me away at my wedding. Without hesitation, he responded, "I've always wanted a daughter. Of course I'll be father of the bride!"

September 30, 1967, Georgetown, Washington D.C—my wedding day. My former roommate and dear friend Libby had moved to Grafenwoehr, Germany, a small Bavarian town with a large US military base where her husband was stationed instead of being deployed to Vietnam. Libby wasn't able to come back for my wedding, but my friend Brenda in New York had graciously agreed to be my maid of honor. Dorothy and Ed Wilhelm, their daughters Cindy and Dottie, and son Paul and his wife Carol arrived from Pittsburgh for the wedding. Bob's brother Paul served as his best man. My resourceful housemates moved a metal radiator cover that stood about four feet high out to the garden and decorated it with fresh flowers. The radiator cover was a perfect makeshift altar. A minister from a local church I'd never attended served as our officiant, and thirteen guests witnessed the ceremony in the garden.

Our reception was a have-cake-and-leave-quick event. We had flights to make—no time for long, heartfelt good-byes. Brenda, Mary Anne (another friend from Booz Allen), Bob and I piled into a car to drive to Dulles International Airport. After dropping off the two gals at Eastern Airlines, Bob and I rushed aboard Pan Am to Rome. In First Class (my last

Wedding with makeshift altar,   Wedding Party, Brenda, newlyweds,
Georgetown, DC, 1967   Paul, 1967

free pass), we drank bottomless glasses of champagne and toasted "To Italy and our honeymoon!" Seven days later, we flew west to Miami for Bob's Esso Inter-America meeting in Key Biscayne, Florida. Three days after that, we boarded Avianca Airlines and flew south to Bogotá.

Newly wed Mr. and Mrs. Robert Wilhelm would be "at home" in the Andes Mountains—for three years.

Bogotá

Located on the Equator at 8,600 feet altitude in the Andes Mountains, Bogotá's climate consists of two seasons: rainy and non-rainy. Its unique setting challenged my cooking, my skin protection, and my never-enough wardrobe.

Security concerns came with Bob's corporate status and directives from US Embassy alerts to expat residents. In response to security needs and to support the local economy, Esso employees were expected to have reliable domestic help, and executives were assigned a vetted company driver. Colombia followed Napoleonic Law: Guilty until proven innocent. Even a minor traffic accident meant go directly to jail and maybe get out later. Esso executives could not be exposed to such risk. The cautions that Esso took weren't overblown, and in fact foretold escalating corporate security issues around the world. As a young bride shedding her past,

I adapted and integrated these concerns into my life. I approached marriage as an exotic, new adventure.

Newlyweds in Bogotá, 1968

In Colombia's Hot Country, 1969

In the Colombian Amazon, 1969

Expat Bride Lessons

The first three years of our marriage and expat life in Bogotá required constant adjustments and produced conflicting emotions. My unwavering need for stable hearth and home convinced me that creating a "perfect" home was the path to happiness. And I responded to a frequent subconscious message, "If something doesn't feel right, just change the setting." In Bogotá, my restless impulse prompted our moving to four different homes—three of them motived and selected by me.

Our first home, Bob's bachelor apartment, was dark and dreary. Naïve about local culture and customs, I was also short on household skills and illiterate in Spanish. Bob had hired a housekeeper named Leonór, who deferentially called him *El Señor Wilhelm.* When Bob introduced me as *"Mi nueva esposa,"* Leonór hesitated but gave me what I thought was a pleasant smile. Soon I'd learn what she really thought of me. Leonór cooked a few family meals, *"Como le gusta à mi Señor,"* meaning "The way my gentleman likes." I didn't take that personally, but it was laundry that did her in. Every day a pristine stack of fresh-folded clean shirts, underwear and handkerchiefs appeared on Bob's dresser. My soiled clothes accumulated in an increasing pile on the dark floor of our closet while my dresser drawers gained empty spaces.

My first expat bride lesson was that even if I wasn't fluent in Spanish, it was possible to fire obstreperous Leonór using hand gestures and facial expressions, and hire adorable, efficient Angelika. She became our devoted, loyal housekeeper.

My second domestic executive decision was to move us out of the dark and dreary bachelor apartment. I took advantage of Bob being away on a business trip and expeditiously moved us to a bright and sunny apartment on the top floor of our building. Guillermo, our designated company *chofér,* met Bob at the airport. On the way home, Guillermo warned Bob, *"La Señora es muy fija,"* meaning she has "a firm way."

The new apartment was fine for a while, until I coveted an even more perfect apartment with tiered balconies and panoramic views of the city. And I convinced Bob we would be supremely happy there. He acquiesced, and again we moved. Looking out over the expansive views of the Andes Mountains from our third apartment in Bogotá, I smiled with satisfaction.

During the years that followed, Bob's rising corporate career would reward him with professional esteem and increasing financial security. Like most other executive wives of that time, I merged my identity into my husband's success. Soon enough, the invitations to Mrs. R. E. Wilhelm flowed from country clubs, women's groups, fashionable social circles, and what would become most important to me, opportunities to become involved with charitable organizations. My contribution, at least the one I acknowledged as inherently mine, tapped into my creativity and intrepid enthusiasm.

Yet every so often, a dark bird of conscience would swoop down and squawk into my ear, "Not authentic! Who are *you*?" I'd duly swat that obnoxious creature away. But that bird was remarkably persistent.

I kept searching for something meaningful to do with my abundant free time (our household help outnumbered Bob and me). There was no denying what I saw whenever I left the safe cocoon of our comfortable apartment—a glaring disparity between the rich lifestyle of the *oligarquía* of Bogotá and the desperate poverty of the crowded barrios. Seldom did I note privileged Colombian women involved in community service. However, there was an abundance of expat women doing charitable work, usually as a group. At the beauty shop and bridge tables, where wealthy Colombian women were the majority, one of them would express what most of them agreed about us. "You Americans always band together for a purpose." I took that as a compliment.

Connecting Long Distance

During our time in Colombia, Bob and I made at least one trip per year to visit his family in Pittsburgh. After each trip I became more aware of just how devotedly local they were to the Pittsburgh Steelers, the Pittsburgh Pirates, and all matters domestic. We supplied "Yes" and "No" answers to their superficial questions about life outside of Pittsburgh. To be fair, Bob's parents and sisters did leave the United States for the first time ever, and they came to visit us in Colombia. Every day, they relished the exotic fruits and vegetables we'd stocked in the refrigerator, and they loved the Colombian *típico* dishes and barbeque served at local restaurants. Although we exposed them to every tourist highlight, I can't remember any interest they showed about Colombian cultural traditions. In private, I nicknamed Bob's parents "Mr. and Mrs. America." Bob smiled and agreed.

•

During that same period, Edith's letters continued to arrive like clock-work. She wrote that our parents were getting the "best of care" and that she'd moved Mother into Dad's house "to nurse them together." With every letter, she asked for money. Mostly out of guilt for not doing my share, I sent Edith monthly checks to cover our parents' care.

Because Mother had never become literate in English and because I'd resisted learning to read or write Polish, we never exchanged let-ters. In contrast, Dad had proudly mastered literacy in three languages— Polish, German, and English. In his quaint, self-taught English, he asked about daily life in Colombia. At the end of each letter, he'd sign off with the same phrase: "Everything in Phoenix going okay."

I took Dad at his word and convinced myself that everything was indeed fine in Phoenix. I justified putting off a visit to my parents and introducing Bob. This resistance evolved from a childhood mired in my parents' neglect and dismissal of me. I resented that they hadn't been dil-igent and nurturing guardians. In truth, I wanted to stay far away, for as long as possible, from the family I resented and the memories of trauma, deception and betrayals that I'd tried to keep buried.

Search, Settle, and Move

In the meantime, my obsessive standards of perfection led me to a house with a charming garden in a safe and gated community. I convinced Bob that we would be even happier in this home—and I'd handle all the details.

We hoped to take advantage of the forthcoming Easter *puente*, so named because Colombians liked to bridge national holidays with short workweeks leading to long weekends. Given the complicated details of moving into a larger, two-story house and the reality of having already been in Bogotá for three years, we decided to get the company's assur-ance that a transfer wasn't imminent. Bob queried his boss and got his answer: "Nothing that I know about."

With confidence, we plunged into the big move on Friday of the Easter *puente*. By late afternoon Sunday, Bob and I toasted each other with champagne in our beautiful new garden. Less than a month later, however, Bob came home from work one evening and stood in the glass-fronted living room. Without even a glance at the garden view behind me, he said, "I've got something to tell you." Bob's grim expression was ominous. "The company is transferring us to Cartagena."

Bob in Bogota, house #3. We've just moved in but are about to move to Cartagena, 1969

Cartagena de Indias

In 1970, after three years in the Andes Mountains, we moved to Cartagena on the Caribbean coast of Colombia. Bob had been promoted to be the manager of the company's major refinery, located in Cartagena, which was in those days an official corporate "hardship post." Soon enough, I'd learn why Bob was paid a bonus for us to live there.

Quaintly called *Cartagena de Indias*, the ancient city derived its name from Spanish explorers who believed they'd discovered the tropical shores of India. Spanish conquerors followed, pillaged, and fortified Cartagena with walls of stone so formidable that they would survive centuries. Now the picturesque decay of the ancient ramparts has become Cartagena's most popular tourist destination. I was captivated by what lay behind the

high stonewalls: arsenals of cannons; former soldiers' quarters; horse sta-
bles and storage areas that provisioned men and beasts. I imagined that
the rows of tight stalls fronted by ominous iron gates that secured but also
allowed visibility, imprisoned long-ago occupants. Bob and I couldn't
resist pretending we were locked together inside those cells. And I still
laugh at the photo of Bob ass-backward on one of the ancient cannons
lining the ramparts. During those early days together, we were a young
couple in love with each other and our shared adventures.

Ancient walls in Cartagena, 1970   Bob ass backward, Cartagena, 1970

Cartagena of the 1970s somehow reminded me of my fifth grade
murals, then my fantasy depictions of everyday life in ancient Egypt.
Now I was a married woman, living in a real-life mural. Wandering the
historic Caribbean city, I observed crumbling facades of movie theaters
that showed no current movies; booksellers in rocking chairs outside
shops that sold nothing printed in either Spanish or English; retail boutiques filled with oddities from baby clothes to motor oil but no fashionable garments for grown women; strutting exotic beauties parading past
hooting local males, yet having no real *Salon de Belleza*, (beauty shop), to
service them.

I was fascinated by the local ingenuity of countless open garages
converted into makeshift beauty parlors jam-packed with gossiping

local women sipping colas while they rolled each other's hair with giant, plastic curlers piled in communal bins. These animated female portraits revealed more about adaptable women and affectionate friendships than the rapid-fire Spanish TV sitcoms that I couldn't translate fast enough.

However the adversities of daily life in Cartagena chipped away at its tropical charms. Luxury foods, fashionable clothes, foreign-made cars, and household appliances were available either as legal imports at astronomical prices, or through illegal deals with *contrabandistas.* I came to believe that the rampant unpredictability of public services amused only local gossipers:

"Did you hear? The rich Boca Grande folks have no air conditioning. Three days now!"

"Teresita's telephone line is down. How do we tell who is canasta host this week?"

"Anything fresh at *La Carnicería del Caribe?*"

Gone, But No Good-bye

I remember the date—July 7, 1970—when I stood by my post office box, my hands shaking as I read a telegram from Edith:

MOTHER DIED IN HOSPITAL TODAY. CORONARY.
FUNERAL WEDNESDAY. DAD OKAY. EDITH.

How was this possible? It couldn't be true! Hania Olszeska—expelled at age nineteen from a privileged life. Hania, Polish Immigrant Girl—survivor and alone in the New World. My mother the entrepreneur, madcap driver, rescuer of strangers, pathological liar, and seemingly indominable dictator—gone!

I staggered out of the building into the tropical heat of Cartagena. The bright sun blinded me. As had Edith blinded me to Mother's failing health, to her final moments spent in hospital. Edith had made sure that I couldn't reach Mother in time to say good-bye.

However, a power beyond Edith's control told me Mother wasn't finished. I knew she would find a way to deliver her parting message to me. And that true to her nature, Mother's final encore would be unpredictable and dramatic.

Life and Death in a Hardship Outpost

Shortages and Peaches

Life in Cartagena was so slow-paced that I could have time out to grieve Mother's death. Instead, I threw myself into the ongoing social obligations of being the Refinery Manager's wife. A constant flow of corporate visitors arrived in Cartagena, and Bob and I were responsible for entertaining them. Most guests requested Caribbean cuisine and immersion in the city's exotic ambience.

Restaurant dining in Cartagena took patience, fortitude, and a quirky sense of adventure. *El Club de Pesca* was a fishing club with splendid views of yachts along the pier and served its motley customers not-too-savory fish dishes. *La Capilla del Mar* was an ordinary house and not a chapel by the sea. The kitchen concocted French food served with exhaustive slowness while impatient patrons drank a lot of booze under circulating fans ruled by power blackouts. *El Caribe Hotel*, conveniently located across the street from our house, was primarily known for Casanova, the arrogant parrot that was resplendent in color and fluent in pornographic vocabulary. He was also a welcome distraction from the restaurant's mediocre food.

Given the risks of dining out, staging dinner parties at home was a more reliable option. But one that took strategic planning, creative versatility, and good luck.

In a town plagued by food shortages, provisioning for large dinners was hit or miss. The best butcher in Cartagena was *La Carnicería del Caribe*. After only one visit there, I left disgusted by the rancid meat odors. At least once a month, Tomás, our company chofér in Cartagena, transported me and a giant Igloo cooler to the airport in time for the early morning, daily flight to Bogotá.

At the Bogotá airport, I was greeted by Guillermo, my favorite of the company drivers. His rotund figure in a tight-fitting suit, gold-tooth smile beaming, Guillermo waved in cheerful anticipation of the forthcoming hunt-and-shop expedition. At Bogotá's most reliable butcher, *Carnecería de Los Andes*, we deposited my order and the empty Igloo to be packed with iced fresh cuts of beef, pork, and chicken for later pickup.

Next stop was *el barrio de los contrabandistas*, the local black market. Guillermo distributed pesos to ragged street kids paid to watch parked cars vulnerable to vandals. With Guillermo as my watchful guardian, I felt safe. Together we maneuvered through the rows of ramshackle kiosks attended by contraband vendors stashing American dollars into metal cashboxes hidden under the counters. I paid a small fortune for processed foods that I'd never desired or eaten in the States: tinned smoked oysters; dye-injected Maraschino cherries; liquor-filled Swiss chocolates; and stacks and stacks of canned Del Monte Peaches—a serious addiction.

Exhausted by shopping in the chaotic marketplace, I'd direct Guillermo to drive me to the *Salon de Belleza*, where Bogotá's privileged and pampered women were served. While I enjoyed obsequious attending to my nails and hair, Guillermo took his late lunch in a nearby café jammed with ever-patient *chofères*. Their typical favorites were *carne con papas fritas* followed by several local *tintos* of demitasse coffee. With perfected timing, Guillermo retrieved the giant ice-packed cooler from the butcher and drove up precisely when I walked out of the salon. He sped us to the airport, where he shepherded me, and the heavy cooler, through the crowds to the departure gate.

Guillermo bowed with portly elegance and twinkling eyes. "*Hasta la próxima vez*," he bid me farewell.

On arrival at Cartagena's small but crowded airport, tall and gangly Tomás waved from the baggage claim area. His enthusiasm led me to believe that hoisting loads of provisions provided much needed fitness workouts and a break from an otherwise sedentary day as a company driver.

At home, our cook Maisie made quick work of unloading the Igloo and freezing the meats solid enough to outlast the inevitable future power outages. Following my instructions, she stacked my black market Del Monte peaches on the very top shelf of the pantry. Those peaches were precious to me, and Maisie knew it.

Maisie hailed from San Andres Island, 348 nautical miles due north along the Caribbean coast, and duly claimed by both Colombia and Panama. Maisie spoke an endearing patois of English scrambled up with Spanish. Her skin was bronze; she stood six feet from bare feet to sleek head traditionally wrapped in lengths of colorful fabric. Her smile, her hands, and her heart were large. However, it was to Clyde, our constantly hungry Dalmatian, that Maisie gave her true love. She spoiled him like a baby.

Donna, Clyde, and Pineapple Seller,
Cartagena, 1970

My system for staging successful dinner parties involved savvy match-ups of visitors and locals: executive guests; at-home refinery executives and wives; and in-town dignitaries with varying English fluency.

An example of a colorful local notable was Teresita, formidable Canasta player-international doll collector-wife of the refinery's medical doctor. I often invited my favorite expat couple: Meinke, a fiber artist, and husband Hans, a scuba diver—home country, Holland. To orchestrate the long list of idiosyncratic personalities, I devised an annotated host's diary:

E—eats everything
HD—heavy drinker
LD—lively and decorative
WS—watch the silver
LE—limited English
AW—always welcome

One Cartagena evening every guest earned my AW rating. Monsoon season had arrived with a vengeance. The streets flooded. Rainwater poured down the entry steps of our house and covered three inches of the ground floor, entryway, living room, dining room, and kitchen. With that quantity of rain, the flood wouldn't recede for hours. And like clockwork, phone service went down and electric power went dead. I had no idea how, when, or what dinner we'd be able to serve that night. But because I liked a challenge, I never canceled a dinner party because of unpredictable setbacks.

For native *Costeños* following local tradition, dinner at eight meant don't arrive before nine. As they did that evening. Willing to go barefoot, the guests left their shoes at the dry upper landing. The men rolled up their pant legs and the women in long skirts laughed gaily as they knotted and shortened their hemlines. Good humor prevailed. Sloshing through the living room water, they hugged and greeted each other in endearing, coastal-accented Spanish. Toe-splashing and playfulness increased with the quantities of rum drinks consumed.

About a year earlier when Bob and I arrived in Cartagena, we chose this particular house with a mysterious mezzanine platform above the living room that we dismissed as "local quirky." After that night's dinner party, the mezzanine pavilion would forever be considered "architectural genius." Around 10:00 p.m., I commandeered our twelve boisterous guests into a team. Well lubricated with rum, they unsteadily hoisted up the twelve-foot dining table that I'd commissioned from Tobár, a talented Colombian carpenter. It was solid wood and weighed about as much as a local piragua fishing boat. Someone in the group suggested they get a rhythm going by chanting like royal oarsmen along the Nile. If only we'd had cell phone cameras in 1971, I would own a priceless video of twelve swaying, singing, and liquored up guests sloshing through three inches of "the Nile," twenty-four arms stretched up high to transport their load across three marble steps upstream to the mezzanine pavilion. Hysterical laughter and competitive male-female grunting accompanied the ritual lowering of the table to the center of the mezzanine-cum-dining area. This was followed by slow and ceremonious placement of fourteen substantial wood chairs around the table.

The true hero of the evening, voted by consensus, was our cook Maisie.

In our candlelit kitchen (fortunately fueled by gas), Maisie produced a triumph. Due to bottomless pouring of our house specialty, *La Tarena*—a concoction of Ron Caldas dark rum, splash of tonic, squeeze of fresh lime and dollop of fresh orange juice—no one was lucid enough to keep track of time. Likely it was well after midnight when Maisie strolled out of the kitchen and announced, "Señora Donna, *la cena mas sorpresa*—is ready!" Indeed, Maisie's dinner surprised us all.

Barefoot, unflappable, and bearing a series of heavy platters from the kitchen, Maisie forged the shallow waters of the living room and climbed the steps to the dining pavilion. With majestic dignity, she presented herb-scented red snapper caught fresh that day, green *plátanos* slathered in butter, and fragrant mounds of her specialty *arroz con coco*, rice simmered in fresh coconut milk. Inebriated guests inhaled every bite with hoots of "*Brava Maisie!*" resounding up and down the long table.

Then came *el postre*—I couldn't imagine what inventive dessert Maisie would produce. With regal flourish, she placed a glistening silver tray upon the dining table. Fourteen cut crystal goblets sparkled in the candlelight. I leaned in to see that topped by dollops of *crema*, each crystal goblet held layers and layers of golden, delicious Del Monte peaches—*my* golden, contraband Del Monte peaches! As she served each guest, Maisie avoided eye contact with me. Other than Tomás, she was the only person who knew about my addictive cravings for premium priced, black market Del Monte canned peaches. I'd trusted her to keep my secret stash safe. But the night of the flood, Maisie served up my coveted peaches to our guests, at about a dollar per bite. I was furious—and drunk.

La Profesora Doña Donna

In Colombia, I had more time and household help than I would ever have again. And so I searched for extra ways to stay occupied. That's how I found a local artist who, like other women with beauty salons in their garages, decided to hold art classes in her garden. I signed up for the first art class of my adult life. In that *pleine air* studio, I created a fairly decent painting of the Cartagena refinery. Bob so liked the painting that he hung it in his Cartagena office. Along with family pictures on his desk, the painting would go wherever he was transferred. Despite taking an art class and being Bob's official company hostess, I was unfulfilled and yearned for something more. As it turned out, I was also in the right place at the right time.

During our tenure in Colombia, the late 1960s and early 1970s, I was proud of the United States' dedication to international education. In Latin America, under State Department auspices, the United States Information Service (USIS) sponsored well-conceived and well-funded cultural exchange and English language study. Myriads of cultural centers fostered goodwill between the US and thousands of foreign students. In the future, this vulnerable foundation of international friendship would steadily crumble. USIS funding would drop decade by decade until student numbers diminished significantly. However, my time in Latin America came before the fall.

Cartagena had applied to USIS with a cleverly strategic mission— the education of underserved, teenage girls. US funding was approved. *El Centro Colombo Americano de Cartagena* became the city's official school for bilingual secretarial training. Ironically, the entire city of Cartagena had only two paid positions for bilingual secretaries: Secretary to the Major of Cartagena and Secretary to Refinery Manager, Robert E. Wilhelm. The same two bilingual women remained in excellent health and capably filled both positions for decades. Undeterred, socially ambitious parents unofficially promoted El Centro as their version of an elite finishing school for "fortunate" girls. Merely being accepted to El Centro was a social coup, and there was a constant teacher shortage.

When I learned that El Centro needed an English teacher, I applied as the first native English-speaking teacher of bilingual secretaries at El Centro. They paid me a bonus. Five decades later, I can't remember my monthly salary—only that I donated it back to the El Centro Scholarship Fund. Although I didn't realize it at the time, I wasn't really working for the money. My incentive was validation—not as appendage to my husband's elite status in the community, but for my own skills and contributions.

Young and enthusiastic, I sauntered into my Cartagena classroom the first day. Flip top wooden desks were arranged in haphazard rows. The walls were decorated with glossy travel posters contributed by Avianca, Colombia's National Airline. It was nicknamed "Avi-Nunca" by those of us frustrated with its too frequent delays and cancellations.

Like a flock of noisy bright parrots competing for hierarchy, fifteen lively teenage girls chattered and bobbed up and down with anticipation. These gals were going to keep me busy. When they saw me, they sprang up from their seats and formed a giggling circle around me, some chanting in singsong, "*Hola, Señora Doña Donna*," and others squawking, "*Bienvenida Profesora!*" They reached out to touch, stroke and hug me. The girls, daughters of costeña mothers, were accustomed to intimate connection by being up close and personal.

"*Señoritas, hay que sentarse*," I corralled my boisterous flock back to their desks. So began my epoch of teaching English-without-boundaries to the future bilingual secretaries of Cartagena, Colombia. "From this moment, we speak only English in this class. I am Mrs. Donna. You may ask me anything, but every question must be in English!"

Lourdes of bright brown eyes: "Mrs. Doña Donna, how long is you married?

"I've been married three years."

Maria of impish dimples: "When you are having baby, Mrs. Doña Donna?"

"That I don't know—whenever it happens."

Paulina of persistence: "You are with good husband? He is very nice, not so nice? What you say, Mrs. Doña Donna?"

"I say you are way too curious, Paulina."

"What is way too curious?"

"It means you are not being polite."

"Okay, I want be polite. Very much please tell me, Mrs. Doña Donna, what is like with your husband? Why no babies, please?"

"There'll be time for babies later." Although I wasn't really concerned about that, because I still felt like a newlywed.

Those adorable girls personified belief among Latinas, that a woman's core identity was based on marriage and as-soon-as-possible motherhood. As a young, newly married American woman in the early 1970s, I belonged to a generation of women who held onto their traditional beliefs. I didn't question a traditional woman's devotion to her husband and his advancing career. What was good for Bob was good for me. Wasn't it?

Profesora Donna with students,
Cartagena, 1971

Cartagena Driver, Tomas,
and Donna, 1971

There was a shortage in Cartagena during our era there that I couldn't overcome—a dearth of fashionable women's clothing shops. The entrepreneurial spirit of Cartagena hadn't even produced a garage boutique for new (not secondhand) ladies fashions. Were there no talented, imaginative local seamstresses? Not in those days. My longing for pretty clothes had turned into an out-of-control obsession. One evening, Bob came home from the refinery and announced he had a business trip to Miami. Would I like to go along?

"Yes!" I screamed and hugged him. Miami was a clothes addict's paradise. A few days later, when we checked in for the Cartagena/Bogotá/Miami flight, the Avianca agent who lifted my giant, empty suitcase sent me a conspiratorial wink.

In Coral Gables, Florida, where the Esso Inter-America office was located, we stayed at my favorite hotel, the Biltmore. Its glamorous history was memorialized in a hallway photo gallery of celebrated past guests, including vintage Hollywood stars. Another world-renowned feature of the Biltmore was its twice-Olympic-size swimming pool. Esther Williams and her synchronized swimmers had once mesmerized guests peering down from the Biltmore's pink stucco balconies. I never took a dip in the celebrated waters—the Sirens of Dadeland Mall beckoned. How easily I succumbed.

Bob didn't believe in room service. His morning ritual, when we traveled, was to have a proper breakfast in the hotel restaurant at a table big enough to spread out the *Miami Herald* and the *New York Times*. After that, he'd return to the room, brush his teeth, hoist his Hartman leather briefcase, and head out with determination to a full day of business meetings.

I thrived on the Biltmore's efficient room service. Gulping down cups of black coffee and a toasted bran muffin, I picked up the phone and summoned valet service to deliver my rental car curbside. Visions of beautiful clothes dancing wildly in my mind, I drove full speed ahead to Dadeland Mall. Never did I imagine that Dadeland Mall in Miami, Florida would be a place of final reckoning for Mother and me.

At the stroke of 10:00 AM, the quadruple glass doors of Jordan Marsh opened to a shopper's fantasy world. I sailed through to a storewide celebration of "Torrid in the Tropics," with a full-scale steel band playing irresistible Caribbean music in the lobby, rhythmic sounds piped via loudspeakers to all floors. I joined a conga line of shoppers ascending the escalator. At Sophisticated Casuals, mannequin maidens dressed in provocative fashions lined the aisles. Their arms, festooned with bangles of rainbow-colored bracelets, gestured toward racks of sun-kissed garments. In record time, my arms were weighed down with dozens of outfits, yet I managed to push open the door of a vacant dressing room and begin my strip-and-choose routine.

Given my insatiable lust for pretty clothes and the very short time I had to shop for them, I soon emerged from the dressing room with my picks and headed to the nearest sales counter. "I'll take these," I said, pointing to a vivid pink flouncy skirt and an off-the-shoulder peasant blouse trimmed with antique-looking lace. The sales clerk cooed, "You'll be dressed like an island princess." She folded and wrapped my purchases in tissue paper, and slid everything into a giant Jordan Marsh shopping bag branded with exotic jungle macaws. With a flourish, I signed the sales receipt, slipped the bag handles over my shoulder and swayed through the sea of fashions to the escalator. Syncopated sounds from the steel band accompanied me out the main doors of Jordan Marsh. Next stop, Burdines!

I was super energized, totally unaware that something festering in my subconscious was about to explode. I entered the main doors of Burdines and was stopped in my tracks.

"Danusia!" There was Mother—legs splayed, red-knuckled hands anchored at the top of her hips—right in front of the Estee Lauder counter.

I frantically surveyed the shoppers around me. Did they see what I saw?

"Danusia, I need you now!"

No one around me was staring at the stocky woman who had barged into Burdines to disrupt and disturb.

"Mamusia, what are you doing here?" I hissed.

True to habit, Mother ignored my question and swirled away. She headed straight for the escalator. I had to get there before she could, yet again, sabotage my quest for pretty clothes. But I wasn't the little girl whose party dress, loafers, bathrobe, and patent leather Mary Janes Mother could steal and give away. Now, I was a grown-up, married woman who could buy her own pretty things. *Mother doesn't have power over me anymore.*

In a wild dash, I leaped the ascending steps two at a time. Reaching the second floor, I thrust myself deep into the rows of Chic Women's Casuals without even glancing back.

Soon enough, Mother's familiar sour odor filled the air. She was lurking nearby. My breaths got short and sharp. Moisture slicked my palms. The clothes hangers wouldn't behave in my fumbling fingers. In that tender time so long ago, I didn't understand what was happening to me—that my symptoms were the onset of a full-fledged panic attack. I'd never had such an episode before (and would never again).

Frantically, I grabbed anything that caught my eye. I heaped one item after another over my arm until my shoulders drooped from the weight. Swooping up the Jordan Marsh bag of earlier purchases, I rushed into the dressing area. A willowy sales woman was tidying up one of the vacated rooms. Her plastic nametag read "Laureen."

"I'll be glad to help you," she said, her tone oozing friendliness. "Let's hang all of your lovely selections right here in this room." How gracefully she gestured me into a pale green dressing room. One by one, she smoothed and hung each garment around the room. Reaching for the handle of the louvered door, she said, "Let me know if you need any help." Before closing the door, she took a final quick scan of me and the hanging clothes. Did she sense how unraveled I was, or did she think I couldn't afford to buy that many items?

Taking in long, slow breaths, I shut my eyes for a few moments and began to assure myself: *Mother is gone now . . . Mother is gone now . . . She can't punish me anymore.* I opened my eyes to check—no sign of her. Yet her unmistakable smell had followed me into the dressing room. I reached over and locked the door, certain that Mother was nearby.

I put my handbag on the pink slipper chair, and dropped the Jordan Marsh bag on the floor next to it. Peeling off my sweaty clothes, I began my strip and choose routine again. "Yes" to this, "No" to that, "Maybe" to the rest. Mechanically, I worked my way through the outfits. I tried on a moss green dress with white eyelet. It was fabulous but the belt felt snug. I'd brought in two sizes, so I pushed the silky garment up along my stretched arms to puddle around my head. *Maybe if the dress was too large and the belt fit, I could just switch belts . . . would that*—a soft knock interrupted my switching belts.

My body tensed. *Oh my God, it's Mother! But she wouldn't knock? Mother would just barge in.*

"Lovely lady, how is everything working for you?"

"Just fine, Laureen," I said. "If I need anything, I'll let you know."

Her footsteps faded away. Relieved, I slumped down onto the pink chair. Sweat had built up on my forehead and under my arms. I bent to salvage a discarded sheet of cardboard from the floor and fanned myself furiously. The insidious sour odor overwhelmed me. I closed my eyes for a second and an image flashed through my head: Mother, the hated leather belt around her hand, like a viper ready to strike.

Fear shot through me. I fumbled into my clothes, heaped a bundle of "takes" over my arm, grabbed my handbag, and gripped one handle of the Jordan Marsh bag. *Mother would be furious to see how many new dresses I'm buying.* The bag gaped open. My state of panic would blur the details of what happened next. Did I purposefully place the green-and-white dress in the Jordan Marsh bag with no intention of paying for it? Or did I passively watch as it slithered from my arm into the Jordan Marsh bag? Or, did I not know it had happened at all? My sole focus was on Mother and my fear of what was happening. Why was she there? What did she want from me?

My face was burning hot. Waves of fear coursed through my brain. Slowly, I opened the dressing room door. I scanned for Mother—the corridor was deserted. Time to escape!

Laureen waited near the cash register. With a swoop, I piled the garments onto the raised counter. "I'll take all of these."

Laureen's eyes glowed bright and she began to sort the clothes. "A lot of beautiful things here, a perfect summer wardrobe." With practiced efficiency, she folded the clothes, read the prices and punched corresponding amounts onto register keys.

"What a lucky lady you are." Laureen's lilting voice sounded envious.

"Yes, I love these tropical colors because I live in the Caribbean."

She arched her eyebrows. "So that's everything?"

"Yes, I've bought enough." Without a glance at the Jordan Marsh shopping bag looped over my left arm, I fumbled in my handbag, found my wallet, and handed her my VISA card. With a smile, I signed the bill for $482.00.

"I hope you enjoy your beautiful new fashions." Laureen brightened her smile and handed me a glossy black Burdines bag filled with my new purchases. Before reaching the down escalator, I glanced back to see Laureen rushing to the dressing rooms. There was a lot to tidy up.

Reaching the ground floor, I approached the Estée Lauder counter with trepidation. *Had Mother followed me?* I held on tight to all my bags and propelled my legs toward the front exit. Taking a deep, slow breath, I left the store and melded into the crowd of mall shoppers. In a few minutes, I'd be in the parking lot, and free of Mother.

But I never got there. Two stern-faced men intercepted me. One was tall and one was short, both were wearing twin navy blazers. I was astonished when I saw their prominent badges with Security spelled out in red. The tall one took firm hold of my arm. "Miss, we must ask you to return to Burdines with us."

They marched me back through the store. I was disoriented and frightened. As the other shoppers stopped to stare, I tried to compose myself. Inside the security office, the tall man confiscated my shopping bags. "Sit here, Miss," he said, his voice stern. He pointed to a chair next to a long, empty counter. "We'll need to verify your purchases."

I had to provide sales slips for everything. But nothing I said could convince the pair from security that I hadn't stolen the green-and-white dress. The tall man offered me the telephone. "You are entitled to make a phone call before we press charges."

I gulped air and swallowed my dread. "I must phone my husband." My hands shook as I scrambled in my handbag for the phone number of the corporate office in Coral Gables. Could anything be worse than having to tell Bob that I was accused of shoplifting? My forehead throbbed. I could hardly focus. A secretary's smooth voice came on the line. Voice croaking, I said it was urgent that I speak to Bob Wilhelm—immediately. A moment later, he was on the line, and I was sobbing, telling him why I needed his help.

Even now, more than five decades later, I remember Bob's response. "Do not agree to anything. Do not sign anything. I'll be right there." In less than thirty minutes, purposeful and defiant, Bob strode into Burdines' security office. Without asking permission from the security guards, he led me into a vacant cubicle.

"Tell me what happened." His voice was firm and patient, his hand soft on my shoulder.

"Bob, my mother was in the store," I trembled as I spoke. "She was waiting for me." I told him everything I had seen and everything that had happened. Bob could have thought I needed psychiatric care, yet he showed me only soothing calmness. And he took charge.

With the security officers, he was commanding. Bob identified his company (SONJ then was the second largest corporation in the world) and his position (the head of their major oil refinery in Colombia). He instructed the store officials to check our extensive shopping record, many thousands of dollars. He demanded to know the total of the as-yet unpaid garment in dispute. The short security guard pawed through the stack of clothes and receipts, fumbled midway, and dropped a garment on the floor then scrambled to retrieve it.

"Here you are, sir." He held up the culprit items. "One green-and-white dress and an untagged white belt. Looks like the total is $129.47."

Bob glared at the security men, his brow furrowed—an intimidating look that would become only all too familiar during our lives together, and one that had a shattering effect on most people. Bob turned to me. "Did you intend to purchase that particular outfit?"

"Yes," I blurted, "of course I did." I explained that the unpaid items must have inadvertently slipped into my Jordan Marsh bag while I tried to collect my things, gather the Burdines garments, and open the dressing room door. "When I laid all the clothes over the checkout counter, I thought everything was there."

Bob turned to the security men, his face livid with anger. The characteristic furrow between his wide-set blue eyes was pulsing. His voice was loud and demanding. "Why didn't your salesperson help my wife carry her garments out of the dressing room?"

The atmosphere in the security office shifted. Bob had become the accuser and the security men the accused. Within moments, the entire matter was settled. We charged $129.47 to my VISA card. The short security guard handed the green-and-white dress and the belt to me with the receipt. He offered an apology for the inconvenience. As we prepared to leave the security office, Bob stood in front of the two security men, his blue eyes scrutinizing one and then the other.

"You will tell your supervisor that this store will *never* receive another cent from us! You will also inform him of a critical need—for better-trained sales help, able to deliver the *right kind* of professional service to customers." Bob was not a tall man, barely 5'10"—but to me that day, he towered over the two security men. Standing side by side, the short one barely reached the shoulders of the tall one, and both nodded their heads like robots.

Together, Bob and I made our way to the parking lot where I'd left the rental car.

"See you back at the hotel." Bob's voice was gentle. "I'll be there soon." He guided me into the driver's seat, and opening the back door, placed one tropical Jordan Marsh bag on the back seat and one glossy black Burdines bag right next to it.

For Bob the incident was closed. For me, it would symbolize Bob's integrity and wise counsel. Yet, we'd never again talk about what happened that day.

Even though I'd expected Mother to deliver her final message, when she did, I was completely unraveled. Why had Mother come back? Why had I panicked?

Decades later, in personal counseling sessions, I'd re-examine my memories of that encounter. I recognized that festering childhood wounds and the unresolved loss of Mother's power over me had generated a panic attack. Eventually, I'd understand my fantastical way of healing myself and saying good-bye to Mother. However, I had absorbed both her positive and negative influences. The impact that Mother had on my life continued to play out in small and large ways. For instance, in the many homes I'd inhabit in future, all of them had closets filled with pretty clothes, hung on custom rods, behind closed doors. All those doors had proper locks.

No News, Bad News

It had been over four years since my last visit and my vow never to return. I had to see Dad! The summer of 1971, Bob and I booked flights to Phoenix. I wrote Edith that we were going to visit Dad and would arrive within two weeks. However, before we could get there, a telegram arrived at Bob's office in Cartagena. When Bob phoned to tell me, I asked him to read the message—his voice was solemn: "Dad died in his sleep Sept 4th. Funeral Sept 7th. Love Edith."

We expedited departure to Phoenix—I needed to learn what had actually happened during the illnesses and deaths of Mother and then Dad. On landing at Sky Harbor Airport, I phoned Edith and told her that we'd arrive at Dad's house within two hours, and we would expect to meet her and Carl there. For the first time in my memory, Edith's voice was shaky and apprehensive, not at all sounding like the self-assured and domineering sister of my past. Mother's fears and warnings flared in my mind as we drove to our destination—"Edith wants to kill us!" Had Mother been right?

When we pulled into Dad's driveway, sadness flowed over me like the irrigation water that flooded the yard. Bob was to meet Edith and Carl for the first time. Everything was awkward. On the surface, the four of us were polite. Yet tension simmered. The ancient circulating fan was still there, its droning useless against the cloying heat of a living room filled with memories.

Bob and I sat together on the newly slipcovered sofa. Strange how my body found the familiar indentation I'd made sitting on that sofa as a teenager when I'd lived with Dad in this house. And again later sitting there with Mother when she'd delivered the diabolic wedding gift—her confession about my birth mother, Irma Lettrich.

Edith paced the room; her tinted glasses hid eyes I remembered as feral when she turned violent. Carl shifted nervously in Dad's shabby wing chair. Their awkward body language told me something insidious was going on. I turned toward Edith circling the room and avoiding eye contact with me.

"Edith." I deliberately raised my voice, to be heard clearly. "You gave Mother and Dad devoted care." Actually, I had no concrete evidence to accuse Edith of wrongdoing. "I hope they appreciated everything you did for them, and that they left you . . . enough."

"There wasn't anything left. Expenses took it all," Edith stared at Carl rather than me.

"Why didn't you let me know Dad was getting worse?" I asked.

"I did tell you his health was failing, and that you needed to come soon. Didn't you get my letter?"

"What letter? I knew nothing—"

"Edith was a real good daughter and nurse to your parents." Carl interrupted and turned to face me. "She always gave them what they needed." His forced smile seemed fake.

Our conversation was anything but assuring. I took Bob's hand, and we stood up together. Then we walked through the vacant rooms of Dad's house. I was searching for a remembrance. Only a few of his personal possessions were left—how quickly Edith had cleared things away. However, on the bookshelf by his favorite chair in the living room, I found a dog-eared copy of *Mechanic's Illustrated* and his old wire-rimmed glasses.

"Dad wouldn't mind my having these. I'm taking them with me," I announced to Edith, who stood and watched in the front entry hall.

I didn't ask for any more details about Dad's death. Edith didn't offer any. Dad's memorial service had taken place the day after her telegram had arrived in Cartagena. Indeed, she had taken care "of everything."

In Phoenix right after Dad's death,
Carl and Edith, 1971

Bob and I, claiming jetlag, made our hasty exit. Settling into the passenger seat, I inhaled the cloying odor of rotting fruit from the surrounding citrus grove. Slowly, Bob drove the car down the driveway. I glanced back to see Edith and Carl standing side by side at the front door. None of us waved good-bye.

When we reached our hotel and checked in, I could barely contain my emotions until we got to our room, where I collapsed on the bed. Shock, outrage, and despair overwhelmed me.

"Something terrible happened to my parents," I moaned.

"You're right." Bob sat down next to me as I sprawled sobbing on the bed. "The whole thing smells. They're hiding something."

"But how can I prove it?"

"We'll go to probate court in the morning and see if your father filed a will."

At the Maricopa County Court House the next day, the clerk indeed produced Dad's will. The document listed Edith as Sole Surviving Family and Carl as Executor of the Estate, valued at $250,000. Edith and Carl were named as Sole Beneficiaries. However, there was a small but glaring exception:

I leave the sum of $1,000 in my checking account to Donna Wilhelm, a woman I helped to raise.

I was stunned. Dad had actually listed me, not as his daughter, but as "a woman I helped to raise"? Years later, I would discover a contradictory funeral notice that had been printed in the Phoenix newspaper—deceased Joseph Sosinski had been survived by "two daughters."

Bob and I examined Dad's signature in the will. His script looked somewhat familiar to me, legible yet oddly erratic. It had been notarized and dated—two days before his death.

At the records desk when I voiced my doubts about the validity of my dad's will, the compassionate clerk recommended an attorney. Immediately, I telephoned his office, and he was able to meet with us that same day. I engaged him to investigate the circumstances of Dad's will and to verify the balance in his checking account.

A few weeks after our return to Cartagena, a letter from the Phoenix attorney arrived. His research confirmed that there had been a withdrawal from Dad's bank account—one day before his death—and that sum had reduced Dad's account balance to zero. A couple of weeks later, I stood in Bob's office and opened another letter from the attorney—inside the envelope was a cashier's check for $1,000. Evidently, I'd won retribution against Edith and Carl for failure of legal obligation to deliver money designated to me in Dad's will. I felt somewhat vindicated. For Bob, I felt deep appreciation and affection. His support and wisdom during a time of grievous betrayal from my family had been a precious comfort. The attorney included his invoice for legal services totaling $2,500. Without hesitation, I wrote a check for the amount, addressed an envelope to the attorney, and mailed payment.

Edith's missing letter—the one she claimed had warned me about Dad's failing health—appeared a few weeks after our return home to Cartagena. The envelope was postmarked June 24, 1971, and was addressed to the wrong address. A vigilant postal clerk had redelivered it to my correct postal box. Notably, every time Edith asked me for money, she had my correct address. Dad had sent his many letters to that same correct address. What could possibly explain why Edith sent the most critical letter of all to the *wrong* address? Ripping open the envelope, I read the message:

Dad failing fast. Come to Phoenix as soon as possible—Edith.

I came to terms with the truth. Edith had deliberately prevented me from seeing our parents before death. Both Mother and Dad had died under sudden and suspicious circumstances.

Years later via the family grapevine, I 'd learn that Mother and Dad had been financially subsidizing Edith and Carl for decades. Not only had they paid for the house in the desert, but also the intrepid Wagon that Edith drove across America and back and forth to the Hopis. Our parents had been sending regular payments of cash to Edith, no strings attached. Their sustained support of Edith revealed the blatant disparity of how our parents treated their two daughters. I was devastated. Why had Mother and Dad showered Edith with financial support for years, yet had put aside no money to fund my college education? If not for the beneficence of a stranger, I wouldn't have been able to attend ASU. I thought about Mother's impulsive arrivals at my ASU dorm, her contributions of greasy bowls of "good Polish" food—what a pitiful substitute that was, instead of the financial support I'd sorely needed. Mother had been unwavering in one way, and unpredictable in every other way.

However, despite the financial injustice, I'd never doubted being Mother's daughter—in many bizarre ways, for twenty-four years, she'd reconfirmed my place in the family. Also, that I was Theresa's cousin, and Aunt Mamie's niece. In every other way beyond genetics, I'd been Edith's sister. The lies Mother had fabricated during my childhood, when she vehemently denied family rumors about my true birth history, had been exposed in Mother's diabolic wedding gift to me—her confession to the Irma cover-up. Yet, I assimilated the trauma and drama of Mother's unpredictable behavior, as proof of what I needed to believe: that my flawed Mother had never waivered in allegiance to me.

But I had failed my mother. For years to come, I'd lambast myself as callous and oblivious to the mysterious circumstances of her death. Instead, I'd focused on Edith's manipulation of Dad in his final days and the betrayal of being disowned in his will. Why had Dad called me a "woman he had helped to raise"? Instead of naming me as his daughter—a legitimacy confirmed by my Connecticut birth certificate. I'd taken legal retribution against Edith and Carl—why hadn't I also confronted them about Mother's illness and death? Had I been too cowardly or insecure? Was this another example of my habitual emotional shut down to avoid confrontation? Why had Edith's disposition of Mother's Boarding House #3 and the disappearance of all her remaining possessions escaped my scrutiny?

Investing my trust in Edith and Carl would as reliable caretakers had been a grievous error. Surrendering control and care of both parents to them was a terrible misjudgment. For the rest of my life, I'd bear the burden of self-imposed guilt: that I had not loved my parents enough. That I had not intervened in their end of life care. That I had sabotaged any possibility of a final peace between us.

Good-Bye Colombia

The New Year of 1972 brought another transfer and another promotion for Bob—back to the corporate office in New York City. Five years in Colombia had transformed me from a naïve young bride to a savvy corporate wife. I'd learned to host dinner parties, to hunt and gather basic provisions in a city blighted by shortages. I'd learned a third language—Spanish with an accent that sounded somewhat native, at least according to generous locals. I'd managed my local household staff and successfully communicated with them in their language. As La Profesora Doña Donna, I'd taught English to a bevy of Cartagena's teenage girls. My five years of experience in the Andes and the Caribbean, had given me personal growth and some of my best memories.

However, I'd tried and failed at something that was easy (for others)—learning to dance the native *Colombian Cumbia*. Local varieties of the *cumbia* flourished throughout Latin America. Its centuries-old origin traced back to slave dancers pulling their shackles along with rhythmic swaying of hips while keeping their torsos tall and steady. I admired the Colombian version, performed by dancers holding a burning candle aloft in one hand, the other hand embracing a partner as they danced together with sensual allure.

The move to New York City meant leaving behind a circle of Colombian friends. Among them, one couple who would have significant influence on our lives in the future. We'd met Maria Cristina and her husband Ramon in Bogotá. They were among Colombia's most prestigious families. During our early Esso days, Ramon and Bob were colleagues. Both men would have ascending careers in the corporation, Bob internationally and Ramon in his native Colombia. In my view, Maria Cristina and Ramon epitomized Colombia's *oligarquía*. Ramon was tall, arrogant, well educated, and a gifted raconteur with a keen instinct for reading the human psyche—attributes that would bring him fame and notoriety. Long after Bob and I departed Colombia, we'd hear through the company pipeline that Ramon played a key role in top-secret missions of life or death, mediating among a trio of players: the Colombian government;

the wealthy families whose members were seized for ransom; and the ruthless Colombian guerilla kidnappers. Success was calculated by price paid and whether or not the hostage survived.

When Ramon married Maria Cristina, daughter and sole heir of a prominent Colombian family of extraordinary wealth, their union was a merger of Colombian affluence and power. Among the women of its privileged class, Maria Cristina was a rare exception. She had *noblesse oblige*, a dedication to obligation that she fulfilled as director of La Casa de la Madre y el Niño, the most prestigious private adoption agency in Colombia during the years we lived there. La Casa would continue to impact lives of children and parents for an undetermined number of years into the future.

Maria Cristina and Ramon hosted our official good-bye, a traditional *despedida*, at their home in Bógota. During the evening, Maria Cristina floated into the opulent living room, where a circle of Esso Colombiana wives surrounded me, hugging and promising to stay in touch. With a regal smile, she squired me away to the private library. We didn't sit; Maria Cristina preferred to stand. Her excellent posture enhanced the drape of couturier clothes. Maria Cristina firmly took my hands in hers. I remember her long fingers were adorned by rings set with impressive Colombian emeralds. That night, she didn't intend for us to chat. She got right to the point.

"If you and Bob ever decide to adopt a child, remember La Casa."

I was twenty-nine years old. During five years of living in Colombia, I hadn't been concerned about having children. Maria Cristina parting message prompted me to ask myself—is a wife truly fulfilled if she isn't also a mother?

Moving Through It All

Reverse Culture Shock

After five years "away from the flagpole" in Colombia, Bob was back at corporate headquarters in New York City. I've forgotten his new title for that promotion. The first five years of my marriage had been shaped by life overseas. Coming home to New York City, USA. would turn out to be the most challenging of all our moves.

For expats like us, readjusting to "normal" in the US meant letting go of special perks: the elevated status of being Americans abroad. In New York City; no "staff" of maids and a full-time cook. Bob didn't merit a *chofér*. And we'd lost our hardship bonus. Living in New York City, one of the most expensive, demanding, and competitive places in the world, would redefine the term "hardship."

Not only had I left behind my friends, my students, and our household help, but I'd also abandoned Clyde, our adored Dalmatian dog. Not since Great Dog Brutus of my childhood had a canine so captured my heart. It was impossible to imagine Clyde, who lived to run, being led on leash over the cement sidewalks of New York. Bleak with resignation, I'd surrendered Clyde to a 'better life' with Bogotá friends who

lived in a spacious home and large garden. Within weeks after our departure, they had fallen in love with Clyde. I felt relieved that I'd done the
right thing—until a few months later when their letter from Bogotá
arrived. Clyde, they wrote, had discovered an irresistible canine lady in
his new neighborhood and chased her with youthful passion that made
him oblivious to a speeding truck. Clyde died in his prime, a casualty of
tragic love. I grieved as if I'd witnessed the tragedy with my own eyes.

Clyde's death added to the loss of human relationships in Colombia
took heavy emotional toll on me. On the outside, I looked like I had it all
together. But on the inside, I was a mess. At the local A&P supermarket,
I went catatonic trying to choose between twenty-odd breakfast cere-
als. In Colombia, there were never more than four brands of anything on
grocery shelves. Overcoming shortages in Cartagena had demanded my
ingenuity. Back home in the United States, it seemed like I was being
swallowed in the land of plenty.

My strange physical symptoms began with wretched stomach
cramps and loss of appetite. Lifting a cup of American coffee, my hands
trembled. *What's wrong with me?* Panic made me diagnose myself—*I have
amoebic dysentery!* I pleaded with the doctor's phone receptionist, "Give
me give me your first available appointment—any day, any hour."

After myriad lab tests and X-rays, the doctor ushered me into his
office. "All tests have come back negative, Mrs. Wilhelm."

I breathed a little easier.

"What you are going through is a syndrome I'd call Reverse Culture
Shock." The doctor added, "With time and resilience, I'm confident
you'll cure yourself."

I had no clue how to do that.

Bob's salary, though commensurate with his rising status as a young
SONJ executive and the average cost of living in other US cities, was
well below the over-the-top costs of New York City. By the end of each
month, we had spent every penny of what Bob earned. Also, he was
determined to pay off his college loans as fast as possible—MIT and
Harvard Business School were among the most expensive places to be
educated in America. Typical of Bob, he intended to pay back every cent

of those loans in record time. During four years in New York City, he accomplished his goal.

The already high price of a New York co-op apartment was made even more costly by the monthly maintenance fees. Co-op boards could even ask new buyers to pay cash only, despite having a pre-approved mortgage. Like every assignment in Bob's career, we had no idea how long we'd be living in New York City. We decided to rent a gracious apartment in a coveted pre-war building at 970 Park Avenue and 81st Street. Coincidentally, it was right around the corner from where Libby and I had shared our five-flight walk-up apartment. Now, ten years later, I'd be living in a spacious three-bedroom, two-bath with an additional small maid's room and bath. "970," as we came to call the apartment, also had high ceilings, thick-walled soundproofing, and a 24-hour doorman. When we announced, "We'll take it," we took on premium rental costs that would sorely test our budget. As a further hedge against New York City's competitive real estate market, we signed a three-year lease.

At 970, Bob and I became next-door neighbors to an attractive young couple—Max, an ambitious art dealer, and Mary, a charming English woman. Soon we became fast friends, often asked by Max and Mary to pose as art buyers at their client cultivation parties. One such event would prove transformational for me.

While working my way through the crowd at this particular party, a woman's hand clamped with thick silver bracelets clawed at me.

"Hello there," said the gravelly voice of a heavy smoker who blinked at me with thick-lidded eyes. "I'm Madeline Hochberg. I'm with the museum." (As if I was supposed to know whether that meant the Metropolitan Museum of Art around the corner, or the Guggenheim Museum a few blocks north on Fifth Avenue).

I was already feeling disenchanted by the melee of crafty-eyed guests circling and scoping out one another. What I really wanted was to find Portia, our neighbors' well-trained canine lady and give her a good-bye cuddle. But Madeline Hochberg wouldn't stop talking.

"And you? What do you do?" She raised black-penciled eyebrows into jagged slants that told me that I'd been prejudged.

"I've just returned to the States from living in Colombia, South America."

"Well, did you *do* something there or just *live* there?"

"Actually, my husband was head of a refinery in Cartagena. He's in the oil business—"

"My dear," her tone reduced *dear* to a non-entity, "it's what you do that I ask about, not your husband's business. All I know so far is that you've left the Banana Republic."

"Madeline, something tells me that you don't really want to know about me." Giving her a fake smile, I sauntered off.

What I didn't realize then was that Madeline Hochberg's rude arrogance would turn out to be a gift in disguise. Years later, I would thank her in absentia. She had shocked me into a life-changing realization. For Bob, the established, worldwide routine of SONJ eased a smooth transition from doing business abroad to being back in the States. However, I needed to be jolted back. Why had I been brought back to New York City? It was my responsibility to find my own purpose, and only I could carry it through.

By the fall semester, I'd re-enrolled in Hunter College, City University of New York (CUNY). Ten years before, I'd been a single, working woman, and part-time student there. This time, I focused on my natural gifts for art. Mother's disparagement—"Worthless girl with talent for nothing, silly drawing all the time"—no longer had hold of me. Now I had freedom to decide whether to study studio art or art history. I chose both, a double major.

Two years later, I graduated Magna Cum Laude from Hunter, CUNY. Confident and primed for a career in the arts, I made good impressions at job interviews. Within weeks, The Arts & Business Council of New York hired me as a new Project Director.

My boss was a feisty, five-foot dynamo from Brooklyn named Sybil Simon. Thanks to her, a demanding feminist, I was well paid. And my role was clear—I would be responsible for matching volunteers who had business skills and passion for the arts with non-profit arts organizations that lacked management and financial planning skills. I functioned like a marriage maker between business and arts. And I thrived.

Until Bob came home from the office only a few months later with an excited expression on his face. "Honey, I've got news. The company is transferring us to Houston, Texas."

Houston

It was 1976. After four years in one of the world's most expensive cities, we were nearly broke. And we weren't alone. The entire city of New York was mired in financial crisis when we left. Lady Liberty had tirelessly welcomed the constant influx of the tired, the poor, and the huddled masses. She had absorbed and provided public services to a population already exceeding seven million. New York State was so desperate for revenue that, even after we moved to Houston, it tried to tax us as "temporarily absent New York City residents." Fortunately, the claim didn't hold up to legal challenge—we were not lifetime residents of the Big Apple.

In stark contrast, Houston, America's oil and gas capital, was booming. For my first six months there, I woke up every morning and asked myself: *Am I in a real world? Is this normal?* The Houston economic boom would last until 1981, when oil prices plunged and bankruptcies surged. But while we lived there, Bob and I were able to replenish our empty coffers and build our own prosperity.

Although I hadn't been ready to leave my position and colleagues at The Arts & Business Council of New York, yet again I made commitment to Bob as my top priority. When Houston called us, I was inspired to create Donna's Golden Rule—*Don't compare one place to another, and pretend you'll be there forever.* I focused on what Houston had to offer. My research led me to an innovative degree program at the University of Houston—an MA in Art Therapy—an exciting new field within healthcare. I envisioned myself as a professional art therapist who could guide clients with emotional conflicts to use art as a way to express their dilemmas, to explore unhealthy environments and relationships, and to find healthy resolutions.

In essence, I'd been using art as my personal therapy since childhood—beginning with my escape into the world of paper dolls and later discovering confidence and a healthy identity as class artist, silencing peers who'd called me Immigrant Girl. If I became an art therapist in private practice, I could realize a dream come true.

To Bob and most of his colleagues, a corporate wife was a subordinate. In that competitive realm, success and equality were determined and earned by top education, relentless ambition, and extraordinary performance. I yearned for my husband to see me as an equal. And to achieve that, I wanted to have professional credentials.

Halfway through completion of my MA degree requirements, I learned about a promising summer art therapy course at Simmons College in Boston that would count toward my degree program and expose me to other specialists in this new field. I signed up. When I left for Boston, I was filled with enthusiasm. Even though it had been almost twenty years since I'd lived in a dorm with other women, I quickly adjusted to campus life and course work at Simmons. I even started daily jogs around the nearby lake. But late one night in my dorm room, the phone jolted me awake. Groggy and apprehensive, I climbed out of bed, stumbled to the desk, and lifted the receiver.

Bob's voice was loud and clear. "Hey, Babe, sorry to wake you," he said, sounding ecstatic and not apologetic. "I'm getting promoted—to head up the Eastern Region."

"New York City?"

"No, Baltimore. It's the headquarters for Eastern Region."

We'd been in Houston less than two years—fruitful years—when we'd both found satisfaction and stimulation, Bob professionally and me intellectually. I'd found a new field of study and career ambition. Also, Houston had offered an expansive cultural life, and our neighborhood had been warm and welcoming. I'd become attached to our pretty, yellow, two-story house with the private backyard pool that I'd always dreamed about. Why hadn't I skinny-dipped every night like I'd promised myself?

Although getting my degree in art therapy was suddenly derailed, how easily I rationalized the move as another critical step upward in Bob's career. My identity was so intertwined with his success that moving wherever and whenever the corporation demanded seemed as much my job as his. However, this was our fifth transfer in nine years of marriage. And it represented at least two major losses: my budding career and my advanced education. I was also typical of the era when corporate wives outwardly contributed two-for-one to the corporate success of their husbands. Indeed, I was among the elite circle of women married to ambitious, high performing executives in America's top-tier companies. Pampered by material luxuries and increasingly prestigious community status, I forged onward to "our" next assignment.

Obsessed in Baltimore

The Eastern Region headquarters was actually located in Hunt Valley, Maryland, twenty miles outside of downtown Baltimore. Bob wasn't thrilled to be in the rolling hills of horse country. After bustling Houston, the bucolic, suburban setting was uninspiring to both of us. Following my Golden Rule was becoming harder and harder—I had a sinking feeling about this move.

Achieving my graduate degree in art therapy turned out to be a futile aspiration. That innovative field of study didn't exist in Baltimore or nearby Washington D.C. And commuting to Houston for completion of my MA requirements was beyond my scope of marital togetherness. While Bob's career and escalating financial rewards were flourishing, I was consumed by loneliness and pessimism. My incomplete professional identity and unpaid domestic contributions just didn't hold up in my mind or his, at least in my perceptions. My childhood insecurities and Mother's voice came back to haunt me. "You are useless, silly girl . . . no talent . . . not important."

My sexual response to Bob had steadily diminished from the spontaneous romance of our premarital intimacy. I couldn't remember Bob ever asking me what he could do to give me sexual satisfaction. In truth, I'd never told any man what I wanted or needed, sexual or otherwise. How could I express to my partner what I hadn't sorted out for myself? A tragic barrier rose between Bob and me. Neither of us was able or willing to communicate our deep, unfulfilled needs.

Then came the night I had a symbolic dream—of a big clock ticking so loudly that I could hardly stand it. I stuffed the clock under my

pillow. The ticking stopped, but a muffled voice spoke through the pillow. At first I could barely interpret it, but it got louder and louder until
I finally understood the message. "You're getting too old, Donna. There
is no time to feel sorry for yourself. No time to waste."

From then on, every time I passed a mom pushing a baby stroller,
or saw ads for irresistible baby clothes in magazines, I began to picture
myself with my own adorable baby. I had finally realized what truly was
missing from my life—becoming a mother. After all, what could be more
rewarding than caring for a baby? Even more transformational, my joy
and yearning infused Bob's desire to be a father. In a way we'd lost years
ago, we rekindled our passion and purpose and focused on something
we both truly wanted—rather than the singular ambition to build Bob's
career. Our desire to nurture a child together renewed our commitment to each other. This awareness was to become a core vision I would
carry into the future—when aligning together, we could create something more beautiful and meaningful than anyone can achieve alone.

However, there were obstacles. Bob and I hadn't used birth control
for at least five years; I'd already suffered one miscarriage. I was thirty-
four years old and Bob was thirty-seven. Undeniably, we had reason to
suspect fertility problems.

In Baltimore, our best resource for assessment was an infertility
clinic considered state of the art. Although in 1977 America, the medical science of infertility was limited. Bob and I underwent testing, and
the results showed we both needed corrective surgery. My diagnosis was
blocked fallopian tubes.

Surgery for me was the easy part. Post-op demanded my tough
endurance—three weeks of in-patient, precisely timed, excruciatingly
painful flooding of my fallopian tubes to keep them open—the only
available treatment option at that time. Yet even this was easier to endure
than what followed.

My hospital room was painted in bright colors. Bob slept fit-
fully on a sunshine yellow sofa during the many nights I wanted him
nearby. Both of us tried to hide our deep anxiety from each other, as
we awaited Dr. Morris Bowman's report. *What news will he give us? Will*

it damage our newfound intimacy and compassion for each other, or will it bring us even closer together?

"My friends, I wish there was better news." Dr. Bowman's expression was dour. "In spite of our best efforts—" at these words my heart cringed—"Donna's tubes have responded minimally." He said we had less than a five percent chance that even the most tenacious sperm could make its way upstream in my compromised fallopian tubes and fertilize a none-too-young egg, adding, "I'd encourage you to consider adoption." Dr. Bowman gave me a fatherly pat on my shoulder as he surveyed both of us. "It's your best option now." He shook Bob's hand and softly uttered, "Best of luck." Then Dr. Bowman turned away and left us in that superficially cheery hospital room.

For a few moments, we sat in silence. Bob gently reached up to touch my face with trembling hands; his dimpled chin and familiar smile that I so enjoyed comforted me.

"It's all right." He tried to soothe me with tenderness as he wiped my tears away.

Although I couldn't actually give birth, I was still convinced that we were meant to have a baby. Bob and I were emotionally prepared and committed to parenting. Unlike my own parents who had not been. Yet Hania and Juzo had had astounding luck. Hania became a mother not once, but six times—five through convoluted circumstances when she took in the four Holden girls, and decades later when she received me. Mother hadn't bothered to legally adopt any of us. All the lies and deceptions about my birth origins had made me determined that Bob and I would become parents. And do so legally.

Aggressively, we decided to pursue adoption. The clock ticked forward with a vengeance. As Bob moved up the corporate ladder and we kept getting transferred, our chances of agency adoption were evaporating. In those years, private adoptions were rare and risky. Besides, we'd never stayed in a location long enough to develop reliable sources. Five years ago in Houston, we'd had a premonition about our possible infertility and had explored adoption with Edna Gladney, a long-established Texas adoption agency. They'd given us a warm welcome and encouraged us to apply. "Certainly, we can help you, if you're patient," they said. When we were transferred from Texas to Maryland, our application with Edna Gladney didn't relocate with us.

In Baltimore, we had to start the application process again, with a new local agency. "Not much hope," they cautioned us. "Our preferred upper age limit for prospective parents is thirty-five years old for women and thirty-seven years for men. Both of you are at that limit now." We were placed at the bottom of a long waiting list. That hadn't deterred us—we kept hoping that an exception might be made and a baby might come to us. But there were plenty of younger parents waiting. Our call never came.

After three years in Baltimore, Bob was promoted to senior vice president in Esso Europe, headquartered in London. Moving overseas from Baltimore would put an end to any possibility of American adoption—US agencies only served Americans living in the US, not abroad. My emotions went into a tailspin. In terms of U.K. adoption prospects, I saw only bleakness. As expats, I knew our chances would be slim.

However, there were plusses to our move. London was a prime and coveted assignment among foreign postings. Our marriage had faced plenty of challenges. I was determined that Bob and I could find a way to be happy together. By resurrecting Donna's Golden Rule, I vowed to be positive about London. Maybe we'd be there long enough to adopt a child.

London and The Colombian Connection

Where's Our Baby?

London was a city made for walking. The city's verdant parks were irresistible. Our local jewel was the small and perfect Saint Mary of The Boltons Church and gardens, a blissful quadrant of Chelsea within blocks of our new home at 33 Seymour Walk. The 1850's Gothic style St. Mary's Church was encircled by stone pathways and meticulous English gardens.

When I craved window-shopping therapy, I walked from Knightsbridge, past Harrods, Harvey Nichols, and a myriad of small and trendy shops, then onward to Mayfair with its high-end couture fashion houses, posh hotels, and international jewelry stores. If I craved green therapy, I'd nip into Hyde Park or smaller Green Park. On rare sunny days, I'd slow down to gawk at the pale-skinned Londoners of all ages relaxing in those parks—some of them stripped down to their underwear, aka "personals," as if they were wearing bathing suits. Gaggles of uniformed park attendants bent over and popped up among the lounging humans like geese on a mission as they collected small fees for rental deckchairs. In 'Londonese,' they'd ask, "Fees paid, sir? Madam? Thanks ever so much." I pondered whether the collectors were titillated by the uninhibited sun-worshipers.

Each borough of the vast city of London seemed to have distinctive housing, a dominant class of residents, and a unique mix of cultures. I was determined to explore them all. Either via the London Underground or a double-decker London red bus, I'd travel to yet another undiscovered neighborhood then set out on foot. My journeys reminded me of those of London taxi-drivers-in-training. To qualify as an official London cabbie took an entire year of maneuvering on a bicycle through the quirky mazes of every neighborhood in every borough until the candidate could pass the exam to spontaneously take a passenger anywhere in London. I would never be able to unhesitatingly deliver a passenger in my car to any obscure address within centuries-old London.

A voyeuristic urge compelled my late afternoon strolls past strangers indulging in the English ritual of "taking tea." That event could serve multiple purposes: tea might be a simple family supper; it could be an opportunity for social chitchat between friends; it might even be a prelude to a lovers' tryst. For tourists, it was often a sipping and munching experience that made them look rather like "true" Londoners. Clutching my *London A to Z Street Guide*, I wandered past cheap and cheery pubs and tried not to stand out among posh tea takers in the lobby of Claridge's as I closely observed clusters of tourists at the coveted Tea Room of Fortnum & Mason, Purveyor to Her Majesty. *The embracing couple in the corner—are they lovers? Is the woman wife or mistress? The wildly gesturing group of women in embroidered vests, peasant blouses, and voluminous skirts—from what distant land did they come?* Those strolling expeditions were among my favorite experiences of life in London.

However, as an American in a common language country, I often found myself out of sync: English-sized envelopes didn't fit my American stationery; bangers, kippers, smoked eel and Marmite sounded as strange as they tasted; chemists, not drugstores, sold nappies, not diapers. Department store "food halls" were mini cafes—unique emporiums selling coffee, sandwiches, bakery items to take away, full arrays of fresh meat, fish, and game, as well as international cheeses, chocolates, and wines. One could buy dinner in the food hall then head for other departments such as refined ladies, gents' fashions, and fine jewelry. When an Englishwoman hosting an elegant dinner party invited me "to spend a penny," I thought she was organizing a low-stakes bridge game. "Silly me," she said with a haughty smile. "That's our English for your American ladies' toilet."

Despite my determination to adjust well and stay positive, I couldn't let go of my obsessive fixation on motherhood. Time was marching on. I was thirty-seven, Bob was forty—was it too late for us? Of course my fantasies also included clothes. The English climate was unpredictable. Our first summer in London, it was so cold and damp that I never even got out of my winter clothes. What would I wear pushing my adored baby in a proper English pram along the high street? I imagined Bob arriving at the end of his workday to our charming home on Seymour Walk. In my fantasy he jaunted down the cul-de-sac, climbed the steps of our house, and savored the flowers cascading from the window boxes that gave me such pride. Eyes twinkling, I imagine Bob popping through the front door to excited "Daddy! Daddy!" toddlers with chubby cheeks. Of course, he'd also be welcomed by his adoring wife, and we'd exchange passionate kisses.

However, like so many of my anticipations, reality didn't match my fantasies. No adoption agency in London had enough babies for British families, and United Kingdom citizens had priority. International adoption was our only hope. But how? And where? Developing countries had countless abandoned children facing destitute futures. Sadly, even the most determined couples willing to adopt those children had to overcome formidable cultural and language challenges, and face social services plagued by corruption. American citizens like us living in the U.K. who wanted to adopt foreign-born children and bring them into England had to provide volumes of documents and go through an official British home study. Overburdened U.K. social services didn't allot staff resources to foreigners, no matter how qualified expat couples were. The excessive costs of international travel, living expenses, legal fees, immigration fees, and adoption fees were beyond the means of most.

Bob and I, now having built comfortable financial resources, were fortunate exceptions.

Once again, a dream foretold my future. One night, images of babies appeared, all sleeping in their little cots in a row. A mysterious pair of women walked together observing the babies. They stopped at a cot, and one peered down at the sleeping baby, and then turned to the other woman. "Remember La Casa," she said. The other woman smiled at her and nodded. They walked to the next cot, and again the woman stopped, peered down at the sleeping baby, and then turned to the other woman. "Remember La Casa."

I jolted awake in our London bedroom. "Bob," I shrieked, shaking him like a wild woman. "Wake up! It's Colombia!" Bob, who had been sleeping peacefully beside me, sat up with a start. "It's Colombia! We can get our baby from La Casa in Bogotá."

We had spent our first years as a married couple in Bogotá. When we were transferred from Colombia, Maria Cristina and her husband had hosted our farewell party. As Senior Director of La Casa, the most prominent adoption agency in Bogotá, Maria Cristina had nearly divine power to decide the futures of Colombian babies surrendered to the agency for adoption and to make dreams come true for the couples longing to adopt those babies. Memory flooded back to the last time I'd seen Maria Cristina. At the end of that farewell evening, more than a decade before, she'd taken me aside to tell me three words: "Remember La Casa!"

Colombia was one of the few countries in the world that allowed infant children to be adopted by foreigners. Prospective parents were given generous age concessions—Bob, at age forty, and I, at thirty-seven, would still qualify to adopt a baby. We'd lived in Colombia for five years and were both fluent in Spanish. Bob's corporate network was still there and would be invaluable.

December 1980, auspiciously just before Christmas, I placed an international phone call that traveled through three operators and two languages in order to reach Maria Cristina's home in Bogotá.

A sweet voiced maid named Marta answered the phone, announcing I'd reached Maria Cristina and Ramon's house.

"*Hola Marta, habla La Señora Donna de Wilhelm, estoy llamando de Londres.*" How easily I slipped back into Spanish, although my voice quivered as I identified myself. "*Por favor se encuentra la Señora en casa?*" I hoped Maria Cristina was at home.

Long moments passed before a familiar French-Spanish-English accented voice from the past came on the line. "I can't believe it's you, Donna." She sounded surprised. "And you are calling from London?"

"Yes, it's me. We live in London now," I said. We chitchatted for a few minutes, talking about our husbands and their most recent promotions. I told her about our lovely home in Chelsea. "I'm calling about a very special mission," I said. My heart was beating so fast I had to breathe deeply to calm myself. "I remember what you told me when we left Bogotá. Bob and I want very much to adopt a baby. Will you begin an adoption search for us?"

"Of course I will," she responded immediately. Hearing her affirmation, I felt my mouth go dry and my hands get clammy. Maria Cristina was indeed willing to deliver on a promise she'd made more than ten years ago.

Very soon after, Maria Cristina sent hand-written letters of introduction about Bob and me to other couples living in London, all of whom had adopted children from La Casa. This network of couples would evolve into The Colombian Connection. Significant among them were Penny and Jimmy Vaughan. An amazing series of coincidences linked us. During our years in Colombia we had developed a close friendship with the prominent Vaughan Family, members of the privileged oligarquía and owners of a global flower export business. Jimmy Vaughan, we would learn, was the youngest son in the family, and headed the European branch headquartered in London. He and his British wife Penny had two babies adopted from La Casa. Even more extraordinary—they lived on Gilston Road in Chelsea, only a few blocks from our home on Seymour Walk. We were destined to form lifelong friendships.

In the meantime, all I could think about was: *When will we have our baby?*

Adopting Lara

By then Bob was a senior executive whose wife was invited (indeed expected) to join him when business entertaining was significant to the agenda. A few weeks after my phone call with Maria Cristina, I was in Oslo, Norway with Bob, for one of his business meetings. Most corporate wives genuinely adored the perks of such travel: flying on company jets, going on elaborate shopping expeditions, lunching and chatting at trendy restaurants, returning to five-star hotels, and indulging in exquisite spa treatments before dinner. Local wives served as hostesses. Those who were most gracious earned "points" for when the roles reversed and they traveled with their husbands. They became the pampered guests and we became their hosts. Corporate wives were either assets or liabilities. Our behavior and attitude could enhance or undermine our husbands' careers.

After midnight in Oslo the phone rang in our hotel room, on my side of the bed. Groggy, I fumbled for the receiver and heard Maria Cristina's familiar lilting voice.

"Donna my dear, you must come immediately."

My thoughts swirled, Maria Cristina must have called the London office, explained she had critical need to reach us, and someone there directed her to our hotel in Oslo.

"I have a little girl waiting for you in Bogotá.

"Maria Cristina, this news . . ." My eyes filled with tears.

"She is ten months old and beautiful."

"It's incredible. Please, can you wait for just a moment? I need to wake Bob, to tell him."

"Of course, take your time. I'm happy to wait."

It had happened so fast but had taken so long: thirteen years of marriage, five of them trying to conceive; failed fertility treatments; three years trying to adopt, interrupted by two moves. And now, after only one phone call to Maria Cristina and just a few weeks of waiting, an infant daughter was waiting for us.

Nervous that we might get disconnected, I placed the receiver down on the bedside table. Bob was already sitting straight up in bed. "Maria Cristina has a baby for us! Can you believe it? Our baby!" I hugged Bob tightly. I can't remember Bob's words, only that he was also thrilled with the news. We had absolutely no hesitation about wanting the baby. The only issue was timing: How quickly could we prepare our home for the baby and get to Bogotá?

I picked up the phone again and hoped my voice sounded as sure as I felt. "Maria Cristina, we can leave for Colombia in one week." I reached out to Bob. He grasped my hand and rubbed it gently. "Please tell our little girl we will see her very soon." My voice broke. "You have made a miracle for us."

We rushed back to London. My head was spinning. There were a million things to do, and I had no idea how to prepare for a baby in our lives. Most women had nine months—I had seven days. Amazing Penny Vaughan saved me. As my whirling dervish mentor, she shopped with me, calmed me, and tutored me on every detail necessary to prepare our household for a baby. In one week, Bob and I were as ready as we would ever be. At Heathrow Airport we boarded British Airways to Miami, where we connected to Avianca Airlines to Bogotá. Everything else on the route was a blur.

We arrived in Bogotá in January of 1981—more than a decade after we'd lived there. It was the dry season, and golden colors speckled across the Andean city otherwise shrouded in gray mists or drenched by heavy downpours.

Ramon had sent his company car and driver (by then my favorite, Guillermo, had retired). From the airport, we were driven to Maria Cristina and Ramon's home in the secluded and securely gated enclave of Santa Ana, the neighborhood where, years ago, Bob and I had moved in then immediately moved out when he was suddenly transferred to Cartagena. Maria Cristina and her household staff made us feel abundantly welcome. We were to be their guests for the duration of a momentous event—adopting our baby daughter.

The next morning, Maria Cristina left early to prepare for our arrival at La Casa. When the company driver arrived for us, we set out for a day that I had long hoped for but didn't dare expect. Even though I was nervous, my heart was bursting with joy.

Our route took us through the familiar barrios of Bogotá. Sunshine dappled flowers bursting from hand-carved window boxes softened the old brick facades of Spanish Colonial row houses. The narrow streets of modest, sometimes ramshackle, dwellings looked almost prosperous. As we approached the marketplace, lively sounds of humanity blared out like a rock concert. Dark skinned indigenous vendors hawked exotic fruits from their heavily laden baskets. "*Aquí se vende guayaba . . . cherimoya . . . lulo.*" How I'd loved those rhythmic names, almost as much as the sensuous tastes of the fruits themselves.

Savvy street kids in tattered clothes, skinny runners with quick fingers, darted among the crowds: "*Un peso? Me da un peso?*" Donate, or discover later that your wallet had turned into an involuntary gift. This time our vigilant driver had rolled up the front window.

"Bob, do you remember . . . when we first came to live in Bogotá?" Bob didn't seem to be listening, but I couldn't help reminiscing back to when we were newlyweds exploring the same marketplace in downtown Bogotá. Two little parakeets for sale had charmed us. We'd bought them and promptly named them Cromwell and Beowulf. Sitting in the back seat, just like now, our new pets had distracted us. Then the driver, not so vigilant, had left his window halfway open. An opportunistic thief reached in and over the driver's shoulder and snatched Bob's gold Omega watch right off his wrist, so deft and quick, at first we didn't even realize what was missing.

"How naïve we were then, so many lessons to learn," I said. Our eyes met. "Have we learned enough, do you think, to become instant parents?"

Bob smiled and took my hand. He seemed preoccupied with his thoughts. Like my dad Juzo, he was uneasy about sharing his emotions; even during the most dramatic times, he was silent. I wonder now what Bob was truly thinking that incredible morning, the first time we would meet our baby daughter.

A few minutes later, our car reached the entrance of La Casa, where a chattering reception committee descended upon us. Maria Cristina and the key members of the agency staff fussed over us and walked us to a quaint, French-style waiting room. Immediately a young maid, impeccably dressed in a traditional black and white uniform, entered with a silver tray bearing the inevitable *tintos*—aromatic demitasse servings of Colombian coffee. My nervous hands shook, and the small white cup wobbled in its saucer. With each sip of the full-bodied richness, I felt calmer. Colombian coffee always soothed me. To give us privacy, the staff slipped out and closed the door behind them.

We were about to meet our little girl for the first time. Did she know we were coming? Would she be afraid of us? Would she like us? We had a name in mind—Lara Amanda. Would it suit her? I glanced at Bob next to me on the sofa. He didn't seem to notice the Pierre Deux fabrics and the cozy pillows, or the warm sunshine filtering through creamy lace curtains, the tranquil setting meant to relax nervous parents. He stood up and began to pace. Not a man who liked surprises, Bob opened the door to check the hallway. Satisfied that no one was in sight, he closed the door, walked back, and sat down beside me.

Long minutes later, we heard a gentle knocking, and then the door opened.

As if on cue, Bob and I stood up in tandem. Maria Cristina entered the room, holding a small someone against her bosom. "This little girl has been waiting for you."

The child turned her head to look directly at us. Little beads of moisture clung to her forehead framed by light brown hair. Supporting the child's body with one arm, Maria Cristina reached up to smooth away the glistening dampness from the little one's forehead. With an air of beneficence, Maria Cristina stretched out her arms. "Here she is, Donna. Come hold your daughter."

I rushed forward to scoop her up and press Lara to my heart. Her little arms rose instantly up to my shoulders and tiny fingers pressed, with amazing force, into the skin below my collarbone. That day, I believed that this child knew exactly where she belonged. Feeling her warm body meld into mine, I inhaled the sweet baby smell of floral soapiness from a recent bathing by La Casa caretakers.

My daughter safely in my arms, I lost track of everyone else—until the clicks of a camera interrupted my reverie. A few feet away, Bob was taking pictures of those first moments with baby Lara, the small being who would change our lives forever. Bob didn't reach out to hold his daughter. Instead he was absorbed with taking her picture. This was both true to and a departure from his norm. Bob was indeed an accomplished photographer—of architecture and landscapes. But he avoided cluttering his photos with people. Having his own child, however, was a milestone switch to photographing those few people to whom he gave his heart.

A classic image of mother and child, photographed by Bob, matted in ivory and framed in silver, became my most treasured portrait of motherhood. Even now, when I ponder the photo of Lara's small head against my cheek, her dark eyes soft yet alert, the precious memories of our first day together return, and I savor them all over again.

Adopting Lara, Bogotá, 1980

Mother of Two

When Lara came to us at age ten months, she was still on infant formula. Her appetite for British baby food, the lumpier the better, was insatiable. Infant food from jars filled her up for a while, until Lara took finger swipes of fresh "Ma Da" food from our plates. After that she never ate another mouthful of baby food.

Soon bored with sprawling and crawling, Lara grabbed onto chairs,

Family of three, London, 1981

tables, or passing human legs. Within a month, she had hoisted herself up to toddling. Her vocabulary grew exponentially, especially her favorite words—"No!" "Won't!" "Want!"—shouted out loud and clear.

La Casa told adoptive parents, "An only child is a lonely child." They favored family requests for a second child. Parents were even allowed to choose the sex of the second child. With such power came frightening responsibility. I adored my feisty daughter Lara, who was turning three years old and showed no sign of wanting a sibling for companionship. How would a younger sister adjust to an older sister with a bossy streak? Would a younger brother introduce a positive dynamic, or stir up conflict with his male energy? Friends with two daughters, or a son and a daughter offered strong opinions about why their choice was the "best choice." Bob and I made our decision based on his male logic, my female instincts, and our fervent hopes that we were making a wise choice.

Early May of 1983, I placed another call to Maria Cristina in Bogotá. No international delay this time.

"Donna, it's good to hear your voice." Maria Cristina answered immediately. "We've been waiting, for quite a while."

"Maria Cristina, we needed time to make our decision. Bob and I hope that La Casa will give us a little brother for Lara."

Again Maria Cristina promised, "I will do my best."

As before, we didn't have long to wait. About four weeks later, Maria Cristina delivered the news. "Your baby son has arrived! He was born here in Bogotá, on May 31, 1983."

Jumping the queue for a baby from La Casa was fortuitous. Dealing with the bureaucracy of three countries was formidable. As before, providing the official Social Services Home Study required by Colombia was extremely complicated. The first time around with Lara, the process had been a nightmare. This time, with baby Nicky, we managed better. Our second home study was finalized, signed, and notarized in two weeks.

Logistics for the momentous second journey to Bogotá kept us stirred up in London. We wanted Lara with us during Nicky's adoption. Cumbersome international travel and the likelihood of Bob having to return early to London for work would leave me in Bogotá to finish the adoption process and bring both children home. Every step would need my full attention. I ramped into high gear and made the brilliant decision to take Tamsin, our mother's helper, with us. Her support would prove vital.

Lara with Tamsin, 1983

In a matter of days, outfitted like voyaging immigrants, we geared up for travel: Bob and I, Lara and Tamsin; four carry-on suitcases and a hefty pile of checked bags; one zip-up bag of toys for Lara; one bulky infant carrier and a super-duper size duffle of infant paraphernalia. It took a pair of drivers along with two Esso Europe company cars to pack, transport, deliver, and unload us and our heaps of baggage at Heathrow Airport.

We were to meet our infant son for the first time at La Casa in Bogotá on the Fourth of July, 1983.

Adopting Nicky

When our baby son became Nicholas Alexander Wilhelm, all records of birth family's health history, birth mother's pre-natal health, and conditions of the baby's delivery were intended to remain closed forever—just as they had when we adopted Lara. However, we did know that some birth mothers needed and accepted La Casa's residential care, and some did not.

Fifteen years later, when Nick was a teenager, it would be confirmed that his birth mother had accepted residential care—meaning she had been under observation by the La Casa staff for a notable time. Surely they would have taken her health history and learned that she suffered from debilitating depression. But the agency's policy—to protect the privacy of the birth mother—was inviolate.

Even if genetic history would or could affect the child, adoptive parents were given no information. In fact, prospective parents from all over the world were not allowed to adopt a child from La Casa until they affirmed the rule and its explicit warning: All records were sealed and unavailable to adopting families—such restrictions would have special significance for our family.

London families with La Casa babies, aka The Colombian Connection, of course compared what little we were told about our children's backgrounds. How fascinating that *all* of us had adopted infants born to unwed mothers from good families. That *all* birth parents were young, bright university students, and that *every* baby's birth had been without complications.

For me, being able to openly discuss sensitive issues about adoption, the very subject that was vehemently taboo in my childhood, was a gift beyond measure. Yet, no matter how much love we had for our children, or the amount of funds we were willing and able to spend on them, none of us had access to our children's genetic or medical background information. Even in a medical or mental health crisis, we would not be given the information that might help them.

How often I would need wise insights as an adoptive mother. If I could have changed anything about adopting my children, I would have had full access to every pertinent record. But would more vigilant observation or earlier intervention based on family of origin records have helped when Lara and Nick faced what should have been predictable challenges?

After two weeks in Colombia, Bob had to return to work in London. I stayed on to finish the adoption process for baby Nicky in Bogotá, along with Lara and Tamsin. Maria Cristina and Ramon had arranged our guest residency at the elite Bogotá Country Club, where we took full advantage of its indoor Olympic size swimming pool. After weeks of swimming in its warm waters and diving off of low and high springboards with Tamsin cheering nearby, Little Fish Lara turned into Prune Girl. Meanwhile, I was fully occupied with tending gleeful baby Nicky and prodding my languished Spanish through Colombian legal documents, adoption procedures, and pre-departure immigration interviews. No obstacle was too great or too small. I had an unlimited reserve of energy and determination to bring my baby son home to London and complete our family.

However, that didn't deter our need for fun. Before we began the journey home to foggy London, Penny and Jimmy Vaughan, with their toddlers Sasha and Alexis, invited us to their vacation home in Abaco, Bahamas. I relished the chance for a sunny respite, but also to introduce baby Nicky as the newest member of The Colombian Connection.

However, just as we began settling into the pleasures of Abaco, baby Nicky developed a high and persistent fever. The local pediatrician was confounded and his lab limited. "Do not travel to London until this baby is healthy," he warned. "As soon as possible, he needs proper diagnosis and care." Only too well, I knew that baby Nicky's "fever of unknown origin" was serious.

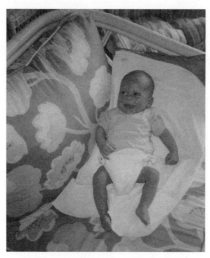

Adopting Nicky, ill in Abaco, 1983

We made immediate preparations to fly to Ft. Lauderdale, Florida. The next day, Jimmy climbed into the driver's seat of the big station wagon loaded with our copious gear, bags, toys, and suitcases. Tamsin and I hugged Penny, but Lara pleaded to stay and play. "Mommy, I not leave Sashi and Alexis!" Tamsin and I cajoled and maneuvered her into the car while baby Nicky, in my arms, was burning with fever. Despite this, he continued to smile like the happiest of babies.

Zigzagging across the runway in Abaco, followed by high-altitude turbulence on Island Air en route to Ft. Lauderdale got us all horribly airsick. As soon as I could compose myself after landing, I stood in the arrivals hall, shouting into a public phone at Ft. Lauderdale International Airport. Working my way down a scribbled list of local pediatricians, I tried to convince doctors' offices to give me an immediate appointment. Without exception, they refused: "No use bringing your child to this office. An infant with fever of unknown origin must be treated at the hospital."

Hailing a taxi, we packed ourselves and our bountiful luggage into the cab, and I instructed the driver to head for the nearest motel with a swimming pool. There I checked in Tamsin and Lara and gave a huge tip to the porter overwhelmed by the volume of our baggage. Hugging Lara and Tamsin, I told them, "Have lunch. Swim. I'll see you soon."

With baby Nicky in my arms, I summoned another taxi and tried to apply cold compresses (stolen wash clothes and ice from the motel) to his tiny sweating body. "As fast as you can," I urged the driver, "take us to Ft. Lauderdale Hospital's emergency entrance!" Nicky's soft brown eyes glowed glassy with fever. But his smiling lips seemed to say, "Just love me."

Once Nicky was admitted, he underwent an onslaught of examinations including a spinal tap that the doctors insisted was necessary. In 1983 a pediatric spinal tap, also called a lumbar puncture, was administered when all other tests proved insufficient to diagnose pediatric leukemia, meningitis, or other serious bacterial, viral, or fungal infections. Now pediatric advancement would assess a baby with those symptoms far less painfully, thanks to sophisticated blood cultures and X-ray imaging such at CT scans. But none of these were available in the early 1980s.

While the doctor performed the necessary spinal tap, Nicky's screams were barely audible from outside the emergency surgery area where I waited. Yet I could still hear them, and I absorbed a mother's pain.

Finally, a young doctor walked out of the surgery and gave his diagnosis: "Your child has pneumonia. He must be sedated and remain on IV meds for several days here in the hospital." He told me I could also stay with my baby in the pediatric wing.

Finding the nearest phone, I managed to make arrangements with British Airways for Tamsin and Lara to fly back to London the next day. Then I phoned Bob. It was well after midnight in London. He listened to my convoluted story of what had put our little baby in the hospital, and duly noted the flight number I gave him for Tamsin and Lara's arrival at Heathrow. Bob assured me that he would meet them and would call me daily for reports.

"When are *you* coming home?" Only then did Bob sound shaken. Yet all I could offer was that my return to London would entirely depend on how quickly our infant son recovered from pneumonia.

It was almost dark in Ft. Lauderdale when a nurse came to the waiting room and told me that my baby had been transferred to the pediatric wing. She directed me to the room where I would keep vigil. Baby Nicky looked so very tiny and vulnerable in what seemed to be an enormous hospital crib. Yet my little son seemed to be sleeping peacefully—if I didn't focus on the beeping wall monitor of vital signs and the IV bottles and plastic tubing delivering vital meds and nourishment into his tiny arms. My sleep was fitful. Each time I woke, the smile on Nicky's baby lips comforted me, but his bright pink cheeks told me his fever was still raging.

The next morning, a nurse came in and announced, "There's a long distance call for you at the nurses' station."

Assuming it was Bob, the only one who knew that we were at the Ft. Lauderdale Hospital, I rushed to talk with him. But when I picked up the phone, I heard the familiar English accent of my friend Penny Vaughan calling from Abaco. Cleverly deducing that I might be at the Ft. Lauderdale Hospital, Penny had cajoled the person at patient information to tell her, a non-relative, that infant Nicky Wilhelm was under treatment in the pediatric ward. Even hearing Penny's voice instantly made me feel better. I must've sounded overwhelmed as I gave her an update: Nicky had pneumonia; Tamsin was taking Lara back to London; and Nicky and I would be in the hospital until he recovered and could travel home to London.

The very next afternoon, Penny and Jimmy walked into Nicky's hospital room—I could hardly believe my eyes. As we hugged, they said that after our conversation yesterday, they'd made immediate arrangements to fly in from the Bahamas to be with us. My friends' incredibly caring gesture lifted my anxiety and filled my heart with joy.

"We couldn't let you wait in this hospital by yourself, darling!" Penny could be affectionate and authoritative at the same time. "Besides, there's a wonderful Caribbean restaurant right down the street."

I laughed and cried at the same time. As long as Penny and Jimmy were with me, I knew everything was going to be okay.

At Home in London

Life in London with two active young children shifted me from romantic fantasy to everyday reality. Bob's travel to Esso's vast European, Middle East, and Asian markets meant there would be many evenings when he couldn't come home for dinner with the children and me. Instead of our warm kisses of welcome that I'd imagined, our marital closeness had disappeared. More and more, I'd come to depend on Penny and Jimmy for support. When I observed their affectionate ways with each other, I envied them for what Bob and I didn't have. Jimmy admired Penny and treated her as his equal. Two principal men in my lives—Bob and my father Juzo—couldn't or wouldn't show admiration and appreciation, neither in world nor physical gestures, for their closest family members. My husband Bob evaluated people against rigid standards of performance and intolerance of human foibles. In contrast, I'd been raised in Mother's boarding house, where every day heavily accented, vulnerable immigrants moved in and out. My tolerance for human idiosyncrasies, and indeed my fascination with cultural differences, would stay embedded in me for the rest of my life. During our marriage, Bob's my-way-or-no-way judgment about people reopened my unhealed wounds from childhood when Mother disparaged me as "silly girl, no talent," and callous classmates belittled me as "Immigrant Girl."

Family of four, London, 1983

Yet, in spite of our inherent differences, Bob and I also created wonderful memories together in London. One of them took place during our

Thanksgiving dinner party at Seymour Walk when Bob and I hosted the Vaughans and their friends "American Kip and English Mike." I'd come as close as I could to producing a traditional Thanksgiving meal of roast turkey, cornbread dressing, and Americanized veggies—despite the major difference that in London, turkey is considered a game bird and tastes nothing like a commercially-grown American Butterball. After copious glasses of wine, my husband Bob turned into a standup comedian. He joined Kip in spinning out spontaneous, risqué, irreverent, and hilarious interpretations of American Thanksgiving. When self-controlled Bob revealed his capacity for uninhibited humor and joy, that expression was deeply endearing to me.

Seymour Walk, London, 1985

Lara smelling flowers, London, 1985

The continuity I experienced during five years in London gave me a rare and precious sense of security and belonging. We were able to live during that time in the same small but charming house in Chelsea. Usually when executive families were moved abroad and chose a house or apartment, it was the company that purchased the property and assumed the profit or loss of selling it during the family's next transfer. In the case of our London assignment, Bob and I assessed a strong local housing market, and we took the risk of buying the house ourselves. That decision would turn out to be one of our profitable real estate investments—as well as a deep emotional investment. After we adopted Lara and Nick, we stayed put because I decided to enlarge the house with a top-floor addition of a playroom for the children and a much-needed guestroom and bath. Downstairs, on pleasant weather days, we dined outdoors in the petite garden, just off the lower ground-floor dining room and kitchen. Lara was thriving at Lady Bird nursery school, only a short drive from home. Within our Chelsea neighborhood, everything we needed was within easy walking distance: family-friendly Italian restaurant and deli; combined newsagent-candy store; chic dress shops; wondrous antique galleries; and our favorite, Cockney fishmonger. Right next to our local cinema was a marvelous bookshop with inviting niches and comfortable chairs where anyone could sit and read without interruption for hours.

For me, so very many aspects of living in London represented a blissful sense of contentment . . . until Bob came home with news that shattered me.

"Babe, I've been promoted!" He was going to head up Esso Inter-America—headquartered in Miami, Florida.

Broken Promises and Crises

I had no heart for starting over. I couldn't imagine leaving the Vaughans and our Colombian Connection. Lara was five, Nicky was two, and I'd soon be forty-two. Since childhood, I'd yearned to belong and feel accepted. In each community where we'd lived, I poured precious time and energy into nurturing new friendships. To lose my deep connections in London seemed intolerable. How could I keep pretending that I'd be anywhere forever when I knew that so many precious and intimate friendships would ultimately become Christmas-card-onlys?

During coming days and nights, I agonized, vacillated, and finally faced my vulnerability. With a heavy heart, I told Bob that I couldn't leave London and that I needed six months of separation—"to focus on the children and think about the future." Even though he was shocked and alarmed, Bob's allegiance to corporate duty was indomitable. We'd been married for seventeen years when Bob left for Miami—for the first time, he went alone.

And for the first time in my peripatetic married life, I had time to grieve the cumulative losses of making friends and leaving them.

I needed to assess my emotional damage and evaluate our marital challenges. Returning to the States after five years abroad would bring changes I couldn't anticipate. I remembered how difficult it had been to come home after years of expat life in Colombia.

After Bob's departure, I was liberated from social obligations to entertain his business associates and corporate visitors. Although there were many other Esso families in London, Bob was younger than nearly all his fellow executives. Primarily because we didn't have children of similar ages in common, I'd had little reason to form close friendships among most of the other Esso wives. Thus, there was no need to explain the personal reasons for Bob's solo departure.

The kids and I continued our comfortable pattern of a social life revolving around the Vaughans and The Colombian Connection. My daily routine centered on the children's activities. In the evening, Lara, Nicky, and I would have early dinner, aka "our tea," followed by bath time and bedtime stories. I so relished those uncomplicated, comforting rituals with my young children. When I felt like going out, Tamsin was there for babysitting. I could leisurely stroll over to the Vaughans for drinks or invite myself to one of Penny's famously eclectic dinner parties. The Vaughans' guests heartily consumed good food and wine as they raucously dissected topics that typical American hosts would shun—inflammatory politics, divisive religious convictions, and titillating gossip.

Even though Bob had grudgingly agreed to my staying on in London with the children for six months, it was only weeks later when he launched another bulldog campaign. Unlike years ago when he coerced me from Georgetown to Bogotá in order to propose marriage, this time his effort was to preserve our marriage.

"I've found a charming house you'll love," he cajoled from across the Atlantic. "It's in Coconut Grove, right on a canal leading straight out to Biscayne Bay."

"Oh, is it a new house?" I asked.

"Well . . ." he hesitated. "It might need just a little work."

I issued a stipulation: I'd pack up the London house as soon as possible and travel with the children to Miami—if Bob would agree to participate together in marriage counseling. He agreed, and I trusted him.

Immediately, I began to shut down Seymour Walk and everything else about London that I'd so loved. However, that brief separation had given me a limited dose of feeling competent, authentic, and worthy—a fleeting remedy that nourished my self-worth as a person and didn't rely on my role as a dutiful corporate wife. Fourteen years into the future, I would no longer be able to deny or repress that polarity.

The house in Coconut Grove oozed with vintage appeal. I saw it as a faded beauty left to languish, yearning to be restored by sensitive hands. The dated kitchen begged for new cabinetry, countertops, and appliances. The laundry room needed a complete update. The interior of the house and the second-story guesthouse awaited a total facelift.

However, the allure of everything surrounding the house and the community beyond captivated me. The 1950s turquoise-tiled swimming pool and lush gardens led to a private dock and canal that opened to magnificent Biscayne Bay. Village life in Coconut Grove was an irresistible mix of primarily merchants, artists, and tourists. We had easy access to the historic bayside with its public marina, a preserved historic landmark plantation, and the once- flourishing Pan Am Customs House.

With creative zeal I took on the role of renovation project manager—in addition to full-time mothering of two little kids and cooking all our meals on the outdoor barbecue since the kitchen was nonfunctional. We ate breakfast, lunch, and dinner on the screened-in patio while our dining room was under construction.

Shoving my London wardrobe to the back of the closet, I enlivened my gusto for pretty new clothes—admittedly my obsession, about which Bob never complained. Of course I needed just the right outfits to entertain business colleagues and visitors in Miami!

Yet again, I followed Donna's Golden Rule. I built new networks of friends in the Miami community, and I lined up doctors, dentists, and a plethora of local resources to efficiently run our daily lives. For creative nourishment, I signed up for life drawing classes at the Coral Gables Museum. For physical fitness and sociability, I played a lot of women's team tennis at Royal Palm Tennis Club.

In spite of the bargain Bob and I had made, we both broke it. Bob counted on my making our environment beautiful and that the house restoration project would absorb and distract me—my husband knew me far better than I'd thought. I never held him to his promise. In Miami, we did no marriage counseling.

My dear friend Libby and I had known each other as naïve young women excited about our unknown futures in New York City. Our life-long bond started in a five-flight walk-up apartment. In years to follow, Libby kept devoted track of my peripatetic life. With every new move, I'd phone Libby. "Not another one!" she'd exclaim. I pictured her grabbing a pencil, crossing out the last address, adding a new one in the jumble of entries, and muttering, "No more ink for you!" Libby visited me in many places, including Cartagena, New York, and Baltimore.

Now we two girlfriends sat in the living room of the under-construction Miami house and gazed out at the tranquil views. We could barely see the LaNi, our Bertram speedboat named after Lara and Nicky, that we kept moored and waiting for our next excursion into Biscayne Bay.

Bob was stretched out on the couch, his hands spreading wide the newspaper above his chest. Little Nicky, wanting his daddy's attention, had toddled into the living room, heading straight to Bob. His small arms reached up and began punching fists into the newspaper that blocked access to his dad. Bob leaped up from the couch, his face flushed with temper, and shouted outrageous reprimands at our two-year-old son. Little Nicky burst into tears. Bob stomped out of the room and left a small boy confused and afraid.

Libby was astonished. She'd known Bob since before we were married. "What has come over that man?" she asked.

I must have wavered, as if unwilling to acknowledge what had just happened.

She glared at me. "Haven't you noticed his anger is out of control?"

I was shocked to realize my friend was right. This moment made me suddenly aware of Bob's flaws as a father, and mine as a mother.

"Why haven't you confronted him about this?" she asked.

Instead of being outraged at what had happened, I'd felt embarrassed by what was a pressing wakeup call. How had I excused, or dismissed Bob's behavior? Why was it that I needed Libby to remind me of my responsibilities as a mother—to stand up for myself and for my children?

Back then I lived in denial. In truth, I had plenty of unfinished inner work to do in order to confront Bob's explosive anger. And before I would make the link between my tolerance of his verbal outbursts and my personal history of abuse—Mother's tirades, Dad's violence, and Edith's rage. It would take many sessions of future therapy for me to acknowledge that I'd lugged, like heavy baggage, the insecurities and doubts of my childhood into my adulthood and my marriage.

No doubt Bob, as a husband and father, had also been shaped by his background. Raised in a German-American tradition of conformity to rigid rules and elevated status of the family patriarch, Bob gave intense loyalty to his family and his inner circle. But until one earned such approved status, one was considered a less worthy outsider. In Bob's highly competitive corporate world, his negotiation and success building skills had been fine-honed while his emotional empathy and respect for differences had been neglected.

As parents and partners, Bob and I stacked up our flaws and vulnerabilities, and both of us continued to excuse and dismiss them.

Aboard the La-Ni in Miami, 1986

•

At last the total facelift of our vintage Miami house was finished! The chaotic year of construction mess and stress produced a visual triumph. No more contractors stomping, slamming, hollering, and disrupting. No more sweating at the outdoor barbecue. We had a gleaming modern kitchen. No more disgruntled sighs in the old laundry room—while drying and folding, I could sing out my repertoire. To top it all, an enticing treetop guest quarters was refreshed and waiting to pamper our visitors.

But the Miami story didn't have a happily ever after. I wasn't going to get to enjoy the fruits of my labors. Memory blurs. Was it just a month later when Bob brought home the news? He'd been promoted—to International Headquarters located in far-from-international Florham Park, in suburban New Jersey.

I regressed to childhood times when my mother's dominance and control were in charge of my life. Only now I had Mother Exxon dictating what I did, who I was, and where I lived. *Don't I get an excuse for not celebrating my husband's success? What about all my hard work on the house?* My mind reeled from Mother Hania's orders: "Do it or I punish!"

Efficiently, I packed up the house and the children, in preparation for our trek to New Jersey. Lara was six, Nicky was three, and I was forty-three years old.

New Jersey

As always, the company provided top relocation services to executives and their families. Before the move to New Jersey, I flew up for a blitz week of advance house hunting, knowing I'd be met by a top realtor and that we could expect expedited memberships to country clubs that would best serve Bob's corporate status. Also, I'd have advisors to help navigate school options and admissions for the children.

Sure enough, in New Jersey, Perky Patty (my nickname for her by the end of day one), picked me up at the hotel. She would be my realtor and companion for as long as it took to find the right house and get my family settled.

"Ask me anything. I've got it right here." Patty held a leather three-ring binder, apparently her go-to source book for schools, doctors, hair salons, and you-name-it handouts. We settled into a sleek silver Mercedes. "Hope you're comfy," Patty warbled, glancing at me for affirmation. I nodded with a sigh that didn't come from contentment.

As we drove through New Jersey suburbia, I stared out the car's tinted windows. Most of the homes were New England traditional-style. Each home was separated by a meticulously manicured lawn. *Where are the people, the dogs, and the kids?* Already I missed Miami's hustle and bustle of people casually switching between English and their native languages. Had I left my Golden Rule in a sealed-up packing box to be loaded into a massive moving van filled with furnishings and fading memories of places I'd lived before?

Perky Patty chirped from behind the steering wheel. "You're going to love what I have to show you!"

We had just passed a roadside marker for Short Hills, a New Jersey neighborhood with a reputation for being elite, old guard, and upscale. Perky Patty drove into a white gravel driveway. For the next hour—or was it two?—we toured a two-story converted carriage house and its quaint yet luxurious guest cottage. They oozed charm. We walked the grounds. There was more than one acre filled with verdant lawns, mature trees, gardens, and a glass greenhouse. In the middle of the back yard was a night-lit, screened-in platform tennis court.

"You'll be all set for winter tennis parties, even when it's snowing." Patty sounded like a high school cheerleader. "Just think, a brand new sport for your whole family!"

We bought the house.

Short Hills, New Jersey, would go down in memory as the most incompatible and forlorn of all locations where we lived. Except for a decision that I'd made in New Jersey. At a business dinner party sandwiched between Bob's pontificating fellow Exxon executives, I listened and talked to these *Petroleum News* and *Wall Street Journal* devotees with feigned interest. I was so convincing that I could have quoted the damn journals myself. Whenever there was a token opening for me to contribute something, I'd switch the conversation to arts and culture. And my dinner partners' attention would last mere seconds before shifting down to the inevitable, man-sized beef entrées.

I'd had enough of feeling dismissed by boring men who assumed they were fascinating. How could I transform my conversation from arts-esoteric to arts-popular? My solution was to expand on my arts talent, by adding a new skill and create something tangible. Jewelry! Women loved it, and men understood it.

I decided to reinvent myself by enrolling in a certificate study in jewelry design at New York City's Parsons School of Design. In the 1980s, getting from Short Hills to New York for classes and lab sessions was cumbersome. I had to drive to the Short Hills bus station, park my car, and board a bus that went mid-way to Manhattan. Then I had to switch to another bus destined for New York City's Penn Station, and from there, either grab a fortuitous taxi or huff a long walk to Parsons in Greenwich Village. However, complicated logistics never could deter me from taking on an exciting new challenge. I duly fired up fortitude and perseverance.

At Parsons, I first worked on paper to design jewelry pieces and then master fabrication of materials and the techniques of stone setting, soldering, filing, and burnishing. As the months passed, I grew competent and confident. I created bracelets, brooches, and necklaces, and I infused each piece with personal symbolic imagery. As soon as it was finished, I'd wear it with pride. Women would stop me to ask where I'd bought my distinctive jewelry. "You made that? I want one!"

But I created no collections, no inventory, no illustrations of my work. "Not enough time" was my usual excuse for not building a professional career as a jewelry designer. Bob earned a high salary that increased with every promotion. I had no financial pressure to sell my jewelry and add to our income. Later reflection gave me deeper insights—that I'd enjoyed the luxury to create art for art's sake, freed from need to make art to pay my living expenses. And inherently, I was a one-of-a-kind-designer who shunned mass production. While I loved the design work, I labored at crafting technique so difficult that I never considered any piece as perfect. Instead, I gifted most of my creations to friends and kept just a few favorite pieces for myself.

Donna's Jewelry creations, 1986

I had reinvented myself creatively, but I still retained my principal identity as corporate wife and mother of two. In essence, I relegated my professional jewelry making into that of a "hobby." And for as long as I considered it a "hobby," I clung to my traditional roles that I put as my top priorities.

Family issues were far more challenging than designing jewelry, and I needed stress relief. In aptly named Short Hills, I began to power walk through neighborhoods and local parks. As my heart rate rose up and down, my brain worked through emotional dilemmas.

For years, I'd been trying to help my daughter gain self-confidence and learn to trust herself and others. I hoped that promoting Lara's sense of security would foster better relationships with her peers and lessen her insecure but strong-willed behavior. Lara had come to our family when she was ten months old. Even though the adoption agency kept all birth history records closed, I never stopped speculating about the mystery of Lara's critical first nine months. Had she bonded with anyone? Did she have a loving caretaker? Or, did she have someone unreliable, or even worse?

Eventually, I'd seek help from a family counselor. Because I didn't have any factual information about Lara's birth history and first months,

I had to rely on pediatric developmental theory. According to the family therapist, the description of my first moments with baby Lara contained a significant clue. On our first day together, I'd been ecstatic that my little girl immediately "just knew" and trusted me. Yet the therapist had a different theory—a child of ten months who accepts a total stranger (in my case, an adopting mother offering abundant love) might not have had anyone significant enough to leave or grieve. How desperately I wanted to keep believing that Lara had instinctively trusted me, right from the start. But no matter how lovely the memory was, it didn't soothe either of us when my daughter was troubled.

Every day after school, my young daughter's angst came home with her. During Lara's primary years in Miami, her teachers and testing had affirmed her learning difference, officially classified as "auditory processing." In New Jersey, Lara was a bright child attending Deerfield Elementary, one of the area's most competitive public schools. Not only was Lara facing increasing academic obstacles, but she also had trouble fitting in with her judgmental peer group. How well I recognized the dilemmas of girlhood—being an outsider wanting to be accepted by the "in girls."

On the plus side for me, during those years when I hoofed through the neighborhoods of Short Hills—my well-exercised legs did look fabulous.

My friend Libby had moved back to New York City. She'd been escaping city's summer heat and bustle by retreating to the low-key town of Normandy Beach, New Jersey. Given our New Jersey transfer, Libby convinced me to rent a vacation house for my family on the Jersey shore—it was easy to decide that what was right for Libby was very likely right for me. Soon enough, in the town of Normandy Beach, I found a delightful rental cottage with a small back yard. The cottage overlooked the bay beyond and the walkway pier, ideal for fishing and leaping into the water for a swim.

Lara spent happy days at the local Normandy Beach kids camp, where crafts, games, and the outdoor communal playground kept her so busy she'd come home exhausted and proud of herself. Libby and I loved spending afternoons together, sitting on the front porch of the rental

Lara on dock of our Normandy Beach house pier, 1990

house. We gabbed and sipped white wine while Nicky pedaled his starter bike like mad up and down the driveway. Libby's two sons were teenagers who preferred hanging out at the beach with their own crowds instead of with their mom and her girlfriend.

Little Nicky, super confident and fearless in his physical abilities, whizzed past Libby and me, and shouted, "Mommy, Mommy, when do we take off the training wheels?"

I tried to be an attentive mom, but some things were more dangerous than Nicky falling off his little bike. Should there be a time when I momentarily wasn't nearby and Nicky wandered out on the pier, what if he accidently fell into the bay? Lara, in contrast, was a natural water baby about whom I had no worries. Bob had taken her to the Chelsea-Fulham pool in London so often that she'd learned to swim almost before she'd started walking.

Although Nicky knew how to dog paddle because he'd had a lot of practice in our Miami swimming pool, we still had some training to do. Again and again, I lectured Nicky. "You must never, never go out on that pier alone!" I told him. "But if you disobey me and you fall into the 'big water,' paddle hard to the stairs and climb right up."

Even as a little boy, Nicky showed intensity of focus. I could always tell by his alert eyes that he was paying close attention. To his childhood teachers and me, Nicky's extraordinary focus and his deep, froggy-sounding voice gave the impression that he was older than his years.

Sure enough, there came an early evening when guests were coming, and I was in the kitchen preparing snacks. I thought Nicky was nearby, playing inside the house. Instead, my four-year-old son had managed to slip out the back door, trot down the pier, and lean over to see "fishies." Sure enough, Nicky toppled over and fell into the bay. Standing at the kitchen sink, I heard Nicky's froggy voice. A little seaweed-encrusted creature dripping copious water was running straight to me. "Mommy, I done it!" he shouted. "I fell in and I climbed up."

My heart nearly stopped. But young Nicky had listened well. That memorable day, he had saved himself.

Nick, Normandy Beach house,
New Jersey, 1990

When we returned to Short Hills at the end of the summer, Lara began her second grade year at Deerfield. For young Nicky, nearby Farbrook School's pre-kinder program was only a twenty-minute walk from our house. In fine weather, Far Brook kids took their lunches at outside picnic tables among the shade trees. True to its idyllic setting, the school's early childhood curriculum emphasized sensory play. Nicky, however, had his own agenda during his pre-kinder year: "Mommy, I want to learn to read right now!"

Miami Vacation Home

New Jersey was frigid during winter. Some families even had heated driveways that melted the snow and icy rain—no need to salt and plow. More and more, the kids and I missed tropical Miami. Although I'd never forgotten the saga of restoring the house in Coconut Grove and leaving it behind, my thoughts calculated something very different—I wanted an easy upkeep, year-round vacation home. It would take me exactly one house-hunting trip to Miami in order to find the perfect one.

Snapper Creek in South Miami turned out to be just the right location and setting. Within a gated development, I discovered six properties that encircled a small private lake. Five of them boasted large houses that anyone, including burglars, would consider prime. But the sixth home was set well beyond a grove of palm trees and dense, lush plantings. Unless one drove down a circuitous driveway, the house was completely screened from street view. Although the neighborhood was dominated by high-end properties, I'd found the only unimproved, single-story, mid-century Florida house—unoccupied and for sale. I convinced Bob that it was a perfect vacation home. And we bought it.

The layout had just enough room for our family: three bedrooms with adjoining bathrooms tiled in 1950s pastel colors; and a guest room off the eat-in kitchen that still had pristine early modern appliances, well planned counters, and plenty of wood fronted cabinets. Both the kitchen and the living room had full views of the pool and beyond. The property also offered endless potential—perhaps to add a tennis court, an elaborate playground, or maybe a mini golf course? Nonetheless, my energy for another renovation project was sapped. I was determined to keep our modest vacation house free from fuss, worry—and construction chaos.

For holiday breaks and when the New Jersey school year ended, the kids and I flew south to Miami. Bob joined us when he could. Our very first summer in Snapper Creek, I enrolled Nicky and Lara at Gulliver Academy's summer school, which Lara had attended when we'd been full-time Miami residents. For Nicky, I chose an early reading course that seemed ideal for a precocious kid wanting to learn to read—or so I thought. Nicky's teacher called me at the end of his first day.

"I'm afraid Nicky is misplaced in this class." She lowered her voice.

"It's for slow kids with reading problems. Your son is way ahead of everyone."

But Nicky loved that class, and he refused to leave. In just four summer weeks, he learned to read and never stopped.

While five-year-old Nicky attended half-day early reading, eight-year-old Lara spent the whole day at Gulliver summer camp. And five days a week she came home elated. "Mom, guess what! I was picked for a big part in the play!" She beamed as she jumped up and down. "And . . . and . . . I won almost every race in swim competition!" Seeing my joyful daughter celebrate her accomplishments filled me with happiness.

Nicky at Parrot Jungle, Miami, 1991

I'd pick Nicky up at mid-day, and we'd head to his favorite place— the Miami Parrot Jungle. As soon as we went through the entry gate, Nicky rushed to the low picnic tables, opened his little yellow lunch box, and gobbled up everything I'd packed inside. While he ate, he told me all about his day's reading lesson. Afterward we'd visit the bird habitats, even though the summer heat was intense. Tropical parrots in their giant habitats cackled and gossiped. Nick and I decided they were mimicking us humans, and we couldn't stop laughing. One day, I had my camera with me, and I snapped pictures of Little Nicky.

One of those photos is now poster-sized, framed and mounted on the wall of my current home. It's one of my most treasured memories of Nicky's childhood—a healthy, gorgeous boy, face bursting with joy, standing with one small arm bent up as if to salute the sun, the other arm straight down like a staunch little soldier. During times at Snapper Creek and idyllic preschool years in New Jersey, Nicky was the happiest of children.

Exxon Valdez Crisis

Early in 1989, Bob was promoted from Exxon International in New Jersey to Corporate Headquarters in New York City. This meant his round-trip commute from our home in Short Hills would involve an hour's train journey into the city's Penn Station followed by a transit bus ride or half-hour walk to his new office in the Exxon Building at 49th Street and Avenue of the Americas. However, we didn't contemplate moving back to New York City (which I would've loved and Bob would have liked the less-cumbersome commute). We stayed put because Bob was duly warned by his boss—the kingpin decision makers of Exxon were discussing a more "significant relocation." In executive offices, in the mailroom, and at home, Exxon families speculated where and what that meant. However, no one at Exxon anticipated the worldwide catastrophe that was about to happen.

On March 24, 1989, the Exxon Valdez oil tanker ran aground on Bligh Reef in Prince William Sound Alaska. News agencies would later report that the impact ruptured eight of its eleven cargo tanks. No prior US environmental disaster would compare. Eleven million gallons of crude oil poured from the damaged tanker, eventually covering 1,300 miles of coastline and spreading hundreds of miles into the Gulf of Alaska.

The reef region, a previously pristine habitat for salmon, sea otters, seals, and seabirds was remote. Government and industry responders had trouble getting to the disaster, which was only accessible by helicopter or boat. Exxon, for its part, was slow to respond. According to a 2004 *National Geographic* anniversary story, during the first few days of the spill when the oil was spreading slowly on calm seas, Exxon didn't send out crews to skim the oil from the surface. Three days after the tanker ran aground, a storm pushed the oil to the shoreline, destroying habitats and wildlife. Existing response plans were grievously inadequate, and by the time Exxon responded irreparable damage had been done.

At the time of the disaster, public outrage surged against Exxon. A scattered few defended Exxon but the vast majority of the world condemned it. Exxon was largely seen as failing to take accountability for the spill. Exxon families across the globe privately and publicly weighed their personal conscience against the company's response. Our family was no exception.

Bob, a loyal pragmatist, kept his reactions private. I held my tongue in public and shouted out at home against the arrogance of top management for not shedding their hubris, hustling to the disaster region, and gearing up in rubber boots and suits alongside cleanup crews. Such actions would have demonstrated top-down commitment to making things right.

With equal vitriol, I blamed all Americans, including myself, for our consumption of energy with unbound gluttony. How reprehensible I believed the public was to expect companies like Exxon to take all the risks. And immoral, I evangelized, to attack those who filled and spilled while the rest of us kept gorging at the trough.

Acquaintances who learned that Bob worked for Exxon lambasted the corporation, the crisis, and the consequences—to his face. At Exxon, Bob had an open door policy and a reputation for fair and unflinching honesty. While I hated that Bob was now thrown into the harsh fray, I admired his ability to listen. And with anyone open-minded enough to hear them, he presented an astute and objective analysis of the facts. I saw Bob's qualities of ethical leadership as woefully rare in America's brutally competitive business world. Had he been in charge at the time, I feel that the company's response might have left a more positive legacy.

When we weren't preoccupied with the Valdez aftermath, we discussed the rumors about Exxon leaving New York City. A spring evening in 1990, things finally crystallized. Bob took his usual convoluted route from Manhattan to Short Hills and arrived home about 7:00 PM. He found me in the small, rather old-fashioned kitchen that overlooked our large, unused greenhouse. I had no skill or time for gardening, potting, and filling a year-round greenhouse with plants and flowers. Strange that I remember what I was making for dinner that night—baked chicken, roasted sweet potatoes, and green beans with mushrooms.

"Babe, things smell really good." Bob's hug was stronger than usual, and his voice was louder when he was nervous. "We won't need to remodel this kitchen after all." Bob was nearly shouting. "Corporate has finally announced the new headquarters. It's going to be Irving, Texas."

After so many moves, some corporate wives may have preferred to stay put in suburban Short Hills, New Jersey. But I was inherently a big city gal. In spite of Donna's Golden Rule, I'd been longing for urban living. I was more than ready to forge onward to dynamic Texas.

Another move, new home, Dallas, 1990

We're in Texas Now

Dallas Early Years

When Exxon moved its corporate headquarters to Irving, it got a big Texas welcome. Press coverage exploded—Exxon's arrival was considered a major business coup for an oil-friendly region. Thirsty non-profit organizations saw Exxon as a bottomless philanthropic well. Employees who transferred might have imagined they were heading to Camelot when they left a high cost of living area for one with lower-cost, high-value real estate and no state income tax.

As for me, I could retire my Golden Rule. There would be no further need to pretend that I'd be somewhere forever—with this move, I would be. Bob had reached the pinnacle location of Exxon leadership, and as such, Texas would be our permanent home. At the top my to-do list was buying a pair of tooled leather boots and an alluring western hat. In the parking lot of the Galleria Mall in Dallas, I inhaled big breaths of petroleum-scented air and hooted out, "We're going to be here forever!"

Since Bob anticipated a fairly easy commute to Irving, we chose to live in Dallas. Realtors were ready and waiting to find us a perfect home. A charismatic duo, Cheryl and JoAnn, expeditiously produced a move-in-ready, center hall colonial in the family-friendly neighborhood of University Park. The sellers were "real nice Texans" who allowed us to start construction on a backyard pool even before they'd moved out of the house. By the Fourth of July 1990, the kids were swimming in a sparkling new pool.

The next-door neighbors, who had a daughter Lara's age, came over to welcome us to the neighborhood and immediately invited her to go to church with them. I soon learned that "Welcome to the Bible Belt" had less to do with a welcome and more to do with vetting whether you were an insider or an outsider.

When I told Farbrook teachers in New Jersey that Nicky would be leaving, they cautioned that his end-of-May birthdate might cause a new school to hold him back a year. "Nicky is precocious and focused," they affirmed. "He needs to be promoted and challenged." Farbrook's glowing recommendation were assets in interviews at top private schools in Dallas. Among them, Greenhill School offered academic excellence, gender equality, and ethnic diversity. It seemed an ideal fit for Nicky—if he could meet the prerequisite for cursive writing. I enrolled him in a summer crash course in cursive penmanship. He passed and was accepted to second grade.

That fall, I looked forward to upcoming Parents' Night and meeting the teachers Nick liked so much. In Nick's classroom, student compositions were displayed on bulletin boards. I located Nicky's two-page story. I don't remember the title or the theme, but I do remember that his was longer than most of the others, that his cursive writing was wobblier than anyone else's, and that one word—worry—was repeated again and again. In later years, I'd look back and wonder how I'd missed that early clue to my son's anxiety revealed in his second grade story.

As for Lara, she consistently earned above average grades in school. She also showed exceptional ability in the individual sports of swimming and English riding. We would acquire a vacation home in Colorado where Lara, who preferred warmer climates, would shiver but learn to be a competent skier. When our houseguests were familiar friends, Lara interacted and enjoyed their company. But developmental tests showed wide disparities between her high performance and low verbal aptitude scores. In the fourth grade, a clinical assessment had identified Lara as "an intellectually gifted child with auditory processing difficulty." Cutting through the jargon, this described a bright child who heard and integrated things differently.

Pre-teen Lara, Dallas, 1993

There was no official way to assess her social behavior. Yet I knew Lara was suffering from distressed relationships. As a mom, my heart hurt when my daughter went immediately to her room after school. Her sadness and feelings of rejection took a toll on both of us. I was confounded about how to help Lara overcome vicious outbursts between competitive, insecure little girls wanting friends but constantly challenging each other in petty arguments. My daughter was going to have a long road ahead—a rocky journey to build up her self-esteem and confidence. I blamed myself for not being wise enough to guide her. How was I to know how to best help my own daughter when my own childhood had been mired in rejection and loneliness?

Diligently, I pursued opportunities to spend concentrated time with each of my children. Even though Dallas and Miami were equally hot in the summer, the kids and I so loved our carefree vacation home in

Snapper Creek, and Bob enjoyed his tropical breaks whenever he could take time off. The summer of 1992 we enjoyed our simple ranch style home and the lakeside setting. We swam in the pool and went to the beach. We revisited the Parrot Jungle and rode our bikes. We laughed a lot, together. At the end of the summer while packing up and preparing to head back to Dallas, we heard the news of an approaching storm. I wasn't too worried—we'd be safe and back in Dallas by the time it hit.

On August 24, Mother Nature fueled Hurricane Andrew and pointed her wrath at South Florida, with 142 mph sustained winds and gusts up to 169 mph. When Hurricane Andrew lifted the roof off our house in Snapper Creek and exposed everything below to ravaging wind and rain, our property damage was minor compared to many others. Over 100,000 homes were damaged or destroyed. Friends, who owned a beautiful home just a few miles south, had suffered such devastating loss that everything retrievable of value could have fit into a plastic ziplock bag. Worst of all, 26 people died because of the storm.

Post hurricane, every builder-speculator in the area was on the hunt for prime home sites. Because of my dedicated nurturing and pruning of our trees and the erratic path of the hurricane, we didn't lose a single one. Our intact landscaping and superb lakeside location was soon discovered. However, I was burned out on re construction, had no heart to demolish the house and start over. When a builder hauling buckets of cash delivered an extraordinary offer to buy our property, we took it.

My final journey to Snapper Creek was a wrenching good-bye. As I wandered through the rooms, memories of happy family times were everywhere: the four of us eating drippy, messy Florida fruits at the kitchen counter; Bob and I laughing together as we watched the kids' antics in the living room; me cuddling with Lara and Nicky for bedtime stories before tucking them in; and all of us taking turns shouting "Where's Waldo?" to anyone left in the swimming pool. This time I visited each room with a bundle of colored stickers to identify every item: green—ship to Dallas; red—give to friends; yellow—donate to charity; blue—haul to trash.

After I locked the doors for the last time, I mopped my wet cheeks, struggled into my rental car and drove out the long, circular driveway onto the road. No looking back. At last I wouldn't have to witness the bulldozer razing our little house to the ground and clearing the site for its future McMansion.

Miami home post-Hurricane Andrew, 1992

Present Meets Past

In Dallas all of us stayed busy—Bob with work, the kids with school, and me managing home and family. Lara was fourteen when I made a decision for us to visit my dear friend Brenda, then living in Tempe, Arizona. We'd known each other slightly as coeds at ASU, and we'd formed our abiding friendship when we amazingly ended up at Booz Allen in New York. Brenda was the maid of honor at my wedding and an intrepid visitor to Cartagena when Bob was refinery manager. On one shared adventure there, Bob, Brenda, and I bumped and swayed aboard a small prop plane, the only transport for company workers and visitors to remote stretches of Colombia—"flying the pipeline" it was called. Brenda handled the flight a lot better than former Pan Am stewardess, who always got airsick in small and bumpy aircraft.

Brenda and her second husband Keith had moved from New York City to Tempe, where they'd pursued careers at Arizona State University. We'd remained close through decades of sharing the ups and downs of our lives. Our bond of female friendship, more resilient than our marriages, had given us permission to meddle in each other's lives.

That visit to Arizona was my first time back after twenty-three years. I'd planned to show Lara the ASU campus and enjoy a relaxed reunion with Brenda. But my friend couldn't resist stirring things up. Instead of a carefree walk down memory lane, our weekend opened a floodgate to my past and plunged Lara and me into turbulent waters. My daughter was a strong swimmer, but I had no idea that she would also keep me afloat.

On arrival at Brenda's, we were welcomed with hugs and wet doggy kisses from the resident canines. Keith and Brenda had decorated the living room walls with indigenous art, a reflection of their passions. He was an archaeology professor and she a project manager in the archeology office of ASU—both of them loved collecting Native American Art. The intense Arizona heat hadn't changed, but now there was air conditioning to cool us. Sipping iced tea, Brenda and I reminisced about the past and caught up on what was new. Never one to let things get boring, Brenda tossed an emotional grenade into our conversation.

"Since you're here, why don't you try to find Edith?"

I was stunned that my friend would suggest this, considering what she knew about Edith.

"No! I never want to see her again." I glared. "We're finished. How could you even suggest that?"

"Don't you want some kind of closure?" she asked.

"No!"

"It's been decades since your parents died and Edith exposed her hand." Brenda wouldn't give up.

"Some dirty hand." Bile rose in my throat. "She did exactly what my parents warned me about." I tried to stop visceral reaction by pushing the memories back and staying in the present. I glanced at Lara across the room, sitting cross-legged on the floor playing with one of the dogs.

Just like my husband Bob, my friend Brenda had the tenacity of a bulldog when it came to wearing down opposition. Assuming nonchalance, she strolled to a bookshelf, pulled out the White Pages telephone book, opened it on a nearby table, and flipped through the pages to the R section.

"Wow! Here she is." Brenda looked pleased. "Rueger, Edith, 12 Desert Valley Court in Sunnyslope."

In less than an hour, Brenda was behind the wheel of her VW bug, with me scowling in the passenger seat, and Lara jammed into the cramped back seat, her long legs bent into V shapes. We were headed to Edith's address in Sunnyslope.

Lara leaned forward and tapped my shoulder. "Mom, why are you so angry about your sister?"

No longer could I avoid telling Lara the family secrets and betrayals that I'd been trying to forget. "Lara honey, there were so many painful things. When I was around your age and living with my parents in Connecticut, Edith invited me to go live with her in Arizona. I expected her to be loving and caring. She wasn't."

A flood of painful memories roared over me. How could I control my own emotions, protect my daughter, and translate the chaos of my family into a story she could understand? That was the first time I would tell my whole story in one sitting. Brenda just focused on her driving while I talked.

I began with the year I'd lived with Edith, Carl, and Reggie. When Reggie got into serious trouble, Edith wouldn't accept her own mistakes in not looking after and supervising Reggie. Instead she held me responsible for Reggie's bad choices—and because I hadn't tattled on Reggie, my sister threw me out of her house. I told Lara about the magical year of living with Mary Jane in the Sunnyslope cottage, where I was one of "Mary Jane's kids"—all of us loving her and each other almost as much as we loved dancing to rock and roll music. Until suddenly everything changed. Mary Jane's little girl died, and Mary Jane returned to Montana. We never saw each other again. The next year I went to live with my dad—a shocking time when the parent I thought I knew exposed a dark side I'd never expected. I recounted my graduation from high school and the life-change choice I faced. An anonymous benefactor had offered me a scholarship—my only path to college—and at the same time, I had the chance to work for the American government in a distant country called Afghanistan. I decided to take the scholarship and attend ASU.

"You did the right thing, Mom." Lara at fourteen was more confident than I'd been at that age.

I continued my story: two years at ASU, working part-time and taking a full load of classes. Then working full-time and taking classes part-time in order to build up a departure nest egg. Finally, how I left Arizona for a new life in New York City. Judging from Lara's sudden, alert body language, her interest spiced up when I described single life in the city and meeting Bob Wilhelm.

"Was Dad handsome then?" Lara teased.

"Oh, he was handsome," I said, recalling when Bob and I were young. "And he was really smart. Your dad aimed for the stars." I told Lara about his marriage proposal. "Our wedding was small. Aunt Brenda agreed to be my maid of honor." From the driver's seat, Brenda flashed a smile. "Before the wedding I went back to visit my parents in Arizona, to tell them I was getting married and moving to Bogotá."

Lara saw my distressed face reflected in the rearview mirror. "Mom, weren't they happy about your news?"

"Yes, of course," I nodded. "But my parents had their own news—something they'd kept secret from me for twenty-four years." How was I to explain to Lara what I didn't even understand? "My parents decided that it was time to confess that I was not their birth daughter—that I was adopted." I tried to contain old emotions. I waited for Lara's reaction. She didn't seem surprised that I was adopted, but what she couldn't understand was why my parents had kept it a secret.

"Why did they wait so long to tell you?" she asked. Lara had always known she was adopted—as Colombian Connection families, we were completely open to talking about adoption.

Her question was a good one. Even though it was long ago, I still couldn't understand why my parents thought that telling me "the truth" so late in life could actually protect them and me if Edith decided to carry out acts of revenge. I pondered how to teach Lara that most families are protective and loving, not cruel and resentful. *Should I even tell her about Edith's hatred of me, her beliefs that our parents loved me more than her?* But she had asked. And I was already mid-story.

"It had to do with Edith," I said. I described my mother's panic and hysteria, and how it had affected me—that I'd been shocked and confused. I also told her the story of the Holden Girls. I described the saga of how my mother had raised four girls who were unrelated to her. She'd never adopted them, but expected Edith to treat them like sisters. I thought such a story might help Lara understand human flaws.

What I did not tell Lara that day (or any other day) was that I condemned myself for dismissing my mother's hysterical warnings. I'd blamed old age for ravaging Mother's mental health. Ultimately, I decided not to tell my tender fourteen year old that everything my mother had feared had actually happened. That when my parents were under Edith's care, she'd deliberately kept me from seeing them before they died, and that I had no way to know exactly how or why they died. I also chose not to tell Lara that Edith had abused Dad in his dying hours by poisoning his mind against me. I didn't have the courage to say out loud that my own dad had cast me out before he died and that he dismissed me as if I'd been just another boarder in his life.

These things I kept to myself as we drove onward. But recalling these memories had my mind racing—what lay ahead for Edith and me after two decades of silence?

Brenda pulled the VW bug up to Desert Valley Court—we weren't expecting it to be a trailer park. Yet we continued driving along the trailers until we found location #12.

"Oh my!" Brenda exclaimed.

In the middle of the lot stood an old silver Airstream trailer, made stationary by a wood platform built around it. On one side was a battered Ford station wagon with vanity license plates that read E.R. Nurse. On the other side, a wheelchair was draped with a Hopi blanket.

The three of us sat silent in the car, taking in the scene. No one moved. No one spoke. Until Brenda whispered to me, "Just go up and ring the bell."

I looked at her in horror.

"Edith will never recognize you after all these years," she insisted.

"After you get a quick look, just apologize for being at the wrong trailer and leave."

Would I be able to do that? Did I even want to? Mother had modeled making tough decisions. And I remembered Mother's long-ago warnings about Edith, that I'd dismissed. Would I be able to confront Edith now? And feel what—relief? closure? Taking one deep breath after another, I waited for an inner message to surface. And it did.

"I'm going up there," I announced to Lara and Brenda.

Lara climbed out of the back seat and pulled on my arm. "Wait up, Mom—you're not going up there alone. I'm coming with you." My teenage daughter had plenty of her own struggles, and I admired her bravery. Lara's sensitive gesture touched my heart.

Holding on to each other, we walked to the trailer, ascended the short flight of wood stairs, and stopped at the metal front door. My heart was pounding. We didn't knock. We stood and listened. No noise from inside. I stepped away from the door and peered through a grimy window. Inside was a slovenly mess. I couldn't help thinking about Mother's awful housekeeping during my childhood, and Edith's ramshackle house in the desert. The trailer had dirty clothes, pillows, and blankets strewn about, piled high. The built in, bolted furniture was made everything look cramped. A mini kitchen counter overflowed with dirty plates, half-filled bottles, assorted pots. On the coffee table below the trailer window, I saw greasy crumpled paper bags that reminded me of the trash Edith hauled in the wagon after her cross-country treks—garbage she'd expected me to clean up. What I couldn't see in the trailer was any sign of Edith. How had my once vain and scheming sister ended up in such a woeful place? A cold shiver ran through my body. I turned away from the window and tried to collect myself. Like other times in life when I had to confront reality and choose which path to take, I asked myself, "What do you feel? What do you need?"

I took a deep breath of hot, dry desert air. And I felt . . . nothing . . . no need for closure. No need to reconnect with Edith. No reason to knock at Edith's door.

I hugged my daughter close. "Lara, we don't have to be here—it's time to leave all this behind." With our arms around each other, we walked down the platform stairs and away from my past. In the VW bug, Lara and I settled in. Without saying a word to each other, Brenda turned on the ignition and drove us away from Location #12 of the trailer park. I never looked back.

Decades later, a private investigator did some research for me and discovered that Carl had died in Phoenix at age seventy-four. Family gossip confirmed that he'd had a leg amputation. *What a fitting end,* I thought, *for an old dancer.* Had it been Carl's wheelchair next to the trailer?

The investigator also found out that Edith had apparently remarried, though unclear whether once or several times. Her final address was a California nursing home. She died at age eighty-eight, and her death certificate was signed by daughter "Regina" with a surname I didn't recognize. Was she the "Reggie" I'd spent a year with in the Arizona desert? Had Edith and Reggie eventually reconciled? Edith's death certificate named her deceased mother (and mine) as "Harriet Worsheski." Was this misspelling of our mother's name—Olsezska—the natural error of Reggie, who'd never learned Polish or our family history? According to Mother's saga, repeated so many times during my childhood, when she was granted asylum in New York, American Immigration officials had changed her name from Harriet Olsezska to Harriet Olse. When she married Dad, she became Hania Sosinski. My childhood had taught me what Mother would do if anyone mispronounced her name as Worsheski. She'd curse them out in Polish. And Little Danusia would have snickered with laughter.

Troubles Rising

Mid-Life Changes

My growing children had unique genetic backgrounds, strong personalities, and complex behaviors. They'd challenged my parenting skills. My marriage was troubled. And I was having mid-life hot flashes and mood swings. In February, I'd turned fifty.

It was time for my annual medical checkup. I sat in a comfortable upholstered chair facing my gynecologist, Dr. C. His red hair was tinged with gray, and his sparkling blue eyes were focused on me. I was among many patients impressed by Dr. C's charisma and compassion. *D Magazine* ranked him among the best of his peers on the annual list of "Best Doctors in Dallas."

"Donna, you don't have to worry about hot flashes and crazy mood swings." His smile reassured. "We can get you through menopause without this nuisance." Dr. C recommended Hormone Replacement Therapy (HRT). Since the 1930s, America's doctors, despite the lack of conclusive and broad range test studies, had been dispensing HRT to multitudes of their ageing female patients.

Each dose of HRT was like an elixir from the fountain of youth.

My desert-dry vagina transformed itself into a fertile oasis. My terrible hot flashes ramped down to tolerable. Unpredictable moodiness turned into predictable tranquility. Yucky and irksome "monthlies" disappeared.

To celebrate my menopause liberation, I decided to make a gift to the local women's shelter. After stuffing a giant shopping bag with my no longer needed sanitary supplies and assorted toiletries, I took on my overstuffed closet. Culling through my copious clothes and accessories, I assembled two gently worn classy pantsuits, designer skirts and jackets, bundles of silk scarves, and heaps of costume jewelry. Packing everything into my car, I turned up the radio. All the way to the women's shelter, I sang out loud and uninhibited karaoke.

For at least ten years, I'd taken HRT and reveled in my restored vitality. The next decade, a major medical study about the risks of HRT would be published linking its sustained use to increased rates of uterine and breast cancer in pre- and post-menopausal women. It would come too late for me. Back in the 1990s, I was successfully managing choices of HRT—pills, patches, or pellets.

However, I had far greater challenges as a wife and mother. Never in memory had Hania and Juzo shown affection to each other, or to me. Neither had they nurtured my aptitudes or praised my achievements. As role models, my parents had shaped how I viewed myself as wife and mother—with self-doubt and insecurity. Mother and Dad never celebrated birthdays and holidays. When I planned my childrens' birthday parties with perfectionist standards, was I trying to impress other parents more than delight the children? Had I forgotten my bliss of long ago, as one of Mary Jane's exuberant kids who danced like crazy in the Sunnyslope cottage? I could recall only one time and place (which house was that?)—when I'd turned up the radio full blast in the garage, and Lara and little Nicky and I danced until we dropped down laughing and exhausted. Why hadn't I created many more ways to share uninhibited joy with my kids?

Instead I'd overscheduled and outdid myself: volunteering in the kids' schools; cooking healthy family meals on a rigid schedule; competing in serious women's team tennis; relentless looking-good-on-the-outside beauty regimes; and obsessive shopping for pretty clothes. Was my compulsive behavior driven by doubts and old baggage insecurities? I'd been role playing for years: as a meticulous, perfectly groomed, always smiling Pan Am stewardess; as a consummate, subservient corporate wife; as a doting, super mother to my children. What was I trying to prove? I'd struggled and failed throughout decades to know and communicate my boundaries and limits.

The larger picture exposed that everyone in my family was struggling.

Nick

During lower school years, Nicky had excelled in everything. Academically he'd soared; socially he was admired and popular with peers and teachers. At individual sports, junior tennis, skiing and swimming, he thrived. In team sports, soccer, baseball and basketball, his trophies for Best Attitude and Most Valuable Player were some of the few decorations that Nicky allowed in his room, along with stacks of books on his shelves—whether academic or youth adventure stories, he loved reading.

In middle school, Nick (Don't call me Nicky anymore!) showed the compassion and empathy of a loyal friend. When a buddy didn't get picked for the school basketball team, Nick discretely approached the coach. "Choose him," he said, "not me—he loves the game and deserves to play more than I do." The coach added both boys to the team.

From the time Nick was twelve, five days a week, he began his day at 5:00 AM for his early morning gym workouts. In the club lounge, I did feeble stretches and scanned the morning paper. Then drove to McDonald's drive-thru for Egg McMuffins that Nick gobbled on the way to Greenhill, where his young brain was pushed to maximum workout.

After school, Nick would dash along the carpool line and leap into my car. "Hi, Mom, I'm starving," he'd announce and fling his jam-packed book bag over the seat. On the way to tennis practice, we'd stop at the Middle Eastern deli for chicken kabobs to fuel the pounding hours ahead on the courts. Nick developed a near reverence for his tennis coach, who championed physical endurance, mental discipline, and intense hard work. And who, in pursuit of more young disciples for the competitive juniors' program, selected Nick as a role model and mentor. Nick's only time-out was dinner at home, eaten voraciously while maneuvering ice bags on his aching legs and soaking his feet in a tub of ice cubes under the table. Exceeding everyone's expectations imposed a heavy price on my son.

Nick, National levels tennis, 1997

By the time Nick reached high school, he was a remarkable athlete. As a cross-country runner, he had a formidable push at the end of a race. When fatigue took its toughest toll, Nick was the one who could forge ahead of other exhausted runners and win for the team. The cross-country coach wanted him to run every race and increase the team's chances to win the All-Conference trophy—another addition to the crowded trophy case in the hallway that got plenty of attention from passing students, teachers, and parents.

Along with cross-country, Nick delivered superior energy to daily tennis practice and tournament competitions nearly every weekend and most holidays. By the time he was fourteen, Nick's ankles and feet had already begun to break down. Far too often we sat in the waiting room of Dr. Moore, esteemed Sports Medicine MD, where the walls were covered with signed photos of rodeo riders and pro-team players whom Nick recognized and admired.

In the examining room, Dr. Moore issued a warning. "Nick, your injuries are only going to increase."

The cost of two intensely demanding sports plus Nick's love of skiing—hard and fast until the lift closed—had pushed his young body past its limits. Nick stared intently at Dr. Moore. I could almost see his teenage brain processing that he couldn't do it all. With agility, Nick swung his legs from the examining table and stood up. "Okay, Dr. Moore," he said. "I guess that's it."

By the next day Nick had made his decision—to quit the Greenhill cross-country team and concentrate on competitive tennis. Although he had been running cross-country on the school team, his tennis was a non-school-related, national level juniors program. Nick and I discussed what his withdrawal from Greenhill's cross-country team would mean to his coach, his teammates, and to school administration.

"Mom, I'm just a piece of meat to them." Nick's shoulders slumped in resignation.

Nick, Greenhill Cross Country, 1997

Nick quit the cross-country team, but did not tell them why. I couldn't convince my son that it was important to share the medical reasons for his choices. But he stubbornly refused to tell even his coach about the doctor's mandate. Nick assumed most of his classmates would not understand and gave few of them the chance to do so.

His decision to keep silent about his physical overload and medical setbacks, incurred multiple penalties. Nick's abrupt withdrawal from school sports caused retribution from the athletic department and from uninformed teachers. His former cross-country teammates, not knowing why he quit, judged him harshly. Adding insult to injury, Nick was put on academic probation because he got an "incomplete" in athletic course credit. His dad was furious. Bob warned Nick that this would not look good on his college application record. Nick seemed confident when he answered his dad. "I'll handle that when the time comes."

When National Honor Society recommendations were made, in spite of having achieved top grades, Nick was not among the students elected to Honor Society. During a rare lapse in his tightly reined emotions, Nick's eyes looked sad and his voice was unsteady when he shared with me that some students who'd made Honor Society had committed more serious infractions. "Mom," Nick said, "I don't know how quitting a school sport makes me ineligible for NHS."

As a parent, I came to doubt my decision not to intervene on Nick's behalf with the coach and the school administration. I'd thought by staying out of it, I'd foster Nick's self-trust and learning from the consequences of his choices. My hope was that his innate intelligence would teach him to advocate for himself, communicate his own needs, and benefit from life lessons. Instead, I've never felt sure that I made the right decision.

At least six nights a week in his room, the clock moved toward midnight while Nick ploughed through homework and studied for tests. His dedication to tennis and academics left no time for "hanging out." Nick's close friends were a small cadre of tennis buddies and a select few at school. While his academic test scores stayed right at the top, his emotional connection with classmates spiraled down.

Lara

Like her brother, Lara had sensitivity and compassion for others. As a little girl, she was drawn to those who looked and acted differently from the popular in-crowd. As a teenager, Lara had become the outsider yearning to be understood and appreciated, but unable to fit in. I imagined that Lara would have befriended childhood me, the outlier disparaged as "Immigrant Girl." When Lara's volatile relationships with other children demolished her confidence, she covered her insecurity with bossiness.

At home, her oppositional personality lit wildfires, especially with her father, a perfectionist with rigid expectations and a trigger temper. Lara's strong will often provoked Bob's anger and triggered my insecurities. What I feared most was that she'd succumb to temptations of teenage sex, alcohol, and drugs. I hoped my daughter would turn to me for support against teen peer pressure. Yet I felt miscast as family mediator between Lara and her father. How could I be successful in that role when I hadn't learned healthy mentoring from my own parents? To protect my daughter and oppose my husband's outbursts, I had to overcome my own childhood traumas. If I did nothing, the outcome would be a continued cycle of generational parental dysfunction.

One evening after family supper, yet another tumultuous family argument flared: Lara lashing out at both of us as horrible parents; Bob raging; me banishing Lara's privileges shouted out at her; and Nick running upstairs, door slamming. That left Bob and me staring at each other in the living room. Having lost my temper, I was undone.

"Bob, the confrontations with Lara are out of control." I must have sounded desperate. "We absolutely need professional help with our parenting."

"Yes, of course we need to find a plan, one that actually works," he said. "Lara doesn't even know where she's going. I can't talk to her. She just screams or shuts down."

I looked down at my shaking hands. "Lara doesn't budge if she's criticized." Knowing that Bob's anger could escalate, I didn't want to push him over the edge and leave Lara wondering whether her father loved or hated her.

Little Danusia's fears, so long ago. "She needs to feel you care about her, even when she's being outrageous."

"Of course I care!" Bob said. "Don't you see I care?"

"Yes, *I know you care*, but you're not showing it to her." I massaged my hands and felt no comfort.

Counseling—For Whom?

At last, there was some progress—I managed to convince Bob that we needed "parent counseling." But what about the commitment made and broken—to do marriage counseling? Could I leverage our parent counseling agreement? I went on the hunt for competent family counselors. And I found a promising practice, two PhDs, a married couple working in tandem as marriage and family counselors. I hoped that their gender balance might relax Bob's entrenched bias against psychotherapists, and I made an appointment for us.

But he had already passed judgment. "I don't expect much from these people." Bob scowled. "The whole mental health profession is corrupt. They've been swindling a fortune out of corporations like Exxon for decades." As a senior executive responsible for employees worldwide, Bob had become convinced that Exxon's employee benefit plan was abused by inept mental health professionals treating countless employees who, afterward, showed no improved performance. "We've paid through the nose. Not a one of them can be trusted." When Bob made up his mind, he was unflinching.

Nevertheless, we showed up right on time for the appointment. With cool handshakes and appraising eyes, the therapist couple greeted us. They ushered Bob and me into a dimly lit office where the venetian blinds covering the windows had been pulled tightly shut. Small table lamps cast staggered puddles of illumination. We were invited to choose seats among four black leather chairs, flanked by generic end tables. On each table a box of Kleenex stood puffed up and ready. Bob and I gravitated to chairs across from each other. The two therapists sat down next to us, male-to-male, female-to-female. How desperately I wanted them to give us a magic cure for a troubled marriage and my struggling daughter. Could they help us? I focused on the floor-to-ceiling bookshelves along the wall in front of me, filled with journals and academic volumes with complex and baffling titles. My preparation had been the self-help section at Barnes & Noble.

The male therapist cut to the core and addressed both of us. "Tell us a little bit about what brought you here."

I glanced at Bob, who stared down, arms across his chest, hands gripping his elbows so tightly they made dimples in his shirtsleeves. The silence in the room was awkward.

"We behave like our family is a business," I plunged in. "We don't share our feelings. We have lost intimacy." To this day, I have no idea whether Bob was surprised by the fact that we were actually there for marriage counseling.

The male therapist nodded like ours was a perfectly natural situation. He turned to my husband. "And, Bob," he prompted, "what is your impression?"

"If Donna sees a problem, it's *her* problem. *I'm* not to blame. *I'm* not doing anything wrong."

Now, nearly two decades later, what I remember still chills my heart—that my husband dismissed any responsibility for trouble in our marriage. I wouldn't have been shocked by Bob's judging me (I was used to that), but his refusal to acknowledge us as equal partners devastated me. For decades, I'd been clinging to a false hope that a truly loving husband would validate his wife. If my heart was troubled, wouldn't he care?

However, Bob saw no such obligation. He'd made it eminently clear in front of two marriage counselors. Within a half hour, before we'd even gotten to parenting issues, the therapists simultaneously stood up, and the female partner delivered.

"I suggest you may want to work in individual sessions first, and then seek couples' counseling. We can refer you, if you like." She looked directly at Bob. "We specialize in helping couples, but positive change can only occur if each takes responsibility for the issues between them."

Neither of us asked for a referral. Bob paid the $250 bill with his Amex card. The receptionist issued a receipt and directed us to the door marked "Exit Please." As was his habit when faced with something emotional, Bob signaled his need for a time-out. On our way to the elevators, he said, "I need to use the men's room."

In the lobby, my heart was beating so hard that my chest was throbbing out of control. I cupped my left hand over my right and pressed hard against my chest, hoping I could calm my heart.

Yes, I'd used false pretenses to manipulate our single session of marriage counseling. No wonder it had failed and Bob had issued judgment. Neither of us had ever told the other how we needed to be acknowledged, or what made us feel loved. How could we begin to clear up false assumptions or expectations when, in nearly thirty years of marriage, we'd never talked about them? True to habit, I absorbed guilt like a sponge, leaving no room or courage to confront Bob directly and hold him to a promise made years before. Instead, I'd used Lara's problems as a devious excuse to get him into marriage counseling. Were my daughter's challenges also my fault? Was I inadequate both as a wife and a mother? By then, all rational thinking had deserted me. Mother's words echoed in my head: "You no good enough—doing nothing useful!"

Tears welled in my eyes. Immediately, I wiped them to prevent Bob from seeing my sadness. Hiding my vulnerability was my defensive habit since childhood. When Mother hurt me physically and emotionally, I believed she didn't love me. If I allowed her to see how much I hurt, I thought this would give her even more control over me. These flawed convictions traveled with me into marriage. Although I didn't value myself, I expected my husband to treat me as his equal. Bob announcing that I was solely responsible for any problems in our marriage raised the question—what was I going to do about "my problem?"

Beginning of the End

Bob and I had failed at marriage counseling. But I was not going to fail at keeping our family together. I retreated backward to a habitual conviction—*If something doesn't work, change the setting!* The perfect solution formed images in my brain—of a perfect house for our family, a haven of happiness with everything for everyone. On a foldout map, I scrutinized Dallas neighborhoods. In my notebook, I listed my criteria: a lot big enough for a beautiful house and a tennis court; nearby grocery stores, fitness clubs, personal and home services; reasonable distance to Bob's office and Greenhill School. Lara was sixteen and had just gotten her driver's license. She'd be thrilled to drive any distance to high school.

Another concern had to be addressed—keeping my family safe. A few years prior, in 1992, Exxon executive and personal friend Sid Reso had been kidnapped at the end of his driveway in the suburbs of New Jersey. He died while in captivity. Afterward, security was heightened for executive families in Dallas and worldwide—for months we were required to have 24-hour security.

After many reconnaissance expeditions, I found a small, gated community just a few miles away in north Dallas, where there was a perfect double lot for sale. "We'll have everything for everyone," I promised Bob. "If you write the checks, I'll do all the work." We bought the lot. If I planned it right, we'd be able to move into our new home in less than two years, an ambitious challenge that I intended to meet.

With the architect, landscape designer and builder, I adopted what I'd learned from my mother Hania—"Do it right and do it my way!" However, being able to combine beauty, function, and comfort at home had been alien to Mother. My vision was based on what I'd never had in childhood and what I fantasized would make my family happy and keep us together. I created the House Built on Dreams.

Every bedroom would have lovely views and its own private bath (no sharing). There would be a paneled study perfect for Bob, a custom art studio for me, and an expansive dream kitchen. There was no limit to my plan—I added an exercise room to keep us fit; a family room off the kitchen for TV and lounging; a pool table room with space for strategizing and kibitzing; and a tranquil master bedroom with a small, adjoining room for the non-sleeper to cozy up to the fireplace and read or watch TV. In my dreams, we'd have lots of guests—I added a luxurious guest suite. The home I planned was not just for current needs—I projected our golden years together. When Bob and I were too old to nimbly walk up the central and back stairways, we'd use the residential elevator. I designed every landscaping amenity: a night-lit tennis court; spacious swimming pool and spa; jasmine-covered pavilion; open lawn areas;

and native stone terraces that wouldn't overheat during Dallas summers. To top it all off, I would put in a pond where ducks could bob and willows could weep—a tribute to my fond memories of our Florida vacation house.

On the site of the House Built
on Dreams, Dallas, 1997

During my frenzied planning of the House Built on Dreams, our family relationships were turning into nightmares. Lara was in her sophomore year at Bishop Lynch High School, recommended by advisors as a good fit academically and small enough to give students special attention. However, in that high school teenage Lara was attracting the wrong kind of attention from testosterone-driven boys who made her feel like a grown up woman. At home, the confrontations between Lara and her father came to a boiling point.

I needed help. Not from a marriage counselor (I'd given up on that), but for myself as a responsible, loving caretaker of my daughter. A trusted girlfriend referred me to a female therapist who specialized in teen issues. I went there alone and pleaded for professional advice. When I described my fears about my daughter's precarious social choices and the intractable father-daughter conflicts at home, the therapist made dire predictions: that Lara was indeed at risk and that I was a solo lifeboat in turbulent waters. I must face a truth that, in spite of Lara being a potentially strong swimmer and best parenting intentions, my daughter wouldn't reach safe shores without sustained professional help.

Ultimately, Bob and I came together in a heart-wrenching decision. The summer before her junior year, we sent Lara to a boarding school located in northern California. We'd hired a special needs advisor who assured us that it was one of the best schools in the country, specifically designed for teens to develop confidence, courage, emotionally healthy value systems, and ultimately have a strong capacity to face life pressures and become productive adult citizens. Even though Bob and I knew that tough love drove our decision to put our precious daughter into the hands of others because we weren't able to mentor and keep her safe at home, it was still the toughest parental decision we would ever have to make together.

After that, we coped in separate ways, Bob immersed in Exxon, and me obsessively conducting my masterpiece, the House Built on Dreams. Optimistically, we'd have one family year together in our new home, but that was entirely dependent on whether Lara would return to Dallas for her senior year. Again, I morphed into tyrannical clone of Hania issuing orders—no delays tolerated! Amazingly, the contractors delivered. Ten months later the house and landscaping was finished (a miracle in building a custom home). When the last construction vehicle pulled out of the gravel driveway and the final load of sod had been laid, I stood on the terrace overlooking the pond. Feeling like a fairy godmother, I willed that all would be perfect in my fantasy world. My courageous daughter would soon return; our family would be together again.

Lara indeed forged through her challenges at boarding school with courage and fortitude. After one year away, she'd achieved remarkable progress. The school wanted us to keep Lara there for her senior year, but I decided to bring her home. I've never regretted trusting that instinct. Later, I'd credit my mother Hania for modeling strength and fortitude.

Lara came home transformed and infused with healthy confidence, courage, and determination. She re-registered at her former high school to complete her senior year and fulfill remaining graduation requirements.

During that school year, the abundant gardens of our new home were like a Hollywood setting for Lara's senior prom photos. The night included both parental anxiety and glamorous photo ops. Proud parents breathed sighs of relief as they admired teenage offspring who looked grown up and beautiful. Posing like adored celebrities, their immaturity was temporarily disguised.

For Nick's teammates and friends, I staged frequent tennis parties and raucous volleyball tournaments. Greenhill moms wandered through every room of the house, opening even closed doors to check out every detail. "How'd you do it?" I'd hear. "This place is amazing." From another, "Your estate has every luxury, yet it comes off warm and welcoming."

I'd furnished the house with furniture and accessories collected in different times and places: wood crafted bench, trunk, and art from Colombia; oversized mid-century chairs from New York City; antiques from London; tropical lamps and handmade vases from Miami; and oriental carpets from our carriage house in New Jersey. Also, items from our travels abroad including copper cookware, ceramic figurines, an Italian majolica plate collection, a French sideboard, and one of my favorite transformations—a weathered temple carving made into a glass-topped coffee table. Every piece was chosen for function and beauty. Seeing how they seemed to belong together, I affirmed to myself how comfort and beauty could bring contentment and happiness.

Yet, no matter how genuine the compliments from visitors, I didn't take pleasure from their accolades. Shrugging, I'd credit my success to "lots of practice," and praise Bob for his generosity. After all, he'd paid for everything. My innate natural gifts, the aptitudes that came easily to me, were those I most easily dismissed. While many other women might have been overwhelmed by so many decorative choices, I saw affinity within patterns and colors. With little hesitation, I could blend disparate elements into harmony. Along with that creative process, however, I wasn't able to shut down the negative messages imbedded in my psyche since childhood—*You're not worthy! Work harder!*

Our family was finally settled together in our glorious new home. Here the kids would have every opportunity to thrive in safety and comfort. Here, my husband at the peak of his career, would be able to relax, share family time, and entertain visitors. Although I'd also created a space for myself in the House Built on Dreams—an art studio meticulously planned for inspiration and creativity—I would never design a single piece of jewelry there. In fact, I'd never produce art of any kind in our new home.

Facing Reality

Falling Apart Inside

How long could I deny what others saw about me? A girlfriend took my hand after a parent meeting. "Donna, you look so sad and empty."

"Nothing serious," I answered, avoiding eye contact. "Just too many meetings."

At twice-a-week Pilates class, my teacher noticed how unsettled and distracted I'd become. "I'm worried about you, Donna. You're tired all the time."

With a weak smile, I pulled on my warm-up jacket, inside out. "Just a little stress," I mumbled. "Give me some time. I'll be fine."

At home in my beautiful bathroom, the handmade floor tiles were electronically heated. I stood in front of the vanity and tried to feel their warmth. Instead, I cringed. The face staring back at me had dull, bleak eyes, skin the color of gray parchment, and blotched cheeks that looked like decaying fruit. When I stuck out my tongue, it was a horrible white-coated mess. I did the bad breath test—lick your tongue on the inside of your wrist and take a whiff. Mine smelled awful. Based on the tongue alone, Dr. C would probably send me to the lab for testing.

"You're sliding toward disaster," I lectured my reflection in the mirror. "If you break down, Lara and Nick will be the ones to suffer." My thoughts stayed dark. "Don't be like Edith—take responsibility for your children!"

The last thing I could tolerate was to treat my children the way I'd been treated in childhood. In order to break a terrible cycle, I needed professional help. Inside the lower drawer of my night table, I'd kept a journal of languishing insights and vague intentions. Tucked within the pages was a "just in case" list of therapists. I phoned number after number until one practice accepting new patients gave me an appointment.

For the next three months of Mondays, Wednesdays, and Fridays when the kids were at school and Bob was at work, I undertook therapy sessions. My counselor became my surrogate loving parent. Her infinite patience guided me on a precipitous journey—to face my fears, to discover their origins, and along the way, to retrieve something I didn't even know I'd lost.

"Feel your feelings," she encouraged.

Feelings—what were they?

The therapist educated me about eight primary feelings so basic and universal that they're immediately understood and shared by any person, anywhere, in any language—anger, fear, pain, joy, passion, love, shame, and guilt. Each feeling, especially the most uncomfortable, contains a gift—if we know how to unwrap it. For instance, fear, when faced and understood, can provide protection, self-preservation, and greater wisdom.

I learned how the body and the mind work in close tandem. Pain in the body signals stress to the brain. If my chest hurt, I knew my heart was in trouble. If my stomach ached, I felt emotional turmoil. When my head throbbed, it meant I was confused or in doubt about a choice I'd made. However, when I felt a physical sense of comfort and wellbeing, I also knew that my mind was calm and centered.

In addition, therapy illuminated how behaviors produce a broad range of positive vs. negative feelings. An example brought that home for me. When I chose to immerse myself in creative work, my focus and joy was so intense that I lost track of time. In contrast, when I followed "should do" messages—be nice; don't be angry; smile, it makes you look pretty—in response to the judgment of others, I felt wretched. As I looked back at my behavior of past decades, it was impossible to deny consequences of doing what I thought others expected, wanted, and needed from me. In truth, I was living like a shadow of myself.

Each therapy session sapped my energy. On the drive home, I had to force my exhausted brain to focus on the road and find my own driveway. I'd stumble out of the car, shuffle into the house, and stagger up the spiral staircase. When I entered the master bedroom, I'd draw closed the luxurious draperies that puddled to the floor, swishing like silken ball gowns. Almost as soon as I crawled into bed, sleep overcame me. Until the vigilant alarm clock, preset to 2:30 p.m., jarred me awake. Just in time to get to Greenhill, pull into the carpool line and wait for my energetic son to burst into the car, expecting effusive greeting.

Those arduous therapy sessions ultimately produced brutal awareness about myself, my marriage, my parenting—and what I had to change. After more than three decades of living together, neither my husband nor I considered ourselves or behaved as equal partners. I made a pledge—not to spend the rest of my life in a marriage that wouldn't grow stronger and happier. Yet, even contemplating giving up and leaving was excruciating. I'd overcome so many obstacles in adopting and raising two children. I was obsessed about fulfilling my responsibility to them. How could I have believed that creating the House Built on Dreams was a magical way to keep our family together and insure our happiness?

A time for reckoning—I was a critical role model for my children. If authenticity, equality, and willingness to compromise are missing, a marriage cannot survive. And if all dreams are shattered, a responsible person must confront reality.

At age fifty-six, I made the most difficult decision of my life—to divorce. What lay ahead was going to hurt those I loved the most. How would I tell Bob and the children? In what way could I find clear words that my small and precious family would understand? A communication that would keep me from falling apart in the telling. I chose writing— two formidable letters, the first one to Bob and the second one to the children. Each word came with terrible pain. Writing those letter felt like I was undergoing a blood transfusion, with no assurance that I'd survive.

Mid-July, I phoned Bob at his office, my voice was high-pitched with anxiety. "Bob, there's something extremely important we have to do. I need you to come home as soon as you can."

Bob didn't ask me why, and he took me seriously. Less than an hour later, we sat facing each other in the living room designed to foster joyful events in the House Built on Dreams. Bob chose his favorite chair, but instead of relaxing into it, his body was tense, his eyes were filled with worry. I sat on the upholstered sofa opposite Bob, my fingers gripping the edge of the cushion beneath me.

"I've written you a letter." My voice faltered as I handed Bob a white envelope. His hands shook when he took out the handwritten pages and began to read.

The letter expressed my gratefulness: for three decades of marriage; for how he supported and protected our children; for the way he provided for all of us; and for his integrity. Sentences followed to summarize reality about our nine moves in thirty-two years: inevitable recreating and dismantling of our home life, our friendships and our community networks. Each of the nine moves took three years to settle in. That meant that during our thirty-two years of marriage, I'd spent twenty-seven years settling in and only five years of feeling truly settled.

I believed that I'd met this challenge with "dedication and best of intentions." Because I'd invested fully in Bob's career over three decades, I'd relinquished building my own credentials and a professional career of my own. My attempt at graduate study had been curtailed. As consequence of identifying myself primarily through Bob's career and relying on his community status, I'd lost my own identity and emotional well-being. As a couple, we had not examined and strengthened our marriage with conviction, honest communication. Nor had we enlisted help from professional counseling. I now faced the harshest reality of my life—that our marriage was irreparably broken.

As I watched Bob read, my heart filled with sorrow. He let the pages slip to his lap as he read through the letter. Bob didn't look up to even glance at me. He just kept reading.

*I ask you to release me to myself, to end where we are now, to pursue
our lives apart. I am aware of the costs and consequences, especially to
Lara and Nick. Yet this is not a letter to open a discussion. My mind
and my heart are decided. I must have independence to preserve my
integrity and pursue truth—to survive, I must find myself.*

When Bob finished the letter, he slowly gathered the pages from
his lap, refolded them and placed them back into the envelope. No matter how well I thought I knew my husband, I had no idea how he
would react. I wondered whether he would dismiss me, deny me, or flare
with anger. Bob raised his head. For only the second time in over three
decades, the first being the day his father had died—Bob had tears in his
eyes when he cleared his throat and spoke.

"I need to think about this, Donna." His voice was so low that
I strained to hear. He stood up, crushed the envelope as if preparing it for
the trash. In silence, he turned and walked out of the room.

It seemed as if the clock had turned back to a dark and rainy
day very long ago at Old Glendale Farm. A time in childhood when
I yearned to be understood and cherished by my silent and stoic father.
Yet he could not, and did not give me what I desperately needed. In
essence, Bob and I were reenacting that long-ago scene. I had asked for
a divorce. Although, deep within my heart, I wanted Bob to fight to save
our marriage. This was the second time in my life I'd hoped for what a
significant person in my life was unable or unwilling to do.

Telling the Children

Before that summer came to an end, Bob agreed to a separation. But
with conditions: I was the one leaving; therefore, I would have to
find another place to live. On a monthly basis, I was to submit bills
for his approval in order to receive a stipend. The second request didn't
really bother me. Over the years I'd become accustomed to Bob's dil-
igence when it came to household finances. His compulsion to check
the accuracy of others was so different from my naïve assumption that
bills from utilities, banks, and credit cards were always accurate. Indeed,

I came to admire Bob's thoroughness. Later, when I was the one responsible for paying the bills, I would scrutinize and recheck the math. Even
though I reviewed every one, I never found an error.

Bob also dictated when I could tell the children. Lara, nineteen years old in her sophomore year at SMU, had decided to live off-
campus in an apartment shared with a roommate. Nick, sixteen, was heading into his junior year at Greenhill. Simultaneously, there were major,
sensitive negotiations underway at Exxon, a corporation known for its
entrenched, conservative culture. In that world, a senior executive's divorce
could be perceived as a sign of personal failure. Bob asked me to "preserve his dignity" by keeping our personal business private from everyone,
including the children, until after the public announcement of significant
changes at Exxon, or until the end of the year—whichever came first.

Meaning I had to be publicly surreptitious and selective. To very
few persons could I reveal my pending divorce and ask for help with
critical tasks. One of those confidants was a trusted realtor friend
whom I engaged to find my next home. We discovered a builder's spec
house in an ideal location, another gated community only a couple
of miles away. Since the project was in the final phase of completion,
pending interior finish-out, I was able to transform the builder's plans
for a pretentious French chateau into an understated family home
with charming European accents. The house would be move-in ready
by December. Bob never questioned my selection of the house, nor
did he want to see it. He duly transferred funds to my individual
account without restrictions. This behavior was characteristic of Bob's
integrity—a value that I'd always admired.

In September, after classes had started at SMU, Lara returned home
to pack up a few more things she wanted for her off-campus apartment.
I didn't know then that she had discovered something else—my file of
real estate papers that were in the drawer of my desk. For a month, she
kept her find a secret until she confronted me later.

She stood feet planted, eyes wide, hands clenched. Lara, who usually called me "Mommy," or "Mom," didn't that day. "Mother," she
announced. "Something is happening with you and Dad. I want to know
what's going on."

"What makes you ask that?"

"I found stuff about a new house in your desk. Why are we buying a new house?"

My mind swirled. How was I going to keep my promise to Bob and also be honest with my daughter? "You have no right to go looking through my desk." I said. "Don't snoop!"

Lara's eyes blazed. "You're keeping a secret."

"You've been snooping," I repeated back. Her body language told me that my daughter wasn't angry—Lara was worried. I don't remember how I deterred her, only that she backed off. Perhaps she didn't really want to hear the truth.

December arrived and Christmas was approaching. Corporate negotiations hadn't been resolved, but it was indeed the end of year—the deadline to which Bob had agreed. Now I had to tell the children. My childhood recollections of Christmas were bleak, and so I'd always made Christmas a time of joy and sharing for my family. Through the year, I'd search for perfect gifts for everyone, including our dog Lady and our cat Pye Pye. During evenings before Christmas, I'd enter my gift hideout and begin another frenzied session of wrapping parcels and writing individual messages to recipients. For the final year together in the House Built on Dreams, how could I create joy for my children when their world was about to fall apart? A Christmas we wouldn't be celebrating together. There was no way, no words, no holiday paper, and no gift box—to be able to wrap my terrible news in a festive disguise.

Two weeks before Christmas, we gathered in the "family room." Bob sat rigidly on the leather chair in the corner. Nick and Lara settled together on the dark green sofa. I pulled up a chair across from them, a glass coffee table between us. Bob disdained glass tables, but had grudgingly agreed to that one. It would be one of the first things he'd get rid of, along with the draperies I'd designed to puddle luxuriantly on floors throughout the house. After I was gone, he would have them rehung, nice and straight, barely touching the floor.

My hand clutched the second most difficult letter I'd ever written, my fingers nervously rattling the sheets. My children's anxious faces told me they were fearful.

Trying to sound calm, I spoke slowly. "Lara and Nick, I'm going to have to read this to you—after I finish, we can talk together about everything." I looked at Bob and he glared back at me.

Unlike my letter to Bob, which he had read silently. Even though my soul was shattered, I read aloud in a voice I hoped would not falter. How can one explain the hardest decision of one's life? I could only hope in future that my children would understand and forgive me. I read that my marriage to their father was going to end. We did not have what it took to preserve a loving, joyous relationship as husband and wife, and other attempts to preserve it had failed. I read the reason for waiting until now to tell them, and asked them to forgive my keeping it a secret for a while.

At the end of the letter, I tried to express my hope about the future. Their father and I were caring people who had done our best. Neither of us was to blame. I pledged to Lara and Nick that nothing about us as their parents would change. Our time and love would always be for them, whenever and however each of them needed us.

At that point, I looked up at my children. They were clinging to each other, Lara physically trying to comfort her younger brother. I noticed that Bob was staring down at his knees, not looking at anyone. I folded the letter, put it on the coffee table, and I waited for the children's reactions.

Nick responded first, with tears in his soft brown eyes. "You and Dad have been the best parents. All I want is for you both to be happy . . . nothing else." I don't remember Lara's words, but her gestures were eloquent. Sitting close to Nick, she hugged him with both strength and tenderness.

Now it was time to tell them about changes to come. Their dad would be staying in the house. I'd be moving to a new house in a nearby neighborhood that was close to all the familiar places. Although Lara had her own apartment close to SMU, I told her that her own lovely bedroom in my new home would be waiting for whenever she wanted to be there. As for Nick, it seemed best that he live with me until he graduated from high school. However, whenever he wished, he could spend time with his dad.

"We're still going to Colorado for Christmas, but not all at the same time," I explained. In earlier years, we'd made plans to spend the holidays there, with long-time family friends who were our frequent guests for skiing. They knew about the divorce and were supportive, yet they tried not to take sides. "I'll be with you the first week, and your dad will come up for the second week." I'd use that week to return to Dallas and move into the new house. I promised Lara and Nick, "Everything in my house will be ready and waiting for the two of you."

Despite all of my fervent planning, things turned out different than I expected, and much harder than anything I'd imagined.

Alone at Last

I designed my new home to be an oasis of tranquility, a place free from worry and fear. Bob wanted no reminders of my taste left behind and gave me free range to take whatever I wished from "his" house. I arranged for the movers to come while Bob and the kids were in Colorado. Everything I chose was loaded onto trucks and moved to my smaller home in the gated community a short distance away. As I wandered from room to room, I took stock of the furniture, accessories, and art I'd collected during decades of living in and leaving so many other places. Now I needed to put it all together in a different house and create a sense of welcome for my children. To do that demanded my artistic sensibility—and finding other people with skills I lacked.

I hired two women with specialty painting talents to transform my blank walls into textured surfaces evoking a sense of timeless beauty. To reupholster worn furniture, I chose fabrics inspired by ancient artifacts: olive, topaz, terra cotta, and ochre. In every room, I coordinated disparate objects into cohesiveness. Perhaps I was able to do that because my childhood spent in Mother's boarding house had taught me not only to accept, but also to welcome transient souls. No matter how disjointed or troubled our different lives, it is possible to create a sense of peacefulness and feel safe—if only for a while. All of us somehow got through the holidays. When the kids returned from Colorado, Lara went back to her apartment, and Nick moved in with me for the remainder of his junior year.

The summer before his senior year in high school, Nick and I took a trip together—to the Wimbledon Tennis Championships and then to Oxford University in England where Lara was studying at SMU's summer abroad program.

We enjoyed a typically English experience at Wimbledon—watching exciting pro tennis along with eating strawberries and cream, which was served throughout the day. A highlight for Nick was lining up at the

Nick and Lara, UK Wimbledon and
Oxford, 2000

"Players Only" exit doors to take candid photos of his tennis idols. The elite atmosphere of Wimbledon was a striking contrast to the US Open, which we'd attended in the past. At Wimbledon, only ticketed patrons were permitted entry to stadiums and court play. At the US Open, non-ticket holders could attend practice matches free of charge, or they could mill about and watch the tournament sets on big screens placed around the grounds.

Until now, I hadn't taken either of the kids back to London, where we'd lived when they were babies. It was nostalgic returning with teenage Nick to "our house" on Seymour Walk. At least the familiar doorknocker was still there—a pair of impish brass monkeys that I'd discovered in a dusty antique shop and mounted on our front door. But there were no flowers planted and cascading from the window boxes.

After Wimbledon, Nick and I went to visit Lara, who was enrolled in SMU's Summer at Oxford University program. Ambitiously, she'd signed up for *Chaucer's Tales*. None of us could understand old Chaucerian English, but fortunately we discovered Blackwell's, a much-loved book-seller established in 1879 on Broad Street in Oxford. There we found a modern version of *Chaucer's Tales* that would ease Lara through the otherwise incomprehensible course. While most of her classmates took ample time off to tour the continent, diligent Lara would stay put and study. During our brief visit, Lara showed us around the historic campus. To me, the most obvious difference between housing at Oxford and dorm life at SMU were Oxford's lack of creature comforts—Spartan rooms, no central heating, and communal bath and shower facilities with a dearth of shower stalls and an ample number of bathtubs. Americanized Lara craved eating out in Oxford restaurants, otherwise unaffordable on her modest budget. We wanted to treat her and went to several, from coffee shops to full service restaurants.

Later that same summer, Nick and Lara left for the Caribbean, where Bob was celebrating his sixtieth birthday by hosting a family reunion at a tropical resort. When Nick returned just before school started, he announced, "Mom, I need to move back with Dad."

I was stunned and worried. I knew Bob hadn't begun to resolve his anger and resentment toward me, and I urged Nick not to put himself in the line of fire. However, my son went ahead with, what seemed at the time to be, an impulsive decision.

Shortly after Nick moved in with his dad, Lara also made a seemingly spontaneous change. She left her off-campus apartment and returned to live with her Dad.

Later, one of Nick's friends from Greenhill told me about what had happened at Bob's family reunion in the Caribbean. Nick had confided buddy-to-buddy that his paternal grandmother and aunts (Bob's two sisters) had pressured him to take care of his dad—not his mother. I realized that Nick's decision had not been impulsive, it had been manipulated.

My decision to leave Bob had violated an inalienable Wilhelm family rule—duty and loyalty above all else. From their perspective, my asking for a divorce was an unforgivable betrayal. Although I could accept their angry judgment against me personally, I disdained their manipulation of young Nick. If the report from Nick's friend was accurate, then holding an innocent and vulnerable young man responsible for the care of his wounded, but capable, father was unjust and cruel.

In May of his junior year, to celebrate Nick's seventeenth birthday, Bob and Lara had hosted a dinner for Nick and a few of his buddies at the House Built on Dreams. The same friend who shared with me his concern now reported a new worry. During Nick's birthday celebration, Bob had loudly praised Nick's friends for their outstanding high school achievements—those that he emphasized looked good on their college applications. In front of everyone, he then berated Nick for withdrawing from national-level tennis competition and losing his ranking. Bob predicted that Nick's choices would sabotage his chances of getting accepted to an elite college. Nick's friend was far more alarmed by Nick's submissiveness. He'd taken him aside and said, "You don't have to put up with your dad's crappy verbal abuse. It isn't true, and it's cruel."

For Nick, living with his dad indeed proved to be difficult and isolating. Lara was a busy college student and Bob's job demands included travel. Too often, Nick was left alone and unsupervised. However, even with Bob's busy travel schedule, he didn't disregard Nick's uncharacteristic and increasing lethargy and emotional shutdown. Bob telephoned me. "Something has to be done about Nick!"

I took my unresisting son to his internist. The medical exam included a diagnostic questionnaire for depression. Nick checked off nearly every characteristic on that questionnaire. His doctor prescribed a mild antidepressant.

Over time, despite increasing the dosages and switching to other meds with untenable side effects, Nick continued to suffer worsening symptoms, and none of the antidepressants stopped them.

Our family and close friends tried to understand Nick's emotional withdrawal and erratic behavior. In spite of our best intentions, nothing we said or did would help Nick. It felt as if we were witnessing an unstoppable tragedy. My son, once "destined for the stars," was headed down into a dark abyss.

All of us agonized about the cause of Nick's depression. If only I'd had access then to those sealed records from La Casa that protected the privacy of the birth mother, it might have shed light on my son's depression and enabled us to be more proactive with early intervention. In years to come, Nick would be diagnosed as having long-term, treatment-resistant clinical depression. And we would eventually learn that there was a genetic link.

My nemesis from childhood had traveled with me into my new life—a dark creature that attacked when I was most vulnerable—"*You are not worthy, work harder!*" Many sleepless nights, I lay staring at the ceiling. Many days, I wandered blankly through my quiet house. I was a middle-aged woman, now living alone and facing monumental challenges. *How am I going to redefine myself? How am I going to manage life alone?*

My first priority was to learn how to manage my financial resources. During three decades of depending solely on Bob to handle and plan our financial affairs, I'd become financially ignorant. I enrolled in a course in personal financial management. Using gut instinct and perseverance, I hired a team of trusted advisors to mentor me in financial investment, legal matters, and intricate tax implications. Slowly, I grew more confident, and eventually I would become a competent steward of my financial resources and wellbeing.

Meanwhile, Bob and I were still negotiating the terms of our divorce. The joint property laws of the State of Texas would dictate how the assets we'd accrued during more than three decades of marriage would be divided.

Although Bob was a master negotiator who knew how to maintain financial control, he was never underhanded or petty—always a man of integrity. I was able to pay cash for the new house, no mortgage. Bob did not chastise or subject me to nit-picking scrutiny. Nonetheless, my divorce attorney recommended we pursue a temporary financial settlement. But my unwavering intent was to maintain mutual respect and focus on the children's wellbeing. I believed that putting our emphasis on a temporary settlement would only waste energy and stir antagonism between us. Instead, I intended to persevere toward a final divorce settlement as soon as possible. How naïve that was. Our seemingly straightforward division of assets would drag on to incur layers of emotional angst along with ever-increasing legal fees.

By December of 2000, a year and a half after I'd asked Bob for a divorce, we were still legally married. The kids were lashing out their anger and confusion—at each other, at Bob, and at me. I was consumed by an overwhelming sense of my children having abandoned me. And I knew that in turn, they felt I had abandoned them. No matter what, I was on my own, navigating what felt like a formidable mountain, dangerous with cliffs and chasms. If I fell, would anyone care enough to find me? Alone at night in my bed, a menacing tiger prowled my dreams.

> *But the tigers come at night*
> *with their voices soft as thunder*
> *as they tear your hope apart*
> *as they turn your dream to shame.**

One night, my thoughts traced back to the woman who had disappeared from my life fifty-seven years ago—Irma Lettrich. When my parents confessed that she was my true birth mother, I'd had no time or desire to hunt for her. Now I wanted answers. *Why had my birth mother abandoned me? If I looked for her, could I find her? She'd have to be at least in her late seventies by now—was she still alive?* I became consumed by a mission—to search for the long-missing Irma Lettrich. Only now, would it be too late?

---

* "I Dreamed a Dream" from *Les Misérables*. English lyrics by Herbert Kretzmer, based on the original French by Alain Boublil and Jean-Marc Natel.

Finding Irma

Two Envelopes and a Good P.I.

To search for my birth mother, I needed help. *A good private investigator would be helpful, but how do I find one?* My divorce attorney ought to know about P.I. people—I decided to ask him.

"What tangible evidence do you have regarding Irma Lettrich?" my attorney questioned from across the mahogany conference table.

"Not much," I said. "Only these two envelopes—my other mother Hania gave them to me long ago, when she confessed that my actual birth mother was a woman named Irma Lettrich." I placed two envelopes on the polished surface of the table. The first one showed the sender as Harriet S. of Glendale Farms, Hebron, Connecticut (How strange, since Mother rarely went to the farm), and the recipient indicated was Mrs. Irma McMarkwell of Redondo Beach, California. That envelope wasn't stamped. Apparently, it was never sent. The second envelope was torn across as if it had been frantically ripped open. Neither envelope contained any shred of long-ago contents.

"You'll like Angelo Nolfi. He's reliable and smart." My attorney held out Nolfi's business card and said, "I recommend him for your search. And he has a warm heart."

As soon as I returned home, I made a call to Angelo Nolfi. Immediately, he asked for background information. I repeated what Mother had told me about Irma Lettrich, "a poor and pregnant Irish girl," who'd shown up alone and asked for a room at Mother's boarding house—fifty-eight years ago. I explained that my only visual evidence were two envelopes with reference to two cities: Redondo Beach and Pittsburgh.

Two weeks later, Angelo called me back with incredible news—he'd found Irma Lettrich. Never did I imagine this could happen so fast, or that I'd be on the first flight, the very next morning, to Pittsburgh. When I entered the arrival hall of Pittsburgh International Airport, I confronted a line of greeters and hired drivers hoisting up signs with passenger names. A lanky figure stood, empty handed, among them. Although we'd never met before, he broke away from the group and headed straight toward me.

"You're Donna, aren't you?" He extended his hand. "Glad you're here. Angelo Nolfi at your service."

"But how did you recognize me?"

"Well, it's obvious—you look so much like her."

A sea of arriving passengers began to engulf us. Angelo put a protective hand on my shoulder to guide me, and with the other took the handle of my roller suitcase. "There's no time to waste," he said with a quiet sense of urgency. "We're heading to St. Catherine's Hospital. That's where your mother is now."

This news overwhelmed me—why was she in the hospital? I had so many questions for her. Would she be able to answer them?

In the airport parking lot Angelo opened the passenger door of his car for me, stood patiently until I got settled, then circled around to the driver's side. He reached up to the visor clip for his sunglasses. I liked his face—lots of lines, warm eyes.

"No matter what your adoptive parents told you, she's not Irish," he said as we headed for the highway. "Irma Lettrich is first generation Czech American."

I'd grown up believing I was Polish. For the past thirty years,

I thought I was Irish. And now I'd just learned that I'm Czech. So much deception and confusion—why hadn't they told me the truth? Angelo kept talking, and I kept listening. He explained that Irma had married a man with the same surname. Lettrich was as common a name in Czechoslovakia as Smith or Jones was in America. "How's that for a coincidence!"

There was more. In searching national identity lists for females named Lettrich, Angelo had found four. When he checked their current ages and locations, there was only one Irma Lettrich who could've given birth in 1943. Also, there was a clincher for Angelo. "Her address is right here in Pittsburgh, my home territory." Angelo gave an affirming nod, but otherwise kept his eyes on the road.

The convoluted route from the airport to St. Catherine's Hospital reminded me how confusing Pittsburgh had always been for me. No matter where we were living during past decades, Bob and I had dutifully trekked at least once a year to suburban Pittsburgh for his family reunions. Yet, without Angelo driving, I wouldn't have found my way through a maze of mostly working class neighborhoods, until suddenly things looked familiar—I recognized we were passing through Mount Lebanon, the neighborhood where Bob was born and raised and where his family still lived. When Angelo told me Irma's address was only a few miles away, that meant that during all my past visits to Pittsburgh, Irma and I could have bumped into each other at the mall, the supermarket—just about anywhere. Had we ever crossed paths? And if we had, could she have recognized me, as Angelo did so easily at the airport?

But what if we were wrong and this Irma Lettrich wasn't actually my birth mother? I was about to find out—we'd pulled up to the hospital.

My often-restless hands began to shake. I shoved them into my jacket pockets filled with waiting tissues. As Angelo and I entered the lobby, another memory stirred—wasn't this the same hospital where Bob's sister Cindy once worked as a nurse? At the information desk, a blue-haired volunteer wearing a "Hello, I'm Gladys" nametag echoed aloud, "Hello, I'm Gladys."

"Hello," I parroted back. "We're here to visit patient Irma Lettrich."

Gladys scanned a large logbook. "Lettrich, Irma Lettrich . . . I see this patient is in critical, family only status. Are you family?"

Angelo was tall and wiry, and his thinning gray hair and angular features bore no resemblance to me, a petite redhead. We exchanged tacit glances. "Yes," I said firmly, "we're family."

Gladys gave us a smile. "All right, go on up—fifth floor." A sense of relief poured over me, and I smiled back at her.

At the nurses' station, a plus-size woman commandeered the long counter.

"We're here to visit Irma Lettrich." I don't know how confident I'd looked, but I tried to sound that way. The nurse's features were smooth and youthful, but her eyes evoked an older wariness. When she swiveled around to check patient records, I stepped closer to peek and watched her fingers run down a printed list.

"Irma Lettrich is in critical condition, very critical. Only the three family members listed here are allowed to visit. Exactly who are you two, please?" she raised her eyebrows and looked at us.

I noted her ID badge—Leteesha Jones, R.N. "Nurse Jones," I took a deep breath, "you won't find me on that list. My name is Donna Wilhelm," I tried to steady my voice. "Fifty seven years ago, Irma Lettrich had a baby that she gave away—I was that baby.

Leteesha Jones' now alert eyes met mine. And Angelo had stepped closer to me, as if for moral support. I touched his sleeve.

"I've just found *my birth mother!*"

Nurse Jones looked startled.

"This is Mr. Nolfi, the investigator who helped me find her." I explained that he located a Pittsburgh address for Irma Lettrich, and went to her apartment. Instead he found her daughter, Menina Green there. When he told her that he represented a client looking for her lost birth mother named Irma Lettrich, Menina responded that her mother, Irma Lettrich, was at St. Catherine's Hospital. "Please know this," I needed Nurse Jones to understand, "Menina Green gave her permission for Mr. Nolfi to visit Irma Lettrich in this hospital."

Nurse Jones pulled forward a heavy logbook. Her large hand slapped back a page. "Yes, I see that Mr. Nolfi was a visitor last night. He checked in at 6:00 p.m. and signed out at 6:45 p.m. I also see that Mrs. Green arrived right after he left."

"Nurse Jones," I straightened up to every inch of 5 ft, 4 inches. "I'm fifty-seven years old, and only now have found my birth mother. Even if Irma Lettrich is in critical condition, I must see her!"

Nurse Jones stood up and walked around the counter toward us. Her pastel pink uniform was creased and rumpled—too little iron-ing or too many shifts? She far outweighed me and towered over me. "Let me consult with my supervisor. She's authorized to handle this . . . unusual situation." Her tone was gentle, and her vigilant eyes had soft-ened. "Believe me, Miss Donna," she said, placing her hand on my shoul-der, "I do understand how important this is for you. Please wait, just a few minutes."

I looked up at Angelo. His calm demeanor helped me to relax a bit. My attention shifted to the scene around us. Behind the nurses' station a young man in blue scrubs punched robotically at a computer keyboard. A nurse working nearby filled the rest of the tight space as she hunched over a tray of mini paper cups—patient meds? A few yards down the main hallway, Nurse Jones stood in close conversation with another woman, the head nurse, I assumed. Her trim slacks and crisp white tunic were a stark contrast to Nurse Jones' disheveled uniform.

I tried to be patient, but my hands betrayed me. One ring, on my right index finger, had been the first piece of jewelry I'd purchased after my separation—a disk of speckled amber with a platinum knob pierc-ing its center. The ring served as my well-burnished worry bead. While watching the two nurses in the hallway, I massaged the ring and kept twisting the band around my finger. The pair of nurses took turns glanc-ing at Angelo and me. Finally, they headed toward us, the petite nurse in the lead.

"I'm Head Nurse Marian Cooper," she held out her hand and I took it. How warm it felt. Her voice was friendly, her figure slim and comely. She gestured that we follow her down the hall to a private lounge.

At first I was relieved to see the room empty, until I realized the walls and ceiling were blue, and most of the furniture was blue. It brought back painful memories of the Devil in Blue, my abusive sixth grade teacher. Was something awful about to happen?

I chose to sit in the only non-blue chair. Nurse Cooper selected a molded blue chair next to me. Angelo settled in a blue fabric upholstered chair a discreet distance away, next to a table littered with magazines and discarded newspapers. Nurse Cooper asked me to explain why I was there.

I realized I hadn't introduced Angelo. "Nurse Cooper, please meet Mr. Angelo Nolfi, the private investigator who was able to find my birth mother, Irma Lettrich."

Angelo rose quickly, walked over, and extended his hand.

"This must be quite an experience for you, Mr. Nolfi," she said.

"Yes," he glanced down at me. "I've never had a case like this one." He explained that a series of lucky breaks had led him to locate Irma Lettrich in Pittsburgh, his hometown. He'd driven out to her address, a low-income apartment building. When he rang the bell, the woman who answered was Irma's daughter Menina Green. "She prefers to be called Nina," Angelo added as if he were an insider. When she told him that her mother, Irma Lettrich, was seriously ill and in the hospital, Angelo revealed the purpose of his visit.

"Nina was shocked at first. It took her a while to process," he admitted. "But then she gave me permission to visit her mother here, at St. Catherine's. And I did so, last night."

Nurse Cooper asked about that visit.

Angelo paused as if to collect his thoughts. "Well, first I introduced myself as a PI, a private detective." He'd then explained to Irma why he was there—that his client was a woman searching for her long-lost birth mother. Angelo described how Irma had motioned him closer to her bed. He'd bent over to make sure she could hear him and said, "I've come to ask you two very important questions. Did you give birth to a baby girl in Hartford, Connecticut, on February 2, 1943? And if so, what happened to the baby?"

Nurse Cooper showed rapt attention. Angelo described how Irma had shut her eyes and lay still for a few moments, her breathing labored. When she opened her eyes, they were filled with tears. She admitted she gave birth to a daughter that year, on that very day. Angelo had waited for what came next. Irma confessed, "I gave my baby away to my landlady. I'll never forget Harriet. She was so much older. I thought she would be a wise mother."

Angelo then asked Irma one more question. "Do you want to meet the woman we think might be your daughter?"

"Yes, bring her." Irma's voice had been barely a whisper, but he was certain of what she said next. "There were so many phone calls, so many discussions . . ." Then, Irma closed her eyes, without finishing her sentence.

Desperate to add my own words, I interrupted Angelo. "Nurse Cooper, I've flown 1,500 miles to see my birth mother, in this hospital, in a bed only a few steps away." I couldn't stop from rambling on—about my marriage, about Pittsburgh and my in-laws, our annual visits to Pittsburgh during three decades of marriage. I told Nurse Cooper how shocked I was, knowing that during those countless visits to Pittsburgh, my birth mother was only a few minutes away. Then I stopped babbling, because only one thing mattered—Nurse Cooper's decision.

Silent seconds seemed like hours. Angelo and I exchanged glances. Nurse Cooper shifted nervously in her chair. I sensed she had something difficult to say. I took deep breaths, tried to calm myself. The blue of that room had become nearly intolerable.

"I'm afraid there has been a serious development." Nurse Cooper's grim tone frightened me. "Your birth mother can't communicate with anyone now. During the night, she lapsed into a coma. She survives only on life support."

How was this possible? Only last night Irma had been fully conscious. She'd talked to Angelo and asked him to bring me to her. This was so unfair. Everything happening so quickly had been auspicious. I seemed destined to meet my birth mother . . .

"But why has this happened—now?" I shook my head in disbelief.

Nurse Cooper tried to comfort me. "We just don't know. Last night, Irma was alert. Her other daughter, Nina, was here. They spent perhaps

an hour together, before Nina decided to go down to the cafeteria."
Nurse Cooper paused. "Have you met Nina?"

"No, only Angelo has." When he met Nina at her mother's apartment, he asked her whether she wanted to meet me, her half-sister. Oddly,
while Nina had given Angelo permission to visit her mother in the hospital, she refused to speak to me, even by phone. "It's been incredible to
learn that I have a half-sister who doesn't want to meet me."

Nurse Cooper nodded. "By the time Nina returned from the cafeteria, everything had changed . . . during those thirty minutes she was
away, her mother slipped into a coma."

"Nina must've been shocked—like I am now. What did she do?"
I asked the question and wondered what I would've done.

"She told staff that she needed to see her husband," Nurse Cooper
answered. "She left instructions to do what was necessary and to keep her
informed—by telephone. And then she left the hospital. We don't know
when she plans to return."

I began to speculate what might have happened between Irma and
Nina? Had they argued about me? Did Nina vent her anger on her
mother, for not revealing a long-kept secret sister? I knew Angelo's visit
had exhausted Irma. What other stress might have pushed Irma into a
coma? Later on, I would learn that Irma and Nina had a conflictive relationship—a love-hate battle raged between them. But at the time, my
half-sister's behavior was unfathomable to me. *Her mother was dying—how
could Nina desert her at such a critical time?*

My world had turned upside down. Suddenly, a stranger was my
half-sister. I had two sisters, and I couldn't understand either of them.

Nurse Cooper stood up and reached out to take my hand. "Donna,
now that I've met you and heard your story, I believe that your birth
mother is hanging on, waiting for you." Nurse Cooper signaled Angelo
and me to follow her down the hallway.

We stopped in front of Room 57, coincidentally, my exact age. To
the right of the door, the metal slot held a manila folder labeled with the
name of the patient—LETTRICH, IRMA.

Angelo gave his now familiar smile and told me he'd be in the waiting room. Nurse Cooper put an arm around my shoulder. Her subtle,

clean citrus fragrance and physical warmth comforted me. She whispered, "Go in now, and tell her why you've come."

Finding Myself, Finding Meaning

I gazed down at the blanket-wrapped form of Irma Lettrich, so small and vulnerable, almost like a petite child tucked into a giant's bed. Irma's exposed forearms were a pale contrast to the underlying white thermal blanket. Webs of tubing connected her thin arms to the equipment around her. Bracelets of monitor wires encircled her small wrists, and led to electronic boards that beeped and chirped out an atonal concert. Two plastic tethers stretched over Irma's nostrils and connected her to life-preserving oxygen.

I realized how Angelo had recognized me so easily at the airport. My birth mother, seventy-seven years old, had luxuriant auburn hair that spread like silk over her pillow. Not a touch of gray. My natural hair was the same auburn color. Irma's nearly emaciated thinness allowed but few visible creases and wrinkles on her face. The resemblance was undeniable. I could envision that my older self was laying before me in that hospital bed.

Slowly, I peeled away a portion of the covers. A flimsy hospital gown clung to Irma's body. Her collarbones were prominent, like mine. Her nearly translucent skin showed no age spots. I traced the gentle slope of her right shoulder and felt a flutter under my fingers for a second. My heart pounded—*is she waking?* I looked at her face, hoping her closed eyes would open. *Are they hazel, like mine?* Yet her eyes stayed closed. With a heavy sigh, I drew up the blankets, smoothed them, and gently brushed my warm palms across Irma's forearms.

Careful not to disturb the monitor wires at her wrists, I examined my birth mother's hands. Her skin felt incredibly cool. Her fingernails looked like they were crafted by a shared genetic sculptor—our middle fingers were noticeably longer than our other fingers. Like my knuckles, Irma's were irregular and somewhat swollen. It seemed that arthritis had come to visit both of us.

I moved along Irma's swaddled form. At the bottom of the blanket, I tugged at the tightly folded ends and released them to expose her feet.

How small they were. Irma's big toes shaped into familiar opposing curves. Had Irma also forced her toes into unforgiving, pointed high heels, or had genetics dealt us both this oddity?

My mind churned through years of emotional debris, searching for rational meaning. If Irma Lettrich had not abandoned me at birth, would she have given me unconditional love? If she had nurtured me, would I love myself better? Memories flashed by like a black and white movie: four-year-old Danusia and Great Dog Brutus forging through the snow; losing my beloved Grandma S; little Danusia creating a happy family of paper dolls; lonely Immigrant Girl eating lunch alone, not fitting in.

How to describe the woman I became, the man I'd married, and the children we'd adopted? Would Irma have understood and supported me as I made the most difficult decision of my life—in my senior years, to leave my marriage and face life alone?

I stood next to my silent birth mother. The only noise in the room was the steady beeping and whirring of the machines and fluids that sustained her. Had Irma wanted to find me during "so many discussions, so many phone calls?" Who or what might have intervened? Ironic fate and timing had brought me to Irma—but why now, when she was in a coma? This barely alive woman could answer no questions, give no advice, tell me no stories. The only truths I knew were that Irma had given me life. And she had given me away.

I whispered as I leaned close to her ear, "Irma, you won't hear my stories now—there is no need." A strange sense of peace came over me. Finally, I could let her go.

Irma Lettrich, age sixty-three, 1984

Irma Lettrich, my birth mother, died that night. I wasn't with her when it happened; I don't know if Nina was there. What I do know is that Nina gave strict orders to exclude me from attending our mother's funeral. Nina wrote the obituary. It contained no mention of me, no reference to the existence of Irma Lettrich's other daughter.

Donna meets her uncle Bill, Irma's brother,
Pittsburgh, Pennsylvania, 2001

Cancer Comes

Divorce Granted

After two prolonged years of negotiations, Bob and I were at an impasse. My tenacious attachment to our vacation home in Colorado, where our family and friends had built happy memories, had become an emotional barrier—I didn't want to lose those good times. Any successful way to share long-term use of that home was proving impossible. In truth, the mountaintop community that was white and wealthy fit Bob's taste more than mine.

Our best hope for resolution was mediation. Our first attempt, with a male mediator, failed. But our second attempt, with a female mediator, brought us to an agreement. Finalizing the agreement between us took only one day. When all the documents had been signed (ultimately I did relinquish possession of the Colorado house to Bob), the mediator took me aside.

Earlier that day, she'd begun her process by posing a question separately and privately to Bob and me. "Tell me, in a few sentences," she had asked, "what is the force that drives your spouse?" I summarized, without hesitation, what I knew very well about Bob. However, Bob

had refused to give the mediator any information at all about his perceptions about me.

For years, I would try to understand why Bob rejected that question.
Had I spent thirty-two years in a marriage to a man who didn't know
me? With the passing of time and new insights, I came to ponder a different reason. Had Bob followed a rule of negotiation that he'd learned
at Harvard Business School and honed at Exxon?

Don't reveal to the opposition anything that can later be used against you.
One day I hope there will be enough emotional healing between us for
me to again ask Bob the question of what he believed about me. And that
he will give me a true answer.

At age fifty-eight, on the cusp of the twenty-first century, I was suddenly
single in a vast new world of social connection—Internet dating. Among
most of my middle-age girlfriends, meeting men on the Internet was
new and fearful territory. For me, it beckoned like an exotic new world
to be explored. Enthusiastically, I set out on an Internet dating safari.

Donna's online dating photo, 2001

The single woman I'd been decades before, the young secretary
who worked in conservative Booz Allen's executive recruiting department,

never saw or imagined reading or posting an online profile. Now that I was middle-aged, the Internet world was not only prolific, it existed with few restrictions. Anyone could post a profile and lie—about their background, age, and appearance. Many did just that. Re-crafting the golden rule in my peripatetic life, I set guidelines for my approach and expectations for Internet dating: 1) Be honest—craft a profile to attract men with my values, interests, and priorities, not to appeal to theirs; 2) Run credit checks and vet interesting candidates; 3) establish deal breakers—dishonesty, poor writing and a coercive agenda.

Internet dating for me was a confrontation with my truths, my instincts, and my choices. I needed to set boundaries, but also to push beyond my comfort zone. During a decade of exploring the online world, I did meet plenty of men looking for love. Some were deceitful. Many were honest. All of them had stories to tell. With a few, I made meaningful connections.

While I was starting my new life, New York, the city that I knew and loved, was devastated by the 9/11 attacks. I still had friends there. I had dined at Windows on the World. Libby, my first roommate in New York City of long ago, was a nurse at Memorial Sloan Kettering. Medical personnel across Manhattan waited for survivors who never came. Like millions of people glued to the television as the towers came down, I was riveted, aghast, and terribly confused. How would this atrocity change the world?

The Doctor Calls

I was in a relationship with Bobby, an earnest and charismatic man. We'd been dating a few months when my body began telling me something new and alarming. After years without a period, I suddenly had odd and erratic bleeding. Dr. C had me come in immediately for a pap smear. The results looked normal, but the bleeding wasn't.

"Let's do a D&C," Dr. C advised. "It's the standard treatment to scrape out the uterus and get you back on track." He sent samples to the lab for biopsy—a routine procedure. It would take a week to receive the analysis.

In the meantime, I planned to attend a post-wedding celebration in Florida for my newly remarried girlfriend Pat. We'd known each other for years, beginning when our sons were students and friends at Greenhill School. Pat had met Tom while taking Latin dance lessons, and they turned out to be a beautiful match on and off the dance floor. A few weeks before, I'd been a guest at their intimate at-home wedding in Dallas. The touching ceremony brought back bittersweet memories of my own wedding day, more than three decades before, when Bob and I were married in our small garden ceremony in Washington, D.C. I blinked back tears as I watched Pat's graceful figure in vintage satin descending the stairway on the arm of her son, now college age and about to give away his mother in marriage. When Pat placed her right hand into Tom's palm, their loving gesture touched my heart.

The newlyweds' weekend celebration brought together friends from near and far at a charming resort whose buildings were clustered along mangrove-lined waterways near Sarasota. I'd invited Bobby to join me. In our hotel room, getting dressed for the evening party, my cell phone sent out my incoming ring tone—the theme song from "Chariots of Fire." The caller ID showed it was Dr. C, most likely calling about the results of my biopsy. I answered the phone, reached for the hotel message pad and pen, and then sat down at the desk. Kind and sensitive Bobby pulled up a nearby chair and sat with me while I made my notes: *Biopsy shows malignancy. Dr. C recommends hysterectomy. Make appt. with nurse's office. Surgery should eliminate need for further treatment—no reason to worry.*

At the end of the phone call, I pleasantly said good-bye to Dr. C, folded my notes into a hotel envelope, and stored it the zippered compartment of my suitcase nearby. "Time to join the party!" I announced. Even though my intuition warned that trouble was coming, my gut reaction told me I could rely on my inherent strength. I would face cancer and beat it!

That weekend I immersed myself in celebrating the happiness of my friends. And I pushed the lingering diagnosis to the back of my mind.

Weeks later, Bobby said, "I couldn't believe how calm and methodical you were during the call from Dr. C and how absolutely dazzling you looked that evening." Bobby had a sweet and admiring way. "The rest of the evening you seemed to really enjoy yourself."

After I had the hysterectomy and was recovering in the hospital, my divorce attorney came to visit. "How do you manage to look so healthy?" he asked. "You've just had surgery and your eyes are sparkling."

"I'm just glad it's over," I smiled at the truth.

Then things got complicated. The surgery biopsy showed a secondary trace of cancer in one of my fallopian tubes. Was it an indication of a second and rare form of cancer or a metastasis of the first cancer? No original tissue samples from the D&C were left. Dr. C had cauterized the area, making it impossible to compare cancer biopsies. The Dallas surgeon who did my hysterectomy was opposed to follow up chemo and radiation. He believed that my surgery was sufficient and warned me that exposing my vulnerable abdomen to the toxic flood of chemo, followed by burning radiation, would forever compromise my gastro-intestinal system. He would be right about that.

I thought about my past medical decisions when I'd blindly relied on trusted physicians instead of asking skeptical, relevant questions such as: What substantial research has been done? Would you recommend this option for your own wife or mother? What long-term side effects do I need to consider?

More than twenty five years before when Bob and I were living in New York City, I'd had a miscarriage. My highly regarded gynecologist at the time had not recommended a D&C to clean the internal area. Now facing cancer, I agonized about possible causes. Had the residue left behind in my body after my miscarriage developed into cancer? Or had it been something else? Was the cancer caused by something I had done, or something I had taken such as Hormone Replacement Therapy? Or was I genetically predisposed?

None of those questions had answers. And now I faced a life-threatening decision about whether my cancer surgery alone would be sufficient. Again, I turned to the advice of respected doctors. I pursued a second, a third, and a fourth opinion. Yet no matter how many opinions I sought, there was no majority consensus among the doctors, no conclusive recommendation.

What I came to trust most was advice from loyal, longtime Exxon friends. Ed was undergoing treatment for a much more invasive and ultimately fatal cancer, yet he insisted his wife, Ruth, accompany me to world-renowned MD Anderson Cancer Center in Houston, where he was being treated and where I was seeking my fourth opinion. We visited MD Anderson twice. The first time, my oncology lab reports from Dallas got lost and didn't reach the consulting doctors at MDA. The second time, I personally retrieved the records and took them with me. Ruth and I sat with the team of doctors who considered the reports, discussed options among themselves, and came back to us—with their non-agreement. The decision about what post-op treatment to choose, if any at all, was left entirely up to me. It was Ruth and her firsthand experience with her husband's cancer that provided the greatest insight: "If you don't do aggressive post-surgery chemo and radiation and the cancer returns, how will you feel? Can you rationalize taking that risk?"

I chose the aggressive follow-up treatment. My odds were favorable—I had Stage 1 cancer, early diagnosis, confined to a closed endometrial area. Based on my decision, the doctors at MD Anderson prescribed four cycles of chemotherapy followed by recovery time, and four cycles of radiation. The full treatment period would be January through April 2002—a total of four months. In terms of intensive cancer treatments, mine would be relatively short.

Next, I had to decide where to receive my treatment—MD Anderson was renowned for its state of the art cancer care, but Dallas also had excellent oncologists; many trained at MD Anderson and were perfectly capable of administering my post-op protocol. I chose Dallas and the secure comfort of home. Conveniently, I could travel to UT Southwestern Medical Center and nearby Parkland Hospital for my doses of chemo and the subsequent course of radiation.

For the chemo sessions, I seldom went alone. Often, a willing buddy settled into a comfortable chair in the private cubical while I stretched out on a reclining lounger. The chemo flowed into my system through a surgically implanted port in my left arm. Because human veins collapse from toxic stress, the durable plastic port was inserted before my first chemo treatment. During the long hours of each chemo treatment, I welcomed the distraction of chatting with my friend or laughing together about inane sitcoms playing non-stop on the wall-mounted TV screen.

At home I stood in my master bathroom brushing my luxurious auburn hair, my lifelong source of vanity. With each stroke, more layers fell into the porcelain sink. I was going bald. And it was time to go wig shopping. That I did alone—I didn't want my fashionable girlfriends to see my bald head. The "Jane Fonda" wig was my favorite. After chemo, my hair would grow back curly, and passing admirers would compliment my chic and trendy style and ask for my hairdresser's name. I'd smile and tell them who he was. Later, he'd thank me for the new business.

Radiation treatments turned out to be harder than the chemo because they burned and caused intractable fatigue. During these treatments, I didn't ask companions to go along. They'd only waste their time waiting in the guest lounge while I disappeared into the restricted treatment room and got positioned in the X-ray tunnel. To distract myself, I made up stories about the phantom-like masks with identification numbers at the bottom. They were stored on nearby shelves and belonged to patients being treated for cranial or facial cancers. Each mask had eerie openings exposing the precise areas to receive beams of radiation. Since my treatment was to the abdomen, I didn't need a mask. Sometimes, when the radiologist was delayed, my restless mind had creepy thoughts. Did any patient decide to take home their mask after finishing radiation? I wanted no tangible reminder of the treatment that offered only one promise—of anxious years to come.

Time Out

Because the radiation treatments were so exhausting, I needed a break midway through. Fortuitously, my time-out coincided with Nick's spring break, and we went to Colorado. He and his fearless instructor spent their days extreme skiing. When my pain and discomfort grew intense, I lounged and rested. When discomfort lifted, I celebrated at the nearby spa, where the most difficult choice I had to make was between a massage, facial, or herbal wrap. In the evenings, Nick and I played rowdy board games together. My best therapy was having my son with me.

Nick, Greenhill graduate, 2001

Lara was a senior at SMU. After my post op treatments were over, Lara and I took a safari journey to South Africa and Victoria Falls in Zambia—our second time to experience a spectacular waterfall. Years before, with our friends the Vaughans, when all the kids were young, we'd traveled to South America's Iguasu Falls on the border of Argentina and Brazil. There, we'd stripped off as many clothes as possible because the massive flow of water radiated pounding heat during the peak of summer. In

Reunion of the Colombian Connection—(back) Lara,
Sasha; (front) Alexis and Nicky, Iguasu Falls, 1990

Zambia, as experienced tourists, Lara and I put on yellow slickers against the cold sprays.

Our safari camp in Botswana was luxurious. All common areas and individual "tents" were solid structures built high on stilts. Guests felt secure up high while viewing the panorama below—endless tundra and vast roaming herds of wild animals. Staying safe depended on following one rule—phoning the reception area if you planned to transit from room to anywhere else in the camp. A uniformed escort with a loaded rifle would arrive and take the lead, guiding guests along the elevated wooden walkways. The armed escorts may well have assured guests' safety. They also stimulated guests' fantasies that we were all courageous adventurers in the wild. My behavior, however, bordered on reckless.

Our Ele, Africa with Lara, 2002

Daily, "our Ele," an endearing mountain of an elephant, wandered near our stilt dwelling, doing what elephants do best—eating. As herbivores, elephants spend about sixteen hours a day consuming plants, preferably leaves, shrubs, fruits, bark, herbs, and grasses. Elephants need to consume 60 percent more food than their massive bodies actually digest. Thus our Ele was on a relentless mission to consume daily about 300–600 pounds of his or her (not for me to know the difference) herbivore diet.

Whenever I heard our Ele's distinctive munching of the acacia tree next to our walkway, I'd grab my camera and head out the door on my mission. Meanwhile, Lara screamed from behind the closed door, "Mom, don't be crazy! That elephant doesn't know you from a tree. All she wants is breakfast. You're going to be trampled, and I'll be motherless!"

Time to rest and be with my children gave me the opportunity to reflect about those who had supported me. I hadn't been alone. I'd been surrounded by friends, especially Bobby, my stalwart hero. My encouraging and compassionate doctors and gentle and kind nurses enabled every step of my successful treatment and recovery. Even Bob, in spite of our divorce granted on Aug. 1, 2001, had offered to go with me to Houston for one of my consultations.

I acknowledged someone who profoundly influenced how I would battle a life-threatening illness—my mother Hania. When I'd yearned for her to be soft and tender with me, she showed me toughness. Mother couldn't give what she'd never received. If I whined, she'd shout, "No complain! Nobody listen." From her, more than anyone else, I learned to work hard and be strong.

But I was also different from my mother Hania. I was able to ask others for help because I didn't believe that needing help and asking for it was a weakness. When someone asked me for help, I felt honored.

On Becoming

Renaissance

In 2002, I vowed never to take my restored health for granted and never to waste precious time. My divorce was final—never again would I have to ask anyone for permission to spend money. I wanted to help others make the most of their lives. But how could I achieve my mission?

The answer came from Nancy, a trusted friend, who had just completed a year of training in The Philanthropy Workshop (TPW), a donor education program established by the Rockefeller Foundation. On the fateful day of September 11, 2001, Nancy's cohort had been training at the Rockefeller headquarters in midtown, when terrorists attacked the World Trade Center only a few miles away. One horrific event would change America forever. Nancy called me after her cohort graduated, months later in 2002. Her voice was passionate. "September 11th was a tragic wake-up call—TPW inspired us to shape critical philanthropic missions and learn how to make a difference." Nancy urged me to join the next cohort.

I researched TPW's history and achievements. Since its formation in 1995, TPW had evolved as a primary source for international philanthropists seeking to expand donor skills and increase social impact. What intrigued me most was a focus on strategic and global philanthropy.

As a member of TPW Cohort 8, 2002-2003, I began my immersion in twelve months of enlightenment and transformation.

No one in the program seemed to notice my barely emerging cap of virgin hair. The focus was on what each of us brought to the table, not how we looked. Our group epitomized diversity—a mix of women and men of different ages and backgrounds from the US, the U.K., Taiwan, and Canada. Our common bond was altruism—all of us wanted to effect positive change in the world. Workshops were held quarterly, four one-week sessions in different locations—twice in New York City, once in Washington D.C. and once in a developing country for on-site training, ours would take place in South Africa.

Our first session posed key questions and defined our capacities:

- *What matters most in your life and why?*
- *What strengths of social capital and community networks do you possess or need to expand?*
- *How will you administer your philanthropic reserves?*

During my TPW year, I grew committed to somehow, and somewhere, make a significant societal difference. My social capital and community networks were primarily in Dallas, the city where I'd lived longer than any other. Dallas was undergoing a cultural renaissance that I believed would redefine it as a center for arts and culture. My life's journey had been shaped by cultural diversity. Since early childhood, the arts had transformed and transported me. I wanted the power of the arts to be accessible to anyone yearning for creative connections across economic, ethnic, and cultural boundaries.

During my TPW year, I defined four areas for my philanthropic focus: (1) The arts and creative connection; (2) Enlightened learning and global education; (3) Equal opportunity for underserved youths and women; (4) Cross-cultural awareness and collaboration.

I also established my philanthropic budget and considered tax implications. Philanthropic donations in the United States could be funneled through several types of entities: public and private foundations; collective donor advised funds; corporate contributions; and individual charitable deductions. To decide what would fit me best, I considered two primary choices: a private family foundation or a donor-advised fund. A private foundation required a board of directors and an administrative staff. A donor-advised fund didn't report to a board of directors and eliminated the need for an administrative staff. Instead, a donor-advised philanthropy fund would be administered by a paid financial entity such as Vanguard or Goldman Sachs. The funder served as trustee and independent philanthropic decision-maker. I chose to make grants through a donor-advised philanthropy fund—one of my smartest, long-term decisions.

On reflection, I credit TPW training for my evolution from a local charitable check writer into a global, strategic philanthropist. As a TPW alumna, I inherited a global family of hundreds of trained philanthropists. Graduates gained access to annual international workshops, alumni conferences, and travel focused on learning and collaborative funding.

TPW motivated each of us to expand our knowledge through working experiences. I affirmed how my most productive learning took place in the trenches when I allowed others who knew far more than I did to teach me their core needs and identify my capacity to meet them. I affirmed that valuable learning was directly linked to active listening. During my future years working in a multitude of philanthropic initiatives, I recognized that generous listeners dedicated to collaboration and pooled knowledge were effective leaders who achieved extraordinary results.

Firsthand Learning in Iran

One of my most significant learning experiences took place far away from home. September 2005, I journeyed to a country that Americans rarely visited, for a purpose that few had undertaken. Passengers on my international flight dined on Western food and soon-to-be forbidden alcoholic beverages. Before landing at Tehran Imam Khomeini

International Airport. the flight attendant announced, "Ladies, we'll be coming through the cabin to assist with your headscarves and modesty clothing"—a restriction for women only.

TPF journey, Iran, 2005

Officially, Americans weren't prohibited from visiting Iran, yet for many decades and many reasons few Americans entered that country. Historical events dating back to 1979 had created bitter political tensions between America and Iran. During the Iranian Revolution, Islamic fundamentalists deposed Mohammad Reza Pahlavi, the pro-American Shah of Iran whom the United States had long supported. When the Shah came to the US for medical treatment, the fundamentalists demanded his return. The US refused, and turmoil erupted in Iran. A group of Iranian students stormed the US Embassy in Tehran, seizing and detaining more than fifty Americans. Those Americans who did survive were held hostage for 444 days. Consequences during and after that siege are far too complex to summarize here.

Our small group of TPW alumni travelers included three women and one man. My friend Nancy and I were two of those women. All of us had joined a unique donor circle formed after 9/11. The 2001 terrorists' attacks on American soil fueled potent embers of fear and hatred toward anything Islamic. Yet a dedicated few TPW alumni bonded together to examine stereotypes generated by ignorance of the broad and diverse Muslim society. We aptly named our group The Pluralism Fund (TPF). Our shared vision was building peaceful bridges of understanding between America and the Islamic world. Our mission was to promote pluralism, tolerance, and respect for the rights of all—in particular, the women and girls of majority Muslim countries. It was obvious, at least to the members of TPF, that women and girls—statistically the neglected half of majority Muslin societies—had the most to gain and would be powerful agents of change in their countries.

TPF was totally self-funded; not a cent of our financing came from the US government. Our hope was that private donors and foundations in America would believe in our mission and give us their sustained financial support. When I joined TPF in 2004, we decided to stream-line our focus on two countries—Iran and Pakistan. Neither country was getting much attention because, at that time, the US was preoccupied with Iraq and Afghanistan. Each TPF member chose to concentrate on either Iran or Pakistan. Any in-country travel would be to learn, not to proselytize. Our journey was an apolitical, person-to-person, cultural outreach of hopeful intent.

We four intrepid Americans disembarked and made our way to the immigration complex. Along the route, public announcements blared in Farsi—no translation to other languages. During the rest of our visit, we never heard background music, not even traditional Iranian varieties. All music was deemed decadent and was publicly forbidden. During interminable sessions in dreary rooms, agents that I came to call "immigration police" relentlessly scrutinized and interrogated us, in Farsi. We responded by shaking our heads and sending up universal hand gestures for "I don't know." None of us were offered or allowed beverages or food. Long and thirsty hours later, we four Americans were abruptly released.

Trekking through chaotic masses in the reception hall, I hoped for the best but expected the worst—*had our guide given up and left us stranded?* Instead, we were greeted by Mohammad, our Iranian government-appointed guide, whose warm welcome in impeccable English, brought relief and the first smiles of that oppressive day.

Officially, we'd entered Iran as American tourists with one designated interest: "the history and people of Iran." Unofficially, our purpose was learning about women's core activism and how to assist them. Mohammad would be with us for our three-week immersion in Iranian customs and culture. At first, we couldn't have known that our guide was a former activist. Or that he'd faced imprisonment if his risky mission continued. Mohammad's friends had counseled him to use his perfect English and become a tourist guide. As required by the government, all guides were expected to scrupulously report all tourist activities— in essence, to spy on us. Which Mohammad did—until he realized that his subversive activism and our philanthropic mission formed a unique alliance, and our relationship shifted. Thereafter, Mohammad guided us around the duplicity and dangers of pursuing our true mission—to empower the women and girls of his country.

In public, we followed a scripted, predetermined tourism itinerary: supervised visits to Iran's primary tourist centers—Isfahan, Shiraz, the ancient ruins of Persepolis, and a few "shopping" days in Tehran.

Arriving in Isfahan, a city known for scholarly enlightenment, I anticipated a gracious stay at an historic caravanserai, formerly a palatial safe-haven for royal visitors and their entourage. Instead, as women visitors, we received an inhospitable lesson in gender inequality. Three TPF foreign women were immediately ordered to wait in the lobby. While all male Iranians and our one male TPF member were expeditiously accommodated. Since we women were the last to be registered, not enough individual rooms were available. Two of us were required to double up in one of the remaining rooms—translated from Farsi by an arrogant male receptionist as the "finest of quarters." Nancy and I agreed we'd share.

With much fanfare, an attendant led us to quarters designed for a wealthy, and likely male, traveler accompanied by a servant. Nancy was tall, and I was not. So I volunteered to take the Spartan servant's room, with no door, since any servant would be at the master's beck and call, at all hours, day and night. From my cot-sized bed, I was free to admire the opulent, gilded room inhabited by Nancy, thereafter laughingly designated by me as "The Master."

On departure, we women were again sent to stand in the lobby until all the men were served. Meaning we couldn't pay our room charges—until Mohammad intervened, assumed responsibility for us, and enabled us to step up to the front desk. I stored another lesson learned from the city of enlightenment in my suitcase of memories.

While touring the ancient ruins of Persepolis, clusters of curious locals encircled our small group and, in heavily accented English, welcomed us with questions. "Where you are from? America! We are loving you Americans! I am having many relatives in America Los Angeles." True enough, the Iranian diaspora in Los Angeles is so large that it's nicknamed "Tehr Angeles."

TPF Tehran school children, 2005

We spent our remaining days in Tehran. Our group had already submitted a required and detailed itinerary for approval by the government, specifically with whom and where each of us would be, day and night. However, noting that we were there for "shopping" had been a red-flag-alert to authorities. Since taking American dollars put any Iranian at risk, and any returning American or tourist, during that time, was forbidden to bring Iranian-made products into the US.

Mohammad, well aware of the Iranian requirement to identify intended groups and venues, counseled us to list all of them. And, as expected, the government officials forbade us to visit half of them.

However, with typical Iranian versatility, all the women activists from all the organizations—approved and unapproved—made their way to the sessions and met with us. Although doing so, or even being suspected of aligning with American culture or ideology, put the attendees in danger of spontaneous search and seizure in their homes. Many of the women who met with us did have their computers seized, but none were arrested during our visit. Our hope was that they would remain safe even after we left.

How fervently we admired the passion and courage of those women. Although makeup and fashionable sunglasses were discouraged, they displayed feisty irreverence by wearing both in public. All women, residents and visitors, were supposed to hide their hair. Our new friends complied by wearing brightly colored headscarves pushed back to expose almost as much hair as they conceded to cover. We TPF women did the same.

Many of the activists wanted to learn better English, yet none of them could publicly attend English classes. Ultimately, we were able to connect Iranian women with "sisters" in neighboring Turkey, a country where travel was allowed, and where they could attend capacity building workshops. The most determined Iranian activists did go to Turkey and did enroll in English language classes.

On our final night in Iran, we gathered in a Persian restaurant. Some of the women had invited a few trusted and enlightened male friends—all of them were young and seemed so vulnerable. The long war with Iraq had decimated the male population. Over 60 percent of the country's 80 million people were under the age of thirty. When I listened that night to young idealists sharing their aspirations—availability of good jobs, a lifting of Internet barriers, and most of all, an end to their double lives—I was overwhelmed with compassion and sadness.

During staged public demonstrations throughout Iran, everyone was required to chant *"Death to America!"* However, we were told that in safe, private places, the same people freely expressed their passionate admiration for the liberated opportunities in America. Our celebratory evening was one of those revealing private times.

Our Iranian group included dedicated artists yearning to have their works known in America. "Can you take my new play to Hollywood?"

one of them pleaded. "My paintings," another asked, "will you take photos of them and give them to an American gallery?" Sadly, I could do little more than express my hope for the future—that while they were still young and optimistic, doors of communication and travel would open between America and Iran.

My experiences in Iran changed me. I had walked in the shoes of Iranian women. I had dressed in their clothes. I'd witnessed how the women trusted each other and bonded together against oppression and danger. Humbled by my lack of knowledge about Iranian people and culture, at least I'd been able to take a few determined steps—on a fragile and seemingly endless bridge between human ignorance and enlightened understanding.

During the years ahead, TPF continued collective grant making in Iran and Pakistan, primarily in support of women's education and human rights initiatives. We forged cross-cultural connections between donors, grantees, and activists in Iran, Pakistan, and neighboring Turkey. In America, we'd staged Days of Learning—structured seminars and panel discussions between visiting Iranian and Pakistani economists, professors, and artists who interacted through Q&A with local audiences. TPF members underwrote and hosted these events in their home cities. In Dallas, I invited diverse audiences from my community network. I savored the words of my friend who expressed what the event had meant to her. "Thank you for changing my mind and opening my eyes. I had no idea how little I knew and how wrong I was."

The Pluralism Fund's collaborative experience taught me best practices: creating, operating, and sustaining an emerging non-profit organization. I learned the value of setting short- and long-term goals and the need to evaluate impact through well-crafted, ongoing assessment. Emotionally, my learnings were beyond measure. I'd found my place in a universal sisterhood. Together, we'd transcended political, cultural, and geographic boundaries. In an inclusive, rarified atmosphere, we'd listened with open minds, accepted our differences, and found connection through our shared values.

Despite the magnificent vision and seven years of human energy and financial investment, TPF could not overcome formidable challenges: insufficient outside funding; stymied membership growth; administrative overload; and staffing dilemmas. Every member eventually experienced burnout. In 2008, by majority vote, we dissolved The Pluralism Fund.

If I had to name the underlying reason, my answer would be—TPF was a movement too far ahead of its time.

My training with The Philanthropy Workshop and my experiences with The Pluralism Fund fulfilled my life-long quest for enlightenment, connection, and a sense of belonging. Seeds of learning planted in my childhood spent among immigrant boarders were fertilized. My philanthropic life was enhanced by global awareness—that regardless of where we are born or what language we speak, even a brief time shared, in common purpose, has the power to overcome boundaries and foster understanding. Learning, healing, giving—all coalesce in my philanthropic mission.

At last, I've hit my stride.

Epilogue

This book began as letters to my teenage daughter, Lara, away for a year at boarding school. For the first time, she began to ask questions about my past and the parents who raised me. I sent her crafted answers intended to comfort. Yet, the details I'd left out continued to haunt me. I needed to integrate my past with my present and to recognize how significant people and events had shaped my life.

And so I began to write stories: about my childhood among immigrant boarders; about not fitting in; about rejection and family secrets; and about my parents' histories. I described formative passages: coming of age; flights of escape; peripatetic married life; and motherhood. During the process, I came to acknowledge both flaws and the beauty in others and in myself. The most critical revelations asked fundamental questions: Who am I? Where am I going? What am I meant to do with my life? Decades marked by multiple moves, changing roles, darkness and enlightenment finally coalesced. *A Life of My Own, A Memoir*, was the result.

Sculpting my philanthropic identity began with my training in The Philanthropy Workshop that produced enlightenment and transformation. The Pluralism Fund tested what I'd learned in the trenches. My mission to help individuals and organizations achieve their full potential became my aspirational quest. Recently, I've expanded my philanthropic focus to address preventive mental health and to preserve the earth's vulnerable natural resources.

My journey has continued to be paved with challenges. Every day, I've struggled to make strategic and gratifying choices. Although I'm often tempted to say "Yes" to a promising new opportunity, before I make any commitment, I've learned how important it is to consider whether I have time and energy to carry it through. If I came up short, I need to ask myself what would I be I willing to let go? Inevitably, setbacks and detours were lessons to be learned. Self-awareness wove into my most gratifying philanthropic support: give from the heart; stay true to mission; and embrace the creative process.

At Southern Methodist University (SMU), I was an initiating donor for the National Center for Arts Research, now the merged organization known as SMU Data Arts, where data relating to nationwide challenges facing arts organizations is mined and analyzed. Findings are shared with arts leaders seeking organizational vitality. In Dallas, I have served as trustee of the World Affairs Council of Dallas/Fort Worth and as Life Trustee of the Dallas Theater Center. At The Arts Community Alliance (TACA), I founded the New Works initiative and later became its board chair. At KERA, North Texas Public Broadcasting, I was the initiating donor for Art & Seek, now a nationally recognized service that encompasses arts programming, web communication, arts reviews, and regional events calendar.

On reflection, my largest philanthropic investment in the Dallas Arts District was made with good intent, but ahead of its time. I contributed $1 million with a two-fold designation: to establish a Friendship Endowment and for purchase of TESSITURA, a sophisticated shared technology system. The Endowment was intended to subsidize ticket prices and lower fees, thus giving underserved audiences access to world-class productions and offering non-resident arts organizations the opportunity to perform in state-of-the-art facilities. TESSITURA offered data services to an unlimited number of users. It took several years for community development staff to be hired and for expert trainers to be brought on board to help staff understand and use TESSITURA to full potential.

In contrast, my smallest investment transformed young lives beyond every expectation. Bhavani Parpia, an activist for enlightened education, conceived and developed Connect-Teach, a global initiative. Initially, my modest funding supported Bhavani's efforts to implement a technology program that connected and empowered underserved teachers—all of them dedicated to the poorest of the poor, children in India's slums. This program has become a model that Bhavani continues to replicate in other developing countries.

A second low-cost project that I under wrote and Bhavani directed, connected Indian children with Dallas high school students via Skype. The kids shared their daily lives and aspirations, and created photo and poetry anthologies. The project culminated in a short documentary film that we showed in Dallas. Young people separated by chasms of differences—in culture, economics, and opportunity—learned from each other and formed abiding friendships. Surprisingly the Dallas high school students, brought in as mentors, turned out to be inspired and awed by their younger and disadvantaged counterparts. No other initiative I've funded has been so true to my vision and mission, or given me such a pure sense of purpose and connection.

My philanthropic work inspired my daughter Lara to complete The Philanthropy Workshop training and deeply invested herself in community service. After completing her master's degree at SMU, Lara was recruited to teach at The Shelton School for learning-different children, where she had once been a student. Later, she worked for the World Affairs Council of Dallas/Fort Worth. Lara and her husband Stephen, also a graduate of SMU, are dedicated and loving parents to toddler Isabella, whom we cherish and adore. My granddaughter inspires me to be in the moment and to see the world through loving eyes. That three of my treasured people live next door to me is a rare gift.

My son Nick has born the daily burden of treatment resistant clinical depression. He found strength, connection, and stability through his yoga practice and Buddhism. He has domesticated two feral cats and is their diligent and affectionate caretaker. Some years past and with my help, Nick located his birth mother and her extended family in Bogotá, Colombia. He learned that a half-sister and their birth mother both suffer from long-term clinical depression. This discovery presented a bridge to better understand and accept his health issues. It also influenced me to become a fervent advocate that adoptive parents be given full access to their children's genetic profiles. We need all the information possible to help our children thrive.

Nick, Donna, Lara, Steve, and Isabella, Holiday Photo, Dallas, 2018

Bob and I, despite our now infrequent contact, remain on friendly terms. He has remarried and maintains homes in three cities including Dallas. I consider that our three decades of married life represented the best and honest efforts of two people who loved, nurtured, and raised two children. We had a very good run.

I also remarried, but my second marriage proved to be incompatible and brief. If I could give a wedding gift to every marriage, I would endow both partners with sustained emotional health and the capacity to give and receive selfless love. Life-saving awareness forged my journey—if a relationship becomes a well gone dry, one must stumble on alone to survive. Yet, I haven't given up on finding a wonderful man to share remaining senior years—a period of life that I explore with zest as an "Evergreen Passage."

My birth family history has been complicated. After Irma's death, I was able to meet only one relative—her brother, my uncle Bill, now deceased. During the brief years I knew him, Bill revealed his history as a retired steel worker and his delight as a talented bluegrass fiddler. As Uncle Bill, he generously shared with me his music and family photos, also his perceptions about Irma's life and the name of a man who might have been my birth father. Private investigator Angelo Nolfi followed up with the Pittsburgh man, who admitted to having relations with Irma prior to the time of my birth, yet denied being the father of her baby. Although he took Angelo's contact information, he has never tried to reach me. My half-sister Nina refused to meet during the last hours of our mother Irma's life. To this day, she has not changed her mind. I have lost all desire to know her.

My cousin Theresa, now widowed, and her adult children are my only remaining extended family. Theresa and I have been as close as sisters since childhood. As adopted girls, we shared tears and joys, jealousies and squabbles followed by thoughtfulness and forgiveness. Always, we been there for each other.

After our parents died, I severed all contact with my sister Edith. My decision was shaped by the tumultuous year of living with her in the Arizona desert; the mysterious deaths of our parents Hania and Juzo under her care; and Edith's nefarious intervention that forced Dad, on his deathbed, to sign a new will denying me as his daughter. No space is left in my heart for Edith. Public records affirm her death in 2001, at age eighty-seven. I have lost touch with Reggie, cast out by her parents during our high school year together. I have no knowledge of Reggie's current whereabouts and whether she is still alive.

As for my adoptive parents, writing this memoir has enabled me to acknowledge myself and them with much deeper insight. Just as I am complex and flawed, they were multifaceted and imperfect.

My father Juzo was once a courageous young man who saved his Polish family from oppression and led their escape to America. His gifts to me were the restorative times at the farm and inspiring my love of nature. In his senior years, Juzo was a rejecting and silent father who failed to protect me from Mother's rages. His dark demons punished me when I was an innocent teenager. Growing up with a father who withheld affection and harbored misogyny compelled my vow to cherish my own children with healthy love.

My two mothers—Irma and Hania—shaped the child I was, the woman I became, and the person I aspired to be. For reasons I shall never know, a young and unmarried Irma Lettrich surrendered me, her newborn daughter, to someone she hardly knew—her landlady, Polish Hania. Then, for more than six decades, my birth mother disappeared from my life. Until I searched and found Irma—on her deathbed. She would never be able to give me assurances of love or answers to my questions.

My adoptive mother, Hania, neither received nor gave gentle nurturing. Instead, hard work toughened her, and she faced adversity with courage and resilience. Inner demons and volatile emotions haunted Hania, and her unpredictability fueled my struggle between self-reliance and insecurity. The more she dismissed my talents and achievements, the stronger my determination to prove her wrong.

Evolution of the memoir over the course of many years has allowed me to explore the complex facets of Hania's many identities and to process her impact on my life. I have come full circle—from disparagement and denial to acknowledgment of my mother Hania as my flawed hero.

A Life of My Own celebrates a woman's journey marked by reinvention and transformation.

About the Author

Donna Wilhelm is a philanthropist and arts advocate in Dallas, Texas. Her global outreach, as member of The Pluralism Fund, addressed capacity building of women and girls in Iran and Pakistan. In the Dallas area, her board service includes KERA North Texas Public Broadcasting, Dallas Theater Center, SMU Meadows School of the Arts, the World Affairs Council of Dallas/Fort Worth, and mental health initiatives. She is a graduate of the City University of New York with degrees in studio and art history, and her post graduate work in jewelry design was at New York's Parson's School of Design.

www.donnawilhelm.org

La Reunion

La Reunion Publishing is an imprint of Deep Vellum established in 2019 to share the stories of the people and places of Texas. La Reunion is named after the utopian socialist colony founded by Frenchman Victor Considerant on the west bank of the Trinity River across from the then-fledgling town of Dallas in 1855. Considerant considered Texas as the promised land: a land of unbridled and unparalleled opportunity, with its story yet to be written, and the La Reunion settlers added an international mindset and pioneering spirit that is still reflected in Dallas, and across Texas, today. La Reunion publishes books that explore the story of Texas from all sides, critically engaging with the myths, histories, and the untold stories that make Texas the land of literature come to life.